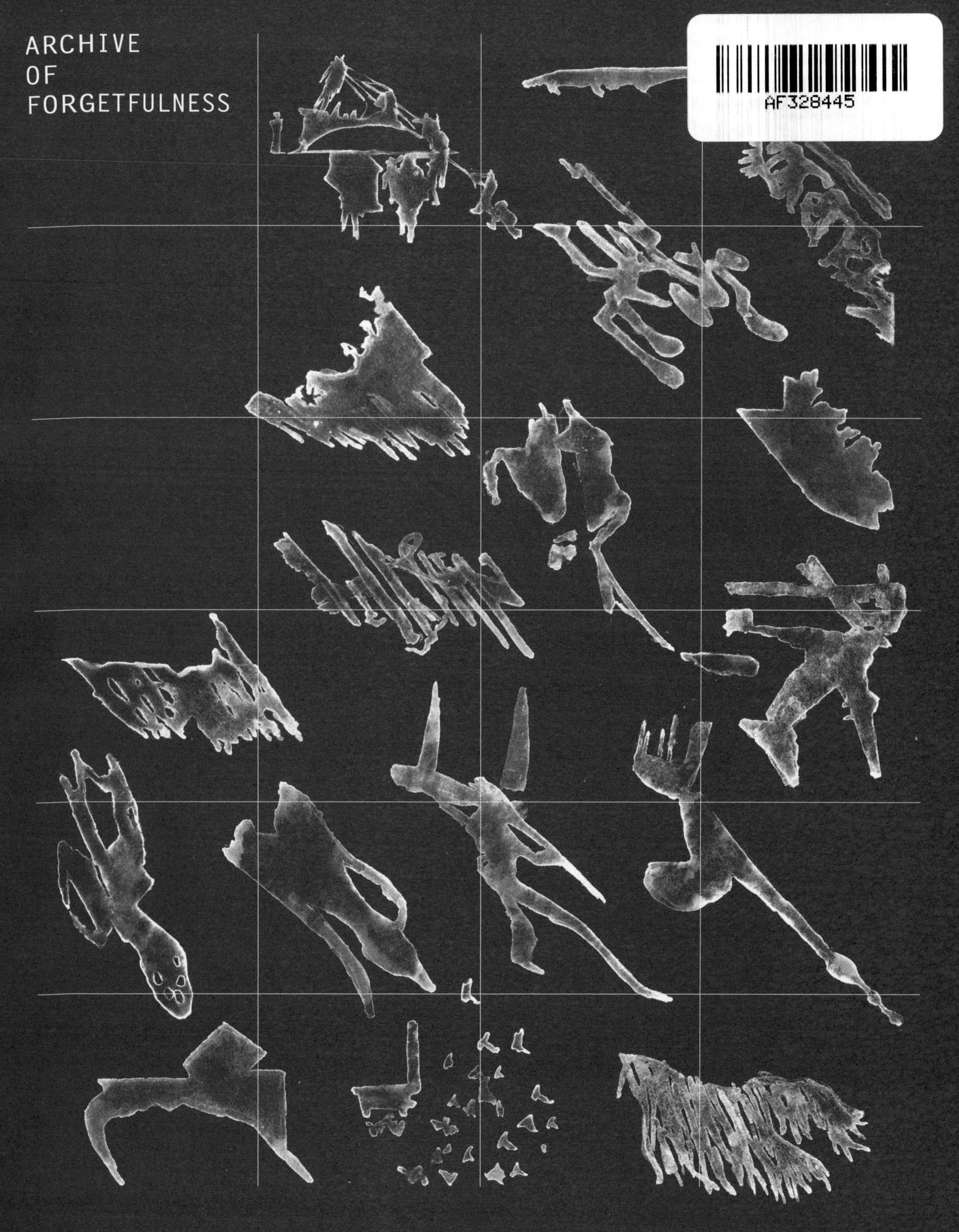

The Goethe-Institut initiated, co-conceptualised and funded
the Archive of Forgetfulness project.

First published by Jacana Media (Pty) Ltd in 2022
10 Orange St, Sunnyside, Johannesburg, 2092, South Africa

ISBN 978-1-4314-3275-2

Design by Fred Swart
Editing by Lara Jacob
Proofreading by Megan Mance
Indexing by Janine Loedolff
Printed and bound by ABC Press, Cape Town

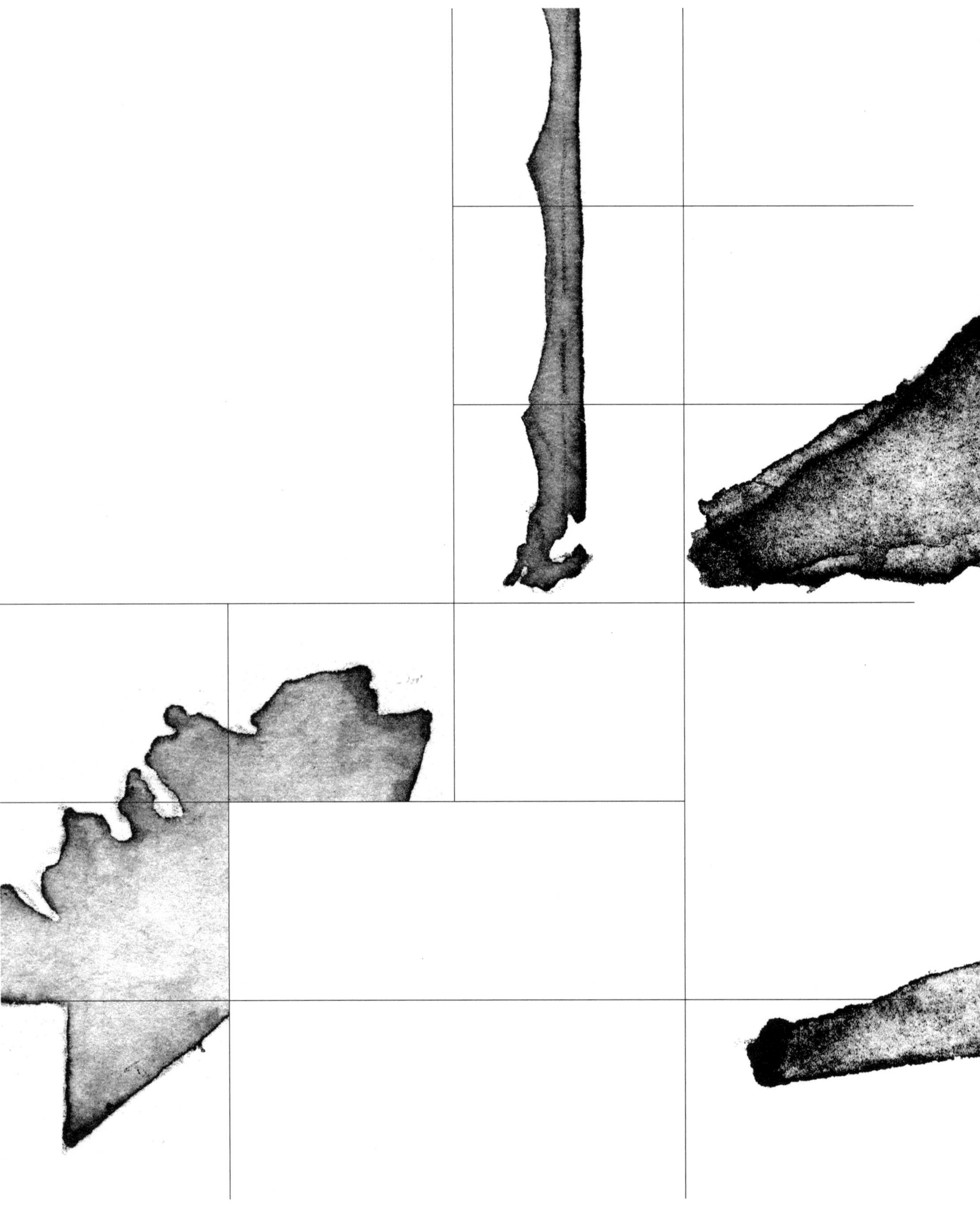

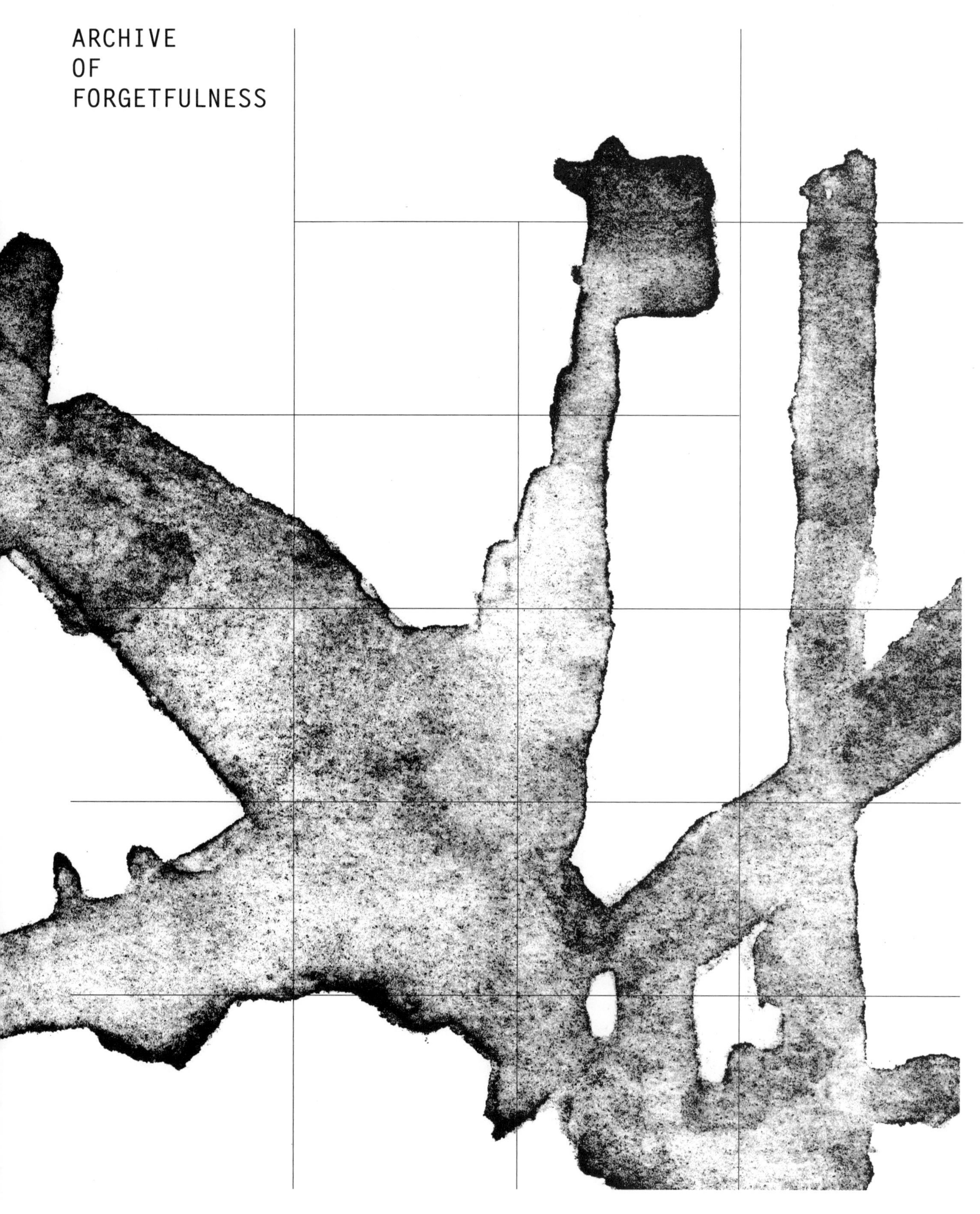
ARCHIVE
OF
FORGETFULNESS

Asma Diakité
& Lilli Kobler

The Sahara does not separate, it connects, as does the Nile. The colonial thinking that divided Africans into 'tribes' and incited them against each other paradoxically brought Africa closer together than was ever the case before the European conquest. A common African consciousness has only existed since the resistance against colonial rule, and it encompasses the entire continent...[1]

The initial idea of *Archive of Forgetfulness* was to investigate the idea of neighbourhoods in local, regional and continental terms, but also in relation to the mobility and neighbourly connections of narratives and concepts. It soon became a project of exploring the neighbourhood of Northern Africa and the Africa that lies South of it, from the perspective of adjacent neighbourhoods, defined by neighbourly connections. Europe's colonial project separated the continent, and while those structures have largely been dismantled, the belief in a split between a supposedly developed and a supposedly underdeveloped Africa can still be read in the contemporary. This imposed narrative, problematic as it is, as well as the often quite complex (self-) understanding of many Africans was where the work began.

In December 2018 several directors of Goethe-Instituts from the whole continent, along with cultural players and experts from those countries, met in Cairo to create a space of open exchange and questions around concepts of neighbourliness, mobility and networks on the continent. A first project idea was born, that kept changing during the course of time, and local and global events. After localised research, mapping and digging during 2019, the crucial driver was the network of artists, activists, curators and experts from different parts of the continent that subsequently met in Kigali at the end of 2019 to continue exploring and shaping the project with further in-depth development during 2020 within local, regional and continental contexts. The expressed aim of the project, initially called Neighbourhoods, was to create work that reaches beyond the mental division of the continent as it obscures reality, and to examine an Africa of multi-ethnic neighbourhoods that already begins at the Mediterranean. This expanded view is preceded by the consideration of an Africa that is characterised by diverse mobilities and migrations; an Africa within Europe's immediate vicinity also offers the opportunity to consider anew the neighbourhoods making up a multi-ethnic, a multicultural Africa and a multi-ethnic, a multicultural Europe.

---

[1] Johnson, D.,'Die unsinnige Zweiteilung Afrikas' (translation by Asma Diakité), *TAZ*, 13 May 2015. Available at: https://taz.de/Die-unsinnige-Zweiteilung-Afrikas/!5008978/.

Beyond the narratives of belonging, identity and self-understanding that were immediately apparent, the Covid pandemic and its forced immobility changed not only the structure of the project, but also surfaced how important mobility and movement is for personal relations, the making of community and neighbourliness. Movement was of central significance in order for culture to flow freely from one place to the next, transform, reshape, stay put and move on. Our idea of permeable borders was challenged by a pandemic that to a large extent forced us to imagine spaces in the absence of sensory experience. With the curators Huda Tayob and Bongani Kona introducing the notion of forgetting and remembering as inspired by Mahmoud Darwish's *Memory for Forgetfulness* (1987), the Archive of Forgetfulness centred on remembering as an active part of forgetting and brought forward a collaborative and collective project in three parts that was published as a website in 2020/21. Regional curators Ali Al-Adawy (Egypt), Eric Ngangare (Rwanda), Jumoke Sanwo (Nigeria), Omnia Shawkat (Sudan), Princess Zinzi Mhlongo (South Africa) and Zoubida Mseffer (Morocco) were involved from the early stages in 2019, and the six regionally curated projects released throughout 2021 draw out specificities from their local contexts and the longer conversations around neighbourhoods woven into the fabric of the *Archive of Forgetfulness*.

The contributions from artists, curators and other cultural practitioners from all over the continent interrogate through different forms and modalities what it means to be African in an expanded understanding of that term. The resultant body of work stands as an emblem of the entangled histories of the continent and moreover a revolt against the static borders that encompass, as well as internally constrict, movement. The *Archive of Forgetfulness* therefore holds space for the forgotten - as forgetting helps to remember. And thus this publication presents not only the three parts of this project, but contextualises and entangles them in an array of essays, art works and contextual pieces. Reaching diverse pan-African audiences and creating discourse and community around topics, audiences and neighbours has been extremely enriching and we are hoping this publication can expand and build on this.

We thank the curatorial team of the project for their generosity and insights, and the hard work to uncover the forgotten stories - and to remember ourselves as the neighbours who witness and reflect the journey.

The *Archive of Forgetfulness* is an archive of mobility and infrastructure.[2] The project was launched in the midst of the Covid-19 pandemic and global lockdowns in September 2020, when the frailty of basic urban infrastructure was laid bare, for so many. As states wrestled the spread of the virus, the restrictions placed on movement - from regimented stay-at-home orders to the mass closure of borders - led to widespread immobility. With a heightened sense of being and breathing in this world, these restrictions drew attention to longer and deeper histories of forced immobility and segregation, and of the extractive infrastructures and racial violences made material in how cities across the African continent were planned and imagined. Drawing inspiration from Mahmoud Darwish's prose *Memory for Forgetfulness* (1987), the *Archive of Forgetfulness* questions how we might engage with what exists in the failure of memory, and that which can no longer be spoken, yet also acknowledges forgetting as an active part of remembering.

The *Archive of Forgetfulness* is a collaborative and collective project, long in the making. In its current form, the project has three parts. The first is an eight-part podcast series, *Conversations with Neighbours* curated by Huda Tayob and Bongani Kona and released between September 2020 and January 2021. The second part is the online exhibition in response to an open call. The exhibition was launched in April 2021 and hosts twenty-two projects and five essays. The third part, which unfolded between May and December 2021, includes six projects developed by the regional curators, namely Ali Hussein Al-Adawy, Eric '1Key' Ngangare, Jumoke Sanwo, Omnia Shawkat, Princess Mhlongo and Zoubida Mseffer.

2   The *Archive of Forgetfulness* framing was co-authored by Huda Tayob and Bongani Kona, in conversation with the regional curators. The *Archive of Forgetfulness* core team includes the following individuals in various stages - Lead curators: Huda Tayob (South Africa) and Bongani Kona (South Africa/ Zimbabwe); Regional curators: Ali Al Adawy (Egypt), Eric Ngangare (Rwanda), Jumoke Sanwo (Nigeria), Omnia Shawkat (Sudan), Princess Mhlongo (South Africa), and Zoubida Mseffer (Morocco); Social media manager: Zakiyyah Haffejee (South Africa); Podcast Graphic designer: Graeme 'Boeta G' Arendse; Podcast production: Andri Burnett; Website design and production: Sarah de Villiers, Frederick Kannemeyer. With support from Asma Diakité, Cara Snyman, Lilli Kobler and Jonas Radunz at the Goethe-Institut.

The *Archive of Forgetfulness* holds together acts of remembering. It is a platform for collecting and gathering stories often untold. The various contributions - from the podcasts to artworks, essays and regional curated projects - renew lines of connections, resurface forgotten conversations and establish the beginnings of future collaborations. The project website is a space for interrogating the archival gesture, from the embodied and spoken, to the written and performed. Beginning with an interest in the entangled histories of our lives, the project is framed by a series of questions. We ask what personal and political histories emerge via infrastructures. We question how thinking through deep and recent histories, across water or through the skies, might reveal alternative ways of living. And we ponder on how dreams of freedom, and other worlds that might have been possible, haunt our present, and suggest alternative possible futures.

The *Archive of Forgetfulness* is shaped by convergences and divergences, overlaps and variations in perspectives and positions. Each phase of the project has built on what came before, yet expands into a new offering. The website offers a unique platform to hold the accumulation of these varied works in a moment of simultaneity, to engage with the difficulties of African pasts, the messiness of promise and potential in moments of decolonisation and anti-colonialism, and to explore possibilities for alternative futures. This publication is a catalogue of the works featured on the website, offering traces and shadows of the digital version which remains live for 2022 at archiveofforgetfulness.com. It marks a moment and time, and acts as a physical remnant of the collection of work online, and we, hope, a starting point for further conversations.

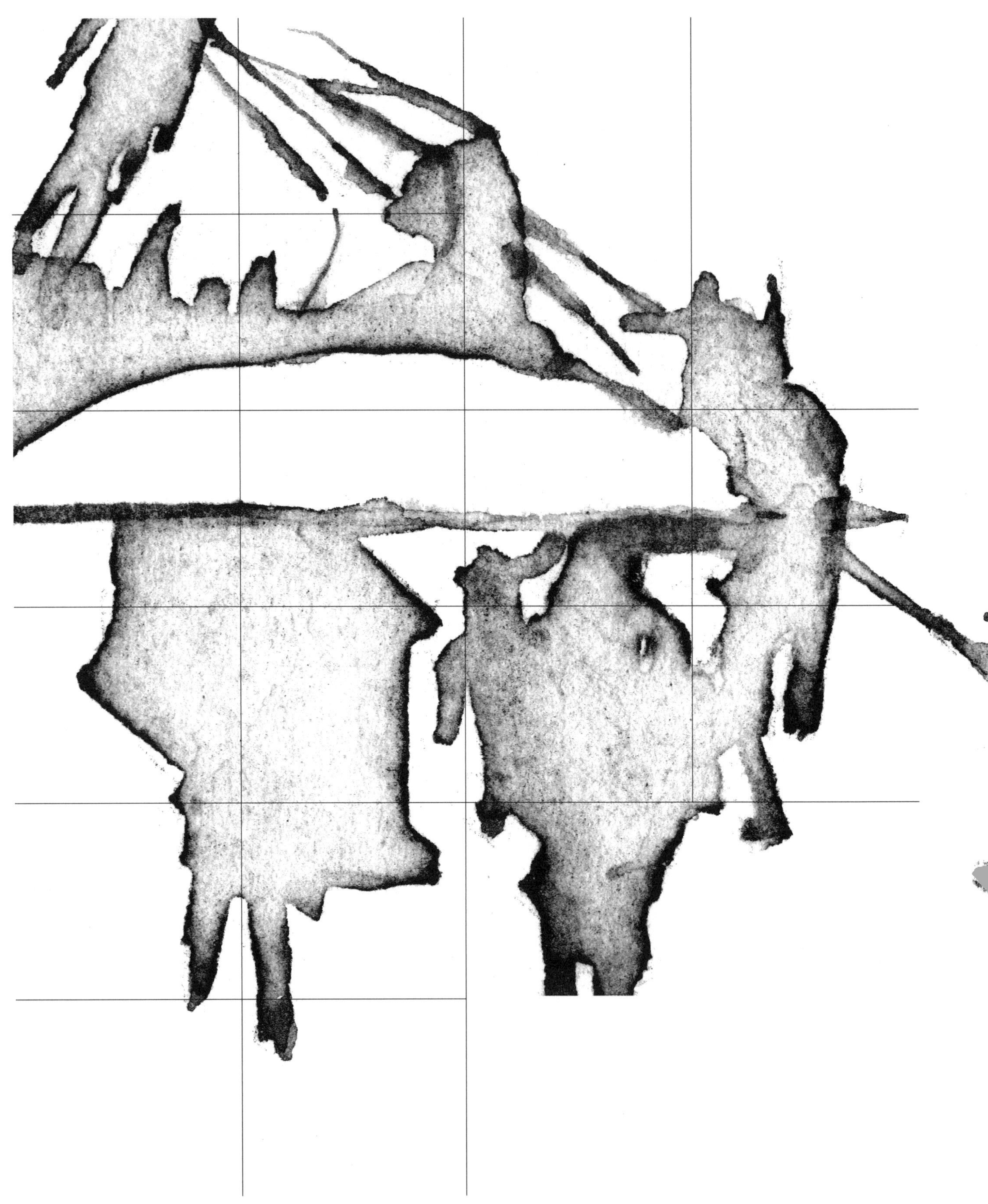

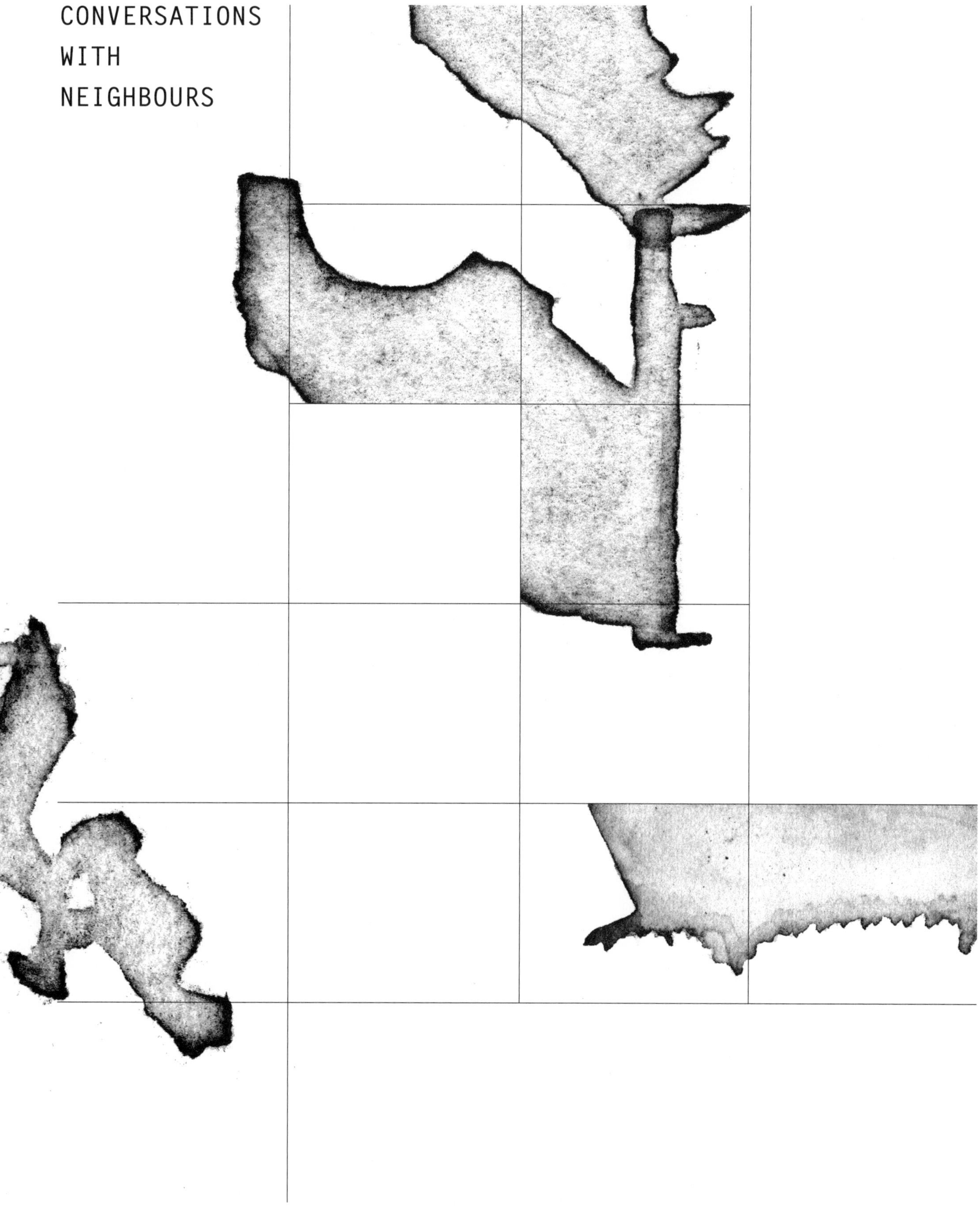

Conversations with Neighbours is an eight-part podcast series.[3] It is an offering of conversations, stories, histories and memories of moving, crossing and living in African cities across geographical and physical borders. Bringing in voices from around the African continent and diaspora, the podcast conversations were a central part of the open call, as provocations on how we might think the past, present and future. The series of eight conversations began with an initial two, which were directly led by earlier iterations of the 'Neighbourhood' project initiated by the Goethe-Institut in 2019 in which the regional curators were all involved. This earlier phase is acknowledged in the naming of this series, which acts as a bridge between earlier iterations focused on the bounded concept of a neighbourhood, to an expanded engagement with neighbourliness across borders, in all its complexities. The first two conversations build on earlier work by the regional curators, and in some ways became a preface for broader and wider themes present throughout the podcast series and wider project. The first episode questions what archives are, and what they might be, suggesting they are spaces of possibility and portals for reimagination. The second episode draws in the widespread contexts of crisis, troubled and difficult times in which artistic and creative practice on the African continent is often undertaken, at times, against all odds. As a starting point for the *Archive of Forgetfulness*, these first two episodes retain traces of earlier conversations and acknowledge previous phases of the project, marking a space for the importance of remembering as an active and engaged process.

The following episodes are each framed by a set of questions that speak to a range of territories and geographies, infrastructures of mobility and archival modalities.

3   The podcast series was curated by Huda Tayob and Bongani Kona, with production support and editing from Andri Burnett, design work by Graeme 'Boeta Gee' Arendse, and design and social media curation by Zakiyyah Haffejee.

These range from conversations which touch on flight, rail travel, overland desert journeys and movement across water. The conversations speak to the immense depth and breadth of the Sahara as filled with history, the poetic territories of the oceanic Swahili worlds, the tangible materiality of road and rail travel and associated infrastructures, and the possibilities of anti-colonial and black flight. The archives spoken to are textual, oral, sonic, auditory and emotional; they are drawn, spoken, heard, felt, experienced and imagined. The careful mapping of these overlapping geographies and archival modalities was central to holding together a pan-African conversation series, with space for the unexpected to take hold.

The episodes include contributions from Nigeria, Egypt, Sudan, Rwanda, South Africa, Ghana, Nubia, Democratic Republic of the Congo, Zimbabwe, Tanzania, Kenya, India, Angola and Morocco. This wide list of countries belies the crossing and re-crossing of borders in the actual contributions, the inclusion of diasporic voices and the fluid positionality of many contributors. The conversations move between the personal and political, possibility and precarity, promises and failures. The episodes draw into conversation an imaginary of borderlessness as sited, specific and ever-present. They acknowledge ways of living with and through movement. They speak to always and already existing archives and forms of knowledge which may be forgotten but are not lost. They invite the audience to listen closely and hear deeply, through broken recordings and imperfect sound, of what might have been and could, perhaps, still be. The following pages share excerpts of transcriptions of the podcasts. These short excerpts from each episode offer a sampling of the questions, geographies and voices you can listen to, and are an invitation to engage further with the contributors involved.

In episode 1, 'The archive is a portal for reimagination', South African architect Huda Tayob speaks to Nigerian curator and story-teller Jumoke Sanwo and Egyptian curator Ali Al-Adawy on epistemological questions around archives, untranslatability and opacity. Sanwo discusses the importance of confronting history and the colonial baggage of dispossession and points to ways of engaging constructively with the 'now' by thinking with and through performance and the body-as-archive. Al-Adawy talks to his interest in the relationship between archives, cinema and contemporary art practices. He suggests that we might think of the archive as an imaginary space of possibility, drawing on the work of Egyptian artist Hassan Khan and the Egyptian rapper Wegz.

Huda Tayob: *'You are opening up questions of how we think of archives as spaces of care or spaces to hold. And where we entrust knowledge. But also by talking through performance, is a suggestion of a different kind of audience interaction with an archive, as central to how an archive is received.'*

Jumoke Sanwo: *'Archive in Yoruba translates to Itoju, and Itoju means to care, to hold. And that's pretty much the meaning of archive in Yoruba language. But I'm also thinking about that in relation to Yoruba concept of time. There's a bit of complexity with how Yoruba engage time. On the one hand there is a belief that there is a circularity to time. There is also that thinking about time in terms of event. So when you're thinking about the future, you think about the future that is always present in the now. And when you are thinking about knowledge, you are thinking about what is being produced now which would be necessary for the future. So when thinking about the concept of archives, and how Yorubas think about time, it is related to the fact that we can only relate to what is produced in the now as ever-present, the most relevant aspect of time, but always related to the future. I think about this in terms of performance, and performance as rooted in the concept of now. [...] Archives are about how a society comes together and looks at certain expressions, customs and holding them. And deciding on what to keep and what to hold. [...] Without some inkling of the past, you cannot have a foundation to produce the now.'*

Ali Al-Adawy: *'Archives are always related to the future more than the past [...] When we look into the archive, as an institution, we have to contend with power. You always find dominant powers who want to keep archives away from those people who are trying to find different approaches to emancipate presents and futures. Because of this, I think of archives in an abstract sense or meaning, as an imaginary space of possibility [...] Archives could be the starting point to make something more critical, more emancipated, for our future and present. This definition of archives is taken from the work of Egyptian artist Hassan Khan. In different artworks, he has introduced this meaning of archives as an imaginary space of possibility.'*

CONTRIBUTORS

Jumoke Sanwo is a storyteller, cultural interlocutor and creative director of Revolving Art Incubator. She works primarily in photography, video art and extended reality (XR), and her work engages the bodily, spatial and temporal realities and complexities in postcolonial societies. She lives and works out of Lagos, Nigeria.

Ali Hussein Al-Adawy is a curator, researcher, editor, writer and critic of moving images, urban artistic practices and cultural history. He has curated several film programmes and seminars such as *Serge Daney: A homage and retrospective* (2017) and *Harun Farocki: Dialectics of images… Images that cover/ uncover other images* (2018). He also curated, together with Paul Cata, the exhibition *The Art of Getting Lost in Cities: Barcelona & Alexandria* (2017). He was one of the founders of *Tripod*, an online magazine for film and moving images criticism (2015-2017) and was part of the editorial team of *TarAlbahr*, an online platform and a publication for urban and art practices in Alexandria (2015-2018).

Huda Tayob is an architect, architectural historian and curator. Her research is focused on migrant, minor and subaltern architectures and the politics of urban space, alongside architectural ghost stories and other archival silences. She is a CCA Mellon Fellow on the project Centring Africa, is co-curator of Racespacearchitecture. org with Suzi Hall and Thandi Loewenson, and was the project manager for the *Archive of Forgetfulness* project. She has been published widely, including in *Eflux Architecture*, *Architecture and Culture* and *Arch+*.

EPISODE 2:
'Art in times of crisis'

In episode 2, 'Art in times of crisis', Cape Town-based writer Bongani Kona speaks to South African theatre director Princess Zinzi Mhlongo, Rwandan poet and spoken-word artist Eric '1 Key' Ngangare and Sudanese co-founder of digital cultural platform Andariya, Omnia Abbas Shawkat, about producing art in troubled times. The conversation moves between the DRC, Rwanda, Sudan and South Africa, raising the difficulties of war and its remnants, and the experience of coming of age in a time of great turmoil. It points to the importance of telling stories that contest history and statehood, discusses forms of silence and organised forgetting, and questions what it means to produce work that can contend with the violence of our times.

> **Bongani Kona:** *'The three of you in one way or another are all storytellers. And I'd like to begin by drawing out some of the stories of your childhood. The theme of our conversation today is art in times of crisis, and in earlier conversations you've all addressed how this moment with the shut-down, curfews, patrolling police and military is in some sense not new. You've all lived through moments of great historical turmoil.'*

Eric '1Key' Ngangare: *'We go through interpretations of time based on who curates narratives. […] My great-grandparents, they moved to Zaire, and my mum was born in Bukavu in 1962, and I was born in Goma in 1981. So that means there's three generations already living in exile when I was born. And the conditions of living in exile mean you don't have access to jobs, to work, to employment […] and at the same time you are treated like a foreigner who came to occupy space that is not their space. But what is interesting is where I was born in Goma used to be part of Rwanda prior to the Berlin partitioning of Africa. So that means until the 1800s it was part of Rwanda.*

[…] Coming to Rwanda in 1997 was returning home, but for me it was really coming to live in Rwanda for the first time. At the same time, I was born in exile in a country that used to be Rwanda, in exile in the country of my father. […] Poetry allows me to make mistakes, to have room, and to be honest, it's just about exploring and the freedom to do and to be.'

Princess Zinzi Mhlongo: *'In 2012 I had received the Standard Bank Young Artist Award for Theatre and in 2010 I had Austria approach me for a young director's project, which meant I had to take a production to Austria. […] Because I was already in mainstream at the time there were many young underground voices reaching out to me, asking what the process is of creating their own work, and unable to make connections with the mainstream. And that is where Plat4orm was born. I had a space that was purely to rehearse my own work, but then I thought as I only rehearsed in the afternoons, I thought let's open a space to artists who have these exciting ideas and new work. […] If as a theatre maker you aren't given a platform to showcase whatever your voice wants to say at that moment in time, it is censored. And theatres are not spaces open to the artist. They are spaces that, in a way, deprive the artist because of how they are managed and run. With Plat4orm, we wanted a space that would be for the artist, where the artist could come with any idea, with any concept, with any medium, we would be that space for them. […] So suddenly we are hearing new voices, we are hearing new stories. […] From that there was a lot of freedom, and a lot of amazing work came from the space.'*

Omnia Shawkat: *'Andariya is responding to two things. One is the disconnect between the different countries starting with our own - Sudan and South Sudan. […] And here we are, we accept the circumstances, we accept where we are at this point in history, but we would like to build bridges. We speak the same language, so many of us can speak Arabic, we share similar heritage, we eat similar food - there's absolutely no reason to cut off our bonds just because we are now two sovereign countries. So it was an attempt to build a bridge between Sudan and South Sudan. […] And then we realised that actually we're so isolated from the rest of the continent, the rest of the world arguably, but more importantly the rest of the continent. And we should reach out, we should connect […] and it seemed that building cross-cultural projects across these two countries and creating positive content written by their own people was a solution that was doable and scalable. And it was something that created an archive on the internet. […] The message is clear that we're building bridges between different communities. […]*

'Culture is the way I'm probing and understanding, and healing and questioning, and being compassionate and empathetic. And also knowing there are things I could never fix or even address in this lifetime.'

CONTRIBUTORS

Bongani Kona is a Cape Town-based writer and contributing editor at *Chimurenga*. He studied creative writing at the University of Cape Town and is editor of the short story collections *Our Ghosts were Once People* (2021) and co-editor of *Migrations* (2017). His work has been broadcast on BBC and has appeared in a variety of publications and anthologies including *The Baffler*, *Safe House: Explorations in Creative Nonfiction* and *The Daily Assortment of Astonishing Things*. Kona was shortlisted for the Caine Prize in 2016 and the True Story Award in 2020/21.

Eric '1Key' Ngangare is an independent poet, spoken word artist, emcee, performer, actor and blogger from Rwanda exploring various formats of storytelling. His work deals with issues of identities - individual and collective - power systems and societal dynamics. His second album *Mwiru* was released in 2021 and offers a mix of genres, styles and languages.

Princess Zinzi Mhlongo is a theatre director and the co-founder of *The Plat4orm*, which for many years provided an alternative space for artists in the theatre industry to develop new uncensored work. She directed her first professional production, *And the Girls in their Sunday Dresses*, in 2008. Since then, her work has toured internationally, and she has received numerous nominations and awards including the prestigious Standard Bank Young Artist of the Year Award for Theatre in 2012. She is a recipient of The Laboratory for Global Performance and Politics 2020-21 fellowship at Georgetown University, Washington DC. In 2020 she launched *Exhibit*, a digital platform that showcases upcoming or unfinished work by an artist seeking funding.

Omnia Abbas Shawkat graduated with a BSc in Biology with a focus on environmental studies from the American University in Cairo in 2008. She has a Master's degree in Environment and Resource Management with a focus on water and climate policy from the Vrije Universiteit in Amsterdam the Netherlands. After six years in development and environmental management, Omnia rerouted her career to become a digital storytelling curator and cultural manager. Omnia is one of two founders of Andariya, a bilingual digital multimedia cultural platform, research and cross-cultural enterprise launched in 2015 in Sudan and South Sudan, and in Uganda in 2018. In 2021, Andariya entered nine new countries in the East and Horn of Africa regions, creating and curating content and common projects.

EPISODE 3:
'What personal and political histories emerge
via infrastructures of mobility?'

In episode three, Egyptian architect and researcher Menna Agha gives voice to the Nubian bonds of kinship that survive the crossing of vast territories between Sudan and Egypt, a practice which rejects borders, ruptures and distances; Congolese novelist Fiston Mwanza Mujila reads to us from his novel *Tram 83* (2014),[4] 'on trains that have lost all sense of time'; South African writer Hedley Twidle shares his journey of traversing the N2 on foot, South Africa's longest highway;[5] and Ghanaian researcher Kuukuwa Manful talks to us of the absences in architectural histories of the African continent.

> **Menna Agha:** *'Habbouba was one of those generations who were born in the beginning of the 20th century. She was not there to witness the 1899 border that was drawn and charted between Egypt and Sudan, in the middle of the village of Adendan, dividing it between Egypt and Sudan, when the one brother became Egyptian and the other brother became a Sudanese citizen.*

---

4   *Tram 83* (2014) was first published in French by Editions Métailié. The English translation by Roland Glasser was published by Deep Vellum, Dallas, in 2015.

5   'Thirteen Ways of Looking at the N2' in *Firepool: Experiences in an Abnormal World* (2017), published by Kwela Books.

Of course this border was a common practice by the British coloniser and it wasn't activated until later in the '50s when Egypt became a postcolonial state. Still, to Nubians, this is an imaginary line that did not disrupt their daily life. […] I see this maintenance of ties as a rejection by Habbouba of the new borders and ruptures and distances. And also I see this as her rejection of a way of seeing the world in which kinship, relationships, active peopling are not the constitutive power that decides spatial relations.'

Fiston Mwanza Mujila: '*In the beginning was the stone, and the stone prompted ownership, and ownership a rush, and the rush brought an influx of men of diverse appearance who built railroads through the rock, forged a life of palm wine, and devised a system, a mixture of mining and trade.*

'Northern Station. Friday. Around seven or nine in the evening. "Patience, friend, you know full well our trains have lost all sense of time."

'The Northern Station was going to the dogs. It was essentially an unfinished metal structure, gutted by artillery, train tracks and locomotives that called to mind the railroad built by Stanley, cassava fields, cut-rate hotels, greasy spoons, bordellos, pentecostal churches, bakeries and noise engineered by men of all generations and nationalities combined. It was the only place on earth you could hang yourself, defecate, blaspheme, fall into infatuation and thieve without regard to prying eyes. Indeed, an air of connivance hung ever about the place. Jackals don't eat jackals. They pounce on the turkeys and partridges, and devour them. According to the fickle but ever-recurring legend, the seeds of all resistance movements, all wars of liberation, sprouted at the station, between two locomotives. And as if that weren't enough, the same legend claims that the building of the railroad resulted in numerous deaths attributed to tropical diseases, technical blunders, the poor working conditions imposed by the colonial authorities - in short, all the usual cliches.

'Northern Station. Friday. Around seven or nine.'

Hedley Twidle: '*N2. Curled up in that tiny alpha numeric are thousands of kilometres, hundreds of service stations, millions of tonnes of concrete. N2 can mean a London bus route; an intelligence officer in the US Navy; an anti-nuclear song by the Japanese indie group Asian Kung-Fu Generation. But for my purposes it is the longest highway in South Africa, which starts at an unfinished flyover near the docks in Cape Town, follows the eastern seaboard of the country (roughly) for over 2 000 kilometres, then bends north and west below Swaziland, to end at the town of Ermelo in the province of Mpumalanga. Major highways are not thought about much. They are pieces of infrastructure that (if working as intended) efface themselves, receding from view in the mirror. In his hidden history of the UK's motorway system, Joe Moran suggests that this bland corporate terrain of tarmac, underpasses and thermoplastic road markings is 'the most commonly viewed and least contemplated landscape' in Britain: 'The road is almost a separate country, one that remains under-explored not because it is remote and inaccessible but because it is so ubiquitous and familiar.'*

Kuukuwa Manful: '*I was always curious about the histories of African architecture, and was never really satisfied with the kind of histories we were taught. Which made it seem like* *there were the pyramids in Egypt and there was Great Zimbabwe, and, if we're lucky, we'll get Gedi or something in Kenya. But then there were dwellings and indigenous buildings. So I was curious about more than that, because I was never satisfied with that. [...] There's an interesting origin story about the Asante people in Ghana, where they came out of a hole in the ground, I think 9 or 12 people were the first to come out. And each of these people represent one of the great clans of the ethnic group. And one of these clans is the Adansi clan, which is literally the building clan. So to them, god gave the power to build. Why would a foundational story of an ethnic group have something about building and architecture and you would now tell me these people never had architecture? […] It just didn't gel.'*

CONTRIBUTORS

Menna Agha earned a PhD in architecture from the University of Antwerp and is an Assistant Professor at the Azrieli School of Architecture and Urbanism, at Carleton University. Spatial justice is an overarching theme in Agha's work, but this is not a choice born of luxury. She is a third-generation Nubian woman displaced by the Egyptian state as part of the Aswan High Dam project in the 1960s.

Fiston Mwanza Mujila was born in Lubumbashi, Democratic Republic of the Congo, in 1981, and writes poetry, prose and theatre. Mujila lives in Graz, where he teaches African literature at Universität Graz and works with musicians in Austria on various projects. His first novel *Tram 83* was longlisted for the Man Booker International Prize and the Prix du Monde, and was awarded the Etisalat Prize for Literature and the Internationaler Literaturpreis from Der Haus der Kulturen der Welt.

Hedley Twidle is a writer, teacher and researcher based at the University of Cape Town. His essay collection, *Firepool: Experiences in an Abnormal World,* was published by Kwela Books in 2017. *Experiments with Truth,* a study of narrative non-fiction and the South African transition, appeared in the African Articulation series from James Currey in 2019.

Kuukuwa Manful is a PhD candidate at SOAS. She curates Adansisem, an architecture collective that researches and documents Ghanaian architecture theory, research and practice and has recently been awarded a British Library Endangered Archives Grant which she will use to digitise an architectural archive in Accra. Kuukuwa's research project examines African nation-building and notions of citizenship through the architecture of West African secondary schools constructed by states between 1945 and 1965.

EPISODE 4:

'What remains of the political and cultural ideas that imagined the African continent as the "utopia of a borderless world"?'

In episode four, Ghanaian architect and scholar Kuukuwa Manful reflects on the place of minor histories in deepening our understanding of Pan-Africanism; Nigerian writer Emmanuel Iduma shares an excerpt from *A Stranger's Pose* (2018),[6] and his search of an atlas of a borderless world; and Egyptian sociologist Sara Salem unravels the workings of coloniality and capital from the vantage point of the sky in a reading from *Fractured Flights* (2020).[7]

6   *A Stranger's Pose* (2018) is published by Cassava Republic Press.

7   Fractured Flights (2020) is published in the Ghost Publication Series and is available at Race, Space & Architecture: https://racespacearchitecture.org/sara-salem.html.

Kuukuwa Manful: *'What really thrills me are those random chance, little notes, these passing mentions of a thing that's not even the main subject of a document. Something in the background of a photo. Or just unfiltered and often unofficial accounts of people and spaces […] I don't know an archive that I will refuse to enter. […] I identify two kinds of ideas of utopia (among Pan-Africanists) - and utopia in the sense of these perfect, imagined communities, nations or spaces where everything was good and happy. So there's these kind of two ways in which it comes up. There's the passed utopia, African utopia, where people either lived really simple lives, content and happy. But also there were these grand kings who these people happily served. This is a very strong idea of utopia in this African context […] well now has passed, but I sometimes call it a future of the past idea of utopia, which is strong in people like Nkrumah and Nyerere where they are thinking of these modern African nations, which are as modern as anywhere in the world but sort of have some innate true African values. So for Nyerere - this comes in his villagisation project. […] Nkrumah is not quite the same, he doesn't have as much nostalgia for that kind of life. […] But he has an imagined idea of what things were like before colonisation, and what things could have been before colonisation. And he's thinking of a modern Ghana where he can almost remake society according to what he thinks people should be doing. So these are the two, the future of the past strand, and a romantic view of the past strand.'*

Emmanuel Iduma: *'Awake or in a dream, face and images and gestures from my travels return to me in great detail. Sometimes it is the wind, sputtering against the window of the car I am in. Or an underfed dog, rummaging through rubbish for a glinting bone. Or a boat unmanned in the middle of a river, seen from afar.*

'I began to exchange emails with a relative who requested anonymity. My first email was a list of all the towns I had slept in during my travels, at least for a night. Towns in which I turned in my sleep unsure of where I was, whether I was bathed in sweat or in tears, or if I lay beside a lover or a travel companion. I hoped, I wrote, that the cities appeared untethered to their countries - an atlas of a borderless world. In the first response I received, I was urged to recount stories of strange sightings, emotions and encounters, remembered or imagined. 'Take me with you on your journeys, my relative replied. Let me go in your place.'

Sara Salem: *'Being part of an Egyptian-Dutch family living in Zambia meant that movement increasingly became part of our lives. This was made possible by both the passport privilege that came with having a Dutch mother, as well as the eventual class privilege that allowed for costly visa and related travel costs for all of us. Looking back, I realise that I understood Zambia and Egypt to be part of one geographical imaginary. My childhood was full of connections between Cairo and Lusaka. I remember Cairo Road, a central road connecting various parts of Lusaka. Even more lucid that these fragmented memories, however, was my realisation of how similar Lusaka and Cairo were, despite the distance between them. I remember being struck, after spending 16 years of my life in Zambia, by how familiar Cairo felt. Not only because of my father or his family, or because of stories I had heard, but because of how similar it was to Lusaka in terms of space. How to explain similar buildings, squares, roads and statues? British colonialism was one answer, and indeed both countries had been British colonies for decades. Another answer was decolonisation, which produced street names that were similar in both cities, as well as familiar motifs of flags, national heroes and prominent figures such as Kenneth Kaunda and Gamal Abdel Nasser. 'Flying between these spaces - leaving one home to visit another - created a material connection between these two spaces as well.*

[…]'But this is also a story of empire. In these maps we see the coloniality of space, in the parcelling out of airspace. The question of who can move and how has always been a question of power. When we think of railways and how they were built across Africa, we see that they were carefully built on the edges of the continent. Built for one purpose: the extraction of resources. There's something about the materiality of maps, whether they are maps of flight spaces or railways, and the visual power of seeing them, that underlies how power is etched into space. We see the railway lines strong around the edges and then fading into the centre of the continent, and how this was linked to extractivism and colonial capitalism. Air space is different; it is abstract, invisible. We know there are constantly planes in the sky, but we don't see them and usually don't hear them. And so flight paths remain somewhat hidden from view; we might know that there aren't many on top of the African continent simply because of our own experiences trying to fly from one place to another.'

CONTRIBUTORS

Kuukuwa Manful is a PhD candidate at SOAS. She curates Adansisem, an architecture collective that researches and documents Ghanaian architecture theory, research and practice and has recently been awarded a British Library Endangered Archives Grant which she will use to digitise an architectural archive in Accra. Kuukuwa's research project examines African nation-building and notions of citizenship through the architecture of West African secondary schools constructed by states between 1945 and 1965.

Emmanuel Iduma is the author of *A Stranger's Pose* (2018), a travel book, and *The Sound of Things to Come* (2016), a novel. His stories and essays have been published widely, including in *Best American Travel Writing 2020*, *Aperture*, *The Millions*, *Art in America*, the *New York Review of Books* and *Artforum*. In 2017 he was awarded an Arts Writing Grant from the Creative Capital/Andy Warhol Foundation for his essays on Nigerian artists. *A Stranger's Pose* (2018) was long-listed for the Ondaatje Prize in 2019.

Sara Salem is an Assistant Professor in Sociology at the London School of Economics. Her research interests include political sociology, postcolonial studies, Marxist theory, and global histories of empire. She has recently published articles on Angela Davis in Egypt; on Frantz Fanon and Egypt's postcolonial state in *Interventions* and her recent book is titled *Anti-Colonial Afterlives in Egypt: The Politics of Hegemony* (2020).

In episode five, Sudanese writer Jamal Mahjoub reads to us from 'Rumble in the Nile',[8] which chronicles the early years of promise heralded by Jaafar Nimeiry's ascent to power in Sudan in 1969, while Egyptian documentary filmmaker Jihan el-Tahri questions why we date African independence to Ghana in 1957 as opposed to the Egyptian revolution of 1952.

Jamal Mahjoub: *'When Jaafar Nimeiri first came to power he seemed invincible. We watched him, young and dynamic, on our old black-and-white Hitachi television, standing up in an open car, riding on the roof of a train, waving an ebony staff, clasping his hands together in fellowship. A man in constant motion. North, south, east, west. He was everywhere and nowhere at the same time. Women ululated, men sang and everyone cheered. He was forever opening new development projects: irrigation schemes, engineering colleges, housing complexes. We saw him leaping over bulls that were laid down in the sand before him, their throats slit in sacrifice.[…]*

'Behind the popular rhetoric, however, so much of what we wanted to believe turned out to be part of an elaborate fairytale. Did we hear what we wanted to hear? What began as an adventure, a bold attempt to unite the nation and work towards the greater good of all, ended in pathetic failure. The broad scale of the vision was whittled down to war and starvation, to persecution, bitter recrimination, paranoia, cruelty, sectarianism and superstition.

The adventure was short-lived, but still, those early years remain a reminder of what might have been.'

Jihan El-Tahri: *'Not dating African independence to 1952 [in Egypt] undercuts the whole of Africa. Basically it means we were not part of Bandung, we were not part of the Non Aligned Movement, because independences happened post that era. How did we get there then? I think the logical questions and the implications of denying Egypt but also the north in general this separation harms us. […]*

'Nkrumah and Nasser were very close. Nkrumah attending the Bandung conference in 1955 was on the request of Nasser. So I think a lot has shifted since the actual days of independence, and the immediate post-indepednence where there was still this collective vision. Up until the creation of what then used to be the OAU, the idea of the Organisation for African Unity, was Nasser, Nkrumah and Sekou Toure with the help and the space of Haile Selassie. This really was east, west, Francophone, Anglophone, north; it was the idea that we all come together because we have this common history. So not dating independence to 1952 I think undercuts the whole of Africa.[…]

'Somehow as Africans we have accepted that there's something called sub-Sahara. Then there's this empty thing called the Sahara. And then there's the North which is another ball game. But, by accepting that the Sahara is an empty lot, we're denying the most profound and most important elements of our culture.'

<hr>

8   This is an excerpt from 'Rumble in the Nile', which was first published in the June 2015 *Chimurenga Chronic* (https://chimurengachronic.co.za/rumble-in-the-nile/), and later in *A Line in the River* (2018) published by Bloomsbury.

CONTRIBUTORS

Jamal Mahjoub is a Sudanese British writer and author of the memoir, *A Line in the River: Khartoum, City of Memory* (2018). He has published eight novels under his own name which cover subjects as diverse as Sudan's history and strife, heliocentricity and explorations of identity. In 2012, Mahjoub began writing a series of crime fiction novels under the pseudonym Parker Bilal. He has won the Prix de l'astrolabe in France, the NH Mario Vargas LLosa award in Spain, and the *Guardian* African Short Story prize.

Jihan El-Tahri is an Egyptian-born writer, director and producer of documentary films. Her films include the Emmy-nominated *House of Saud*, *The Price of Aid* and *Cuba: An African Odyssey*.

EPISODE 6:
'What do lines of flight reveal
of our shared planetary futures?'

In episode six, Zimbabwean architectural designer and researcher Thandi Loewenson digs through filmic and sonic archives and the speculative histories of 'Black flight'; South African architect and scholar, Ilze Wolff, travels from Cape Town to Nagasaki in search of health, care and black peace on earth;[9] and composer Victor Gama speaks to us about the design of new instruments, and tracing the line from Thomas More's *Utopia* to apartheid South Africa's nuclear programme in the unfinished work of Angolan anthropologist Augusto Zita.

Thandi Loewenson: 'To me, [A Tribe Called Quest's] Space Program is a similarly seismic moment in Black radical cultural production. Space here refers to the universe. That untapped pool of asteroid resources, planets to colonise and in which, we are told, a Space Force orbits to provide "superiority" and "command" over this dominion. By implication, this is for some atmospherically over others. It is also the expanse of unknown quantity and delineation in which we find our currently embattled and emplagued planet, largely comprising a dark matter and dark energy of which we know very little. At the end of verse 2, when Q-Tip raps, Imagine if this shit was really talkin' about space, dude / Imagine if this shit was really talkin' about space, dude / Imagine if this shit was really talkin' about space, dude / if you haven't got it by now. […] The Space Program refers to the impossibility of some to even survive in the face of a system in which privatisation and profit reign over production and place, with the associated exploitative dehumanisation of black people this entails.

'Moved you out your neighbourhood, did they find you a home? / Nah cypher, probably no place to / We are presented with a future which looks to the galaxy for more resources whilst talking of sustainability of an extractive way of life, and indeed the extraction of black life. In the last single of a thirty year repertoire of Black sound and 'sonic refusal', to use the terms of the scholar DJ Lynnée Denise, A Tribe Called Quest are clear. They call on us to build. They call on us to make, make, make / make something happen, to make life otherwise, and they show that the scale of the creative

---

9   This is an excerpt from the essay, 'Black Peace on Earth' by Ilze Wolff and Anonymous, which was published in October 2020 as part of Confinement, a project by e-flux Architecture and gta exhibitions, and is available at: https://www.e-flux.com/architecture/confinement/352558/black-peace-on-earth/.

project required for this is none other than that of taking
flight. Of Black flight.'

Ilze Wolff: 'In an early poem called "My Home", Bessie Head
invites us into her home. She writes: "Come and see my home.
It is anyplace where nobody gives orders." It is clearly an
invitation, but she asks that anyone who accepts the invitation
should take a certain responsibility. She asks: "Tread softly—
the walls breathe peace … Deep, dark, black peace and the wind
don't blow."

*'One could imagine that at the time that she wrote
this - the early 1960s - John Coltrane heard her voice from
Serowe, all the way in New York, where he was composing music
like "Alabama" and* A Love Supreme. *In 1966, the John Coltrane
Quartet toured Japan, 20-odd years after the devastating atomic
bomb attacks in Hiroshima and Nagasaki. In Nagasaki, he opened
their performance with "Peace on Earth". It is a performance
considered by many who attended the concert, or who heard
about the performance, as a moment of collective healing. I
think of this story and it makes me remember, as a child, the
sensation of the breath of a beloved parent gently blowing
on a wound that was just inflicted by accident while playing.
I remember, the acknowledgement and care through the act of
blowing is the soothing balm, rather than the application of
the salve or even the administering of the bandage.'*

Victor Gama: *'The Toha is connected to the nest of sociable
weaver birds that exist in the Namib desert, in the south of
Kunene as well, throughout the Namib in Namibia and in the
Kalahari desert. Where you see bundles of nests put together,
one whole bundle can be many, many nests. Can house many
families of weaver birds. They live in a kind of social
community of birds. And it is usually hanging from trees,
or from electrical poles or telephone poles supported by
the pole itself or the trunk of the tree. So it's built
around the trunk or the pole, wherever they can find support.
It's a whole ecosystem. At the same time it's an incredible
sound installation, because the sound of it, of many birds
together, changes throughout the day. The early morning they
all leave to go and look for food; during the day they are busy
reconstructing the nests; at night there are different sounds
because they are coming back - there are lots of things going
on. There are even little snakes that prey on the nests. So
it is a whole ecosystem with a whole sound atmosphere there.*

*'So I was very taken by that, but the other thing
that impacted me was when I started seeing many of these
nests empty in the south of Angola at the border of Namibia,
during the conflict years. Especially during the '80s when
South Africa had invaded the south of Angola and there were
lots of bombings - carpet bombings in the villages and cities
in the south of Angola, especially in Kunene and Kuvango.
So I realised that nature is one of the first to take flight when
there is a conflict, and when there is this level of violence.'*

CONTRIBUTORS

Thandi Loewenson is an architectural designer and researcher currently based at the Royal College of Arts in London. She is also a visiting professor at University of Aarhus, and co-founder of the architectural collective Break Line. She operates through design, fiction and performance to interrogate our perceived and lived realms and to speculate on the possible worlds in our midst.

Ilze Wolff is a partner of Wolff Architects and a co-founder of Open House Architecture, a transdisciplinary research practice. She has taught and lectured internationally including in Switzerland, Germany, Italy, USA, Canada, Japan and India and continues to do so. The work of the practice has also been included at various international exhibitions, including, the Venice Architecture Biennale, Shenzhen Biennale of Architecture and Urbanism, Louisiana Museum of Modern Art, the Chicago Architectural Biennale, the São Paulo Biennale and the South American Architecture Biennale.

Victor Gama was born in Angola and currently lives between Luanda, Lisbon and Bogota. His work of musical composition intersects areas as diverse as music, image, field recording, audio video installation and the design of contemporary musical instruments. Gama has been commissioned work by ensembles and institutions such as the Chicago Symphony Orchestra, the Kronos Performing Arts Association, the National Museums of Scotland, the Tenement Museum in New York, Prince Claus Fonds, the Amsterdam Fonds for the Arts, the Royal Opera House of London and the Kennedy Center in Washington DC.

EPISODE 7:
'How might the global Swahili worlds reframe our thinking of connections across waters?'

In episode seven, Kenyan novelist Yvonne Adhiambo Owuor discusses the deep histories of the Swahili seas and the research that led to her novel *Dragonfly Sea* (2019);[10] Zanzibari architectural student, Halima Ali reads the work of Haji Gora Haji, a Zanzibari poet and seafarer who could navigate from Zanzibar to Yemen through the recitation of poem-maps;[11] and visual artist Meghna Singh draws us into the invisible world of mobile populations immersed in new forms of economic servitude at sea at the docks in Cape Town.

> **Yvonne Adhiambo Owour:** 'To cross the vast ocean to their south, water-chasing dragonflies with forebears in Northern India had hitched a ride on a sedate "in-between seasons" morning wind, one of the monsoon's introits, the matlai. One day in 1992, four generations later, under dark-purplish-blue clouds, these fleeting beings settled on the mangrove-fringed southwest coast of a little girl's island. The matlai conspired with a shimmering full moon to charge the island, its fishermen, prophets, traders, seamen, seawomen, healers, shipbuilders, dreamers, tailors, madmen, teachers, mothers, and fathers with a fretfulness that mirrored the slow-churning turquoise sea.
>
> 'Dusk stalked the Lamu Archipelago's largest and

---

10   *Dragonfly Sea* (2019) is published by Knopf Press.

11   Haji Gora Haji (1933-2021) poem read by Halima Ali is an excerpt cited by Yvonne Adhiambo Owuor in 'In Search of Poem-Maps of the Swahili Seas' (2018). It is an excerpt from Collection of Haji Gora Haji, translated by Zein Abubakar and Dr Mshai Mwangola.

sullenest island, trudging from Siyu on the north coast, upending Kizingitini's fishing fleets before swooping southwest to brood over a Pate Town that was already smouldering in the malaise of unrequited yearnings. Bruised by endless deeds of guile, siege, war, and seduction, like the island that contained it, Pate Town marked melancholic time. A leaden sky poured dull-red light over a crowd of petulant ghosts, dormant feuds, forfeited glories, invisible roads, and congealing millennia-old conspiracies. Weaker light leached into ancient crevices, tombs, and ruins, and signaled to a people who were willing to cohabit with tragedy, trusting that time transformed even cataclysms into echoes.'

Halima Ali reads *Bahari Usichungue (Don't Delve into the Sea)* by Haji Gora Haji (1933-2021):

Ukichunguwa bahari   *Kusafiri huwafiki*
Inamengi yalosiri   *Kuona ukidiriki*
Hata ukiwa hodari   *Hofu itakumiliki*

Bahari ina mawimbi   *Milele hayaondoki*
Kadhalika na vitimbi   *Vilo havidhihiriki*
Kama si rangi na vumbi   *ingekuwa hakwendeki*

Mengi yasoidadika   *Na makubwa masamaki*
Pindi ukisadifika   *Uwonapo hujishiki*
Lazima hutetemeka   *Na mno kutaharuki*

Ikiwa umo chomboni   *Jifanye hubabaiki*
Kaa utuliye ndani   *We la nje hutaki*
Ukitazama majini   *Hapa na hapo hufiki*

Bahari usichonguwe   *Utajitia wahaka*
Omba mola akuvuwe   *Ufike unapotaka*

Be wary before the ocean   *It seduces you into travel*
It remains cryptic   *When you get comfortable*
However intrepid you are   *Be careful*

The sea contains waves   *Ceaseless waves*
Other mysteries and riddles   *Not evident to untrained eyes*
Were it not for the colour and dust   *You would not leave*
Unaccountable things there are   *And giant fish*
When it approaches   *Too great to understand*
You must tremble   *With a sense of urgency*

When you are in the vessel   *Fake fearlessness*
Concentrate on your confines   *Ignore what's beyond your ken*
For should you glimpse the djinns   *There and then your journey ends*

Don't delve too deeply into the sea   *You will worry*
Beseech God's help   *To reach your destination*

Meghna Singh: *'There were nine Indian seafarers on a ship which had been arrested indefinitely. They were on their way to Dubai from Nigeria, and when they came to Cape Town the authorities arrested them, arrested the ship, the vessel. The guys decided not to fly back home, even though they could, because they would not have been paid. So they decided to remain in the vessel until it could move again. And that took a year.*

> […] *'So their story was that their company was located in Dubai. It was registered in Panama. And there was a loan from Singapore which the company had defaulted on. The workers were from India. So they got stuck in Cape Town.*

> […] *'Why is a population, a subaltern population, so used to waiting?'*

CONTRIBUTORS

Yvonne Adhiambo Owuor was born in Nairobi, Kenya. The Kenya-based literary magazine *Kwani?* published her short story, 'The Weight of Whispers', which earned her the Caine Prize for African Writing in 2003. Owuor's fragmented, poetic and emotionally charged style continued with her highly acclaimed debut novel, *Dust* (2014). The book is a recounting of a story of Kenya's hidden pasts through the odyssey of a disrupted family from the north of Kenya. In 2015, the book was shortlisted for the Folio Prize. Several translations are available. Her second novel, *The Dragonfly Sea* (2019), is a coming-of-age story that explores aspects of East African sea imagination in a time of China's return to its milieu.

Halima Ali is a Zanzibari architect, pursuing a Master's degree in architecture at the Architectural Association in London.

Meghna Singh is a visual artist and a researcher with a doctoral degree in visual anthropology focusing on the theme of migration from the University of Cape Town, South Africa. Working with mediums of video and installation, blurring boundaries between documentary and fiction, she creates immersive environments highlighting issues of 'humanism'.

EPISODE 8:
'How might we trace the afterlives of the
trans-Saharan trade routes of the 8th century?'

In episode 8, the last in the series, Moroccan writer and translator Omar Berrada excavates the deep histories of his once-enslaved great, great grandmother; Nigerian scholar Moshood Mahmood Jimba retraces the journey from Ilorin to Timbuktu that inspired him to establish a manuscript archival research group in Nigeria; Moroccan musician Amino Belyamani speaks to us of the healing purposes of Gnawa music in Morocco and speculates on the deep relationship to Ewe music from Ghana. Omar Berrada extends special thanks to M'barek Bouhchichi, Hatim Belyamani and NourbeSe Philip.

> **Omar Berrada:** *'In Zagora, an oasis town in the southeast of Morocco, there is a painted sign that says, "Tombouctou 52 jours - Timbuktu 52 days".*
>
> *'It's like a very old-fashioned road sign. A cliché of turbans and camels, harking back to an era when distance was measured by time, and camels were indispensable travel companions.*
>
> *'The road sign maintains a vision of Black Africa as a*

*separate, faraway place. Far even from some of its parts. But
we know that that distance has been crossed countless times
over many centuries. Zagora, as we know it, is partly made out
of Timbuktu, and Timbuktu, as we know it, is partly made out
of Zagora.*

*'The road sign is a tourist attraction at the desert's
edge. A two-dimensional tool of visual entertainment. It
flattens a rich history. It also neutralizes politics, by
concealing what it actually refers to. In 1591, Sultan Ahmed
Al Mansur's armies left Zagora to go conquer the Songhai.
Which led to the fall of an empire, the exploitation of its
resources, and the enslavement of many.*

'Travel is never innocent.'

Moshood Mahmood Jimba: *'History has it that Timbuktu was
the greatest cultural capital and the biggest centre of
intellectual activities in the whole of Bilad al-Sudan. […]
Historians hold divergent views on the origin of the town.
The most popular is attributed to AbdulRahman al-Sa'dy in his
book Tarikh al-Sudan (1655). According to him, it was founded
in the fifth century of the Hijrah. Some historians argue that
Timbuktu was the name of a black female slave owned by the
Tuareg who used to stay here during the winter. Others are
of the opinion that the Tuareg built a store there for their
goods and later on traders and Muslim scholars from Walata
settled and the town rapidly expanded. […] Perhaps the most
glaring of the glories were those public libraries which were
equipped with the most expensive books in the field of Arabic
and Islamic studies, medicine and philosophy. The libraries
were owned by the scholars of the town who kept their doors
open to students.'*[12]

*[…] 'So from that point my interests in manuscripts
started. And on my way back to Nigeria, I made it a point of
duty that I would replicate what I saw in Timbuktu. Almost
every house in Illorin, my town, every house, it is an ancient
Islamic city, so every house has its own pool of manuscripts
on various aspects of Islamic sciences. So when I returned,
we established the Ilorin history and culture bureau with two
other colleagues. We started collecting manuscripts. And by
the grace of god, I formed the Illorin manuscript group 10
years ago.'*

Amino Belyamani: *'The main instrument which is played by the
lead - the mu'allim, or master - is called the gimbri or
sinter. It has other names, but gimbri or sintir are the most
common names. And it has three strings, it sounds like a bass,
and it has camel skin. So instead of just being a resonating
body […] they hit the skin with the hands too. So it is
percussive and a string instrument. While they are playing the
string, at each stroke there is a hit on the drum head of the
skin of the instrument, which gives it a bass thump.*

*[…]'Gnawa is a healing music. People join these rituals
called lila's, which means night in Arabic. They play these
pieces in an order. There is a repertoire where every set of
songs is part of a colour, which is associated with a spirit
which has its own incense. It is a long and involved night of
different symbolic gestures. […] Essentially the premise is
that you come to these lila's because you have a pain, either*

<hr>

12   Excerpt from Moshood Mahmood M. Jimba's book, *From Ilorin to Timbuktu: Journey Across West
Africa in Search of the African Past* (2010) published by The Nigerian Centre for Arabic Research.

physical or emotional, because you lost a loved one or you miss those who have travelled far away, any kind of pain. That's the reason why you're there. And the master musician will help facilitate the negotiation with the sprits. Its not about exorcism [...] it's all about compromise. It's about the mu'allim speaking with the spirits. [...] It's a conversation with the spirit that is possessing you, and having the spirit at peace. In the gnawa world, they believe that everyone has spirit in them, you have to be at peace with it.'

CONTRIBUTORS

Omar Berrada is the director and co-founder of Dar al-Ma'mûn, a library and centre for artists' residencies that opened in Marrakech in 2010. His work as a curator, writer, editor and translator focuses on the politics of translation and the transmission of knowledge between generations. One of his latest projects is the posthumous publication of the film-maker Ahmed Bouanani's history of Moroccan cinema, *La Septième Porte* (Kulte Editions 2020); other books he has edited or co-edited include the *Album-Cinémathèque de Tanger*, a survey of film in Tangier, and *The Africans* (2016) which deals with questions of race and migration in Morocco.

Moshood Mahmood Jimba was born in 1963 to a Muslim family in the city of Ilorin in North Central Nigeria. In 2012, after six years at Kogi State University, where he headed the department of Arabic and Islamic Studies, he moved to Ilorin to teach at the Kwara State University, where he is currently the Director of the Centre for Ilorin Manuscript and Culture. Jimba specialises in Arabic language and Arabic literary criticism and Arabic-English-Yoruba translation.

Amino Belyamani was born and raised in Casablanca, Morocco, and began playing the piano by the age of six. He is a founding mmber of AXIS TRIO and DAWN OF MIDI wherein he composes, performs, and records original music. Amino's music reflects the diversity of his interests, which usually translates into a blend of complex African rhythms, Arabic melodies, western classical music and jazz. Amino also established Moroccantapes.com, an online archive where you can listen and download Moroccan cassette tapes from the '70s and '80s.

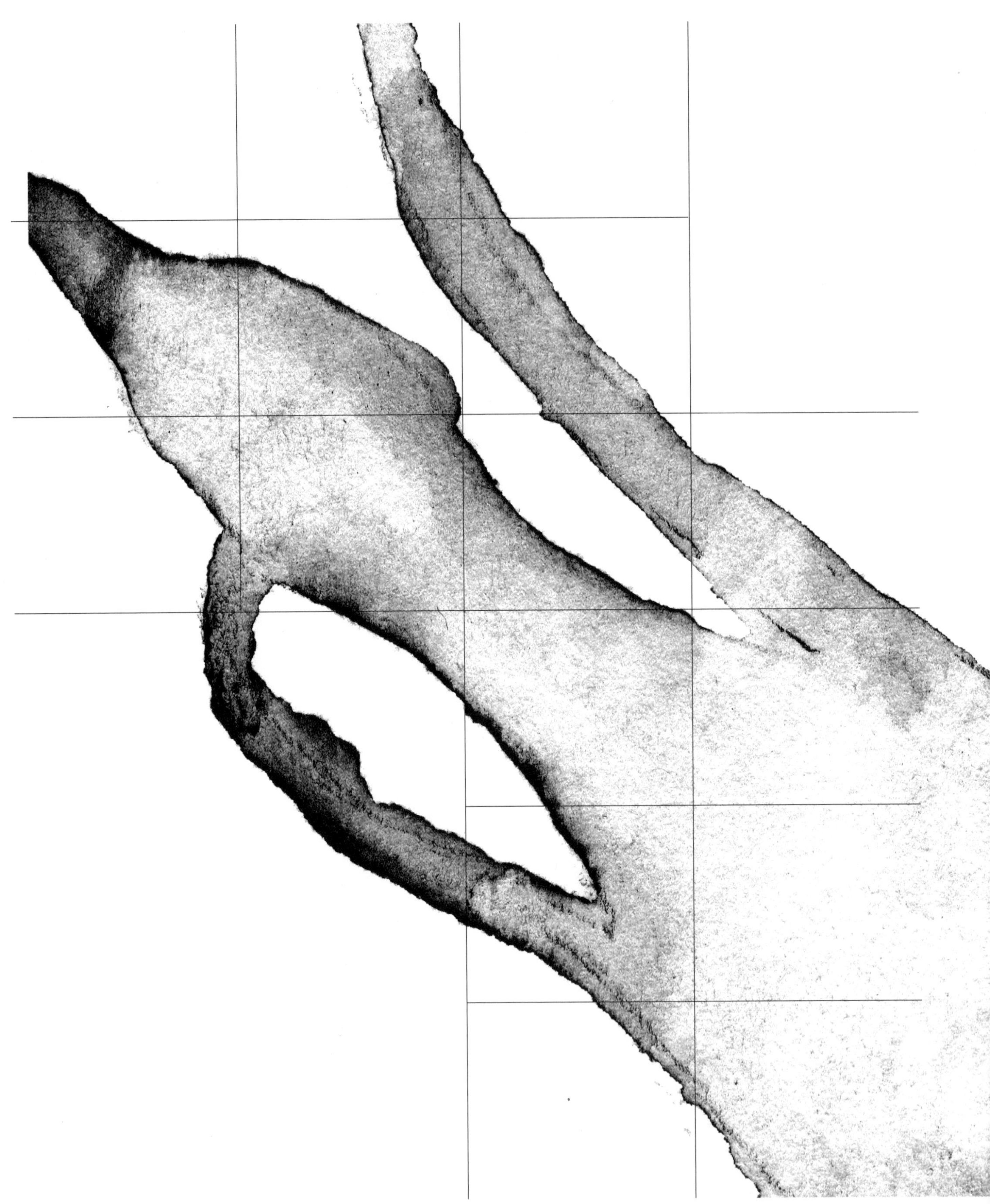

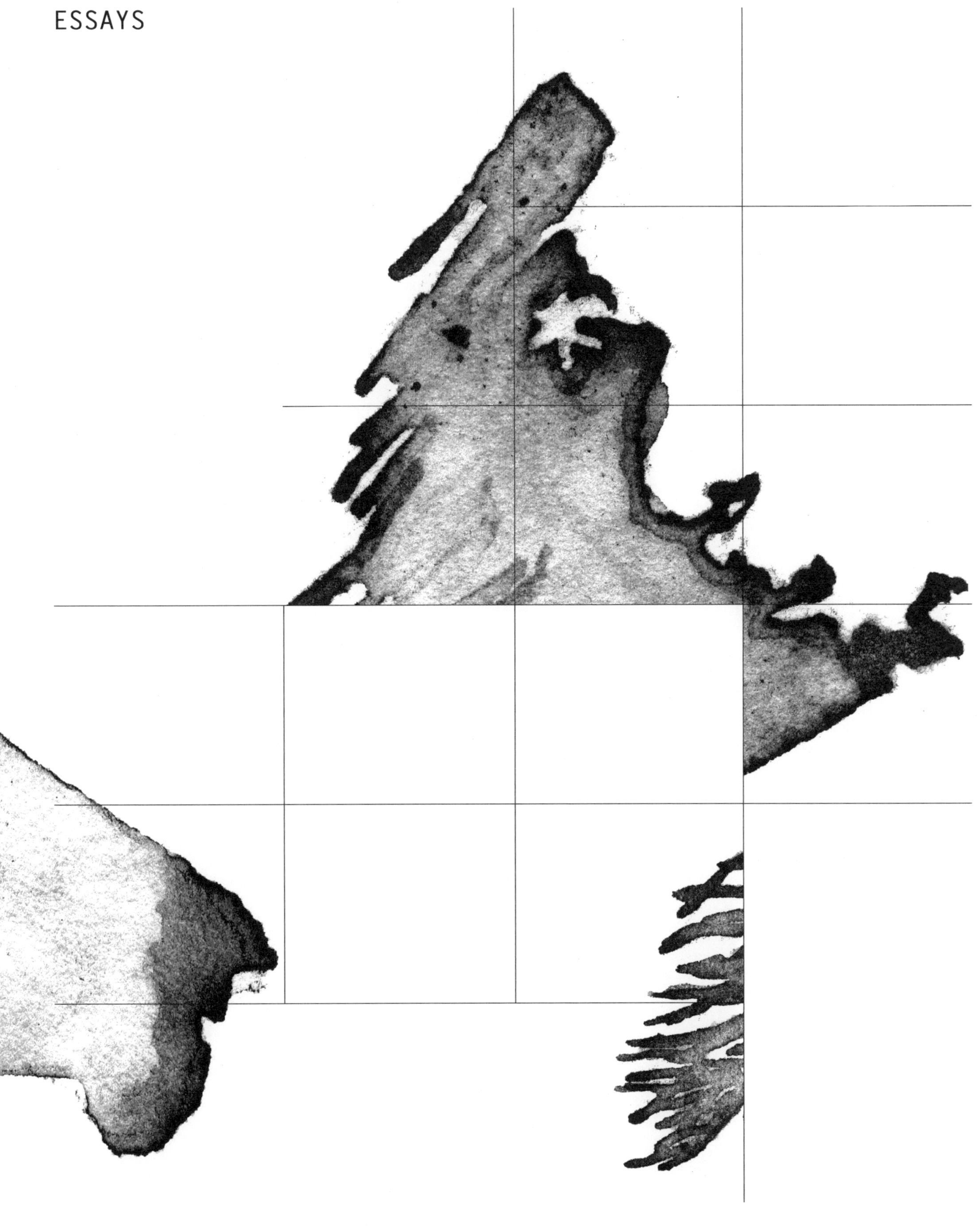

As with the *Archive of Forgetfulness* as a whole, these essays defy the boundaries and categories of clear disciplinary markers. The five contributions gathered here are essays in the sense of opening up and expanding many of the key ideas and thinking in the wider project around archives, memory and borders. Yet, they are also importantly creative works and provocations in their own right, visual essays as much as textual pieces. They collectively question the framing around archives, mobility and infrastructure, drawing out moments of history and time that should not be overlooked and point to methodological and epistemic possibilities around remembering, unearthing and acknowledging radical archival practices and acts of resistance.

'Travessia: Impressões de Viagem' by Maria Gabriela Carrilho Aragão adopts photography and text to recount the author's visit to Ibo Island, Mozambique, in 2001. While this island had been a site of research previously, this particular visit was with her great-aunt to resolve a family matter. The carefully recorded notes are assembled into a loose travelogue, with field notes and personal experiences: they speak to a deeply emotive experience of moving through time and space. The active remembering of a moment of tranquillity offers a sense of peace against the current violence and upheaval which mar the island and wider region. Aragão provokes us to think through the relationship between family archives and architectural histories, acts of remembering in the face of personal and collective loss, and memory as a deeply felt emotion.

In a different approach and engagement with memory, Nkgopoleng Moloi's essay, 'Gestures of Gratitude: Catharina "Groote Catrijn" van Paliacatta', puts forward a provocation and methodology of gratitude as central to how we might engage with the history of those often erased from official archives. As an act of gratitude, her essay excavates the Cape archives for the histories of a formerly enslaved woman, 'Groote Catrijn'. Moloi describes first 'meeting' Groote Catrijn in the Western Cape Archives and Records, in Cape Town, and attempting to follow the traces and footsteps of her history from the Iziko Slave Lodge, a national museum, to the Prestwich Memorial, an ossuary for a slave burial site, to Gallows Hill and the Museum van de Caab in Franschhoek. Her essay draws out the haunting and ever-present relationship to slavery in the Cape and suggests, in return, a series of gestures as a way to remember, recollect and recognise these often forgotten lives. Here memory and remembering of deep pasts is presented as a methodology against forgetfulness, in acknowledgement of difficult and often silenced histories.

With Margarida Waco we travel to Bagamayo in Tanzania through her essay 'Counterpoints: Extraction, Race and Global Capitalism'. Waco's writing draws out generations of extractive infrastructures and racial violence, from the history of Bagamayo as a slave-trading outpost in the 19th century, to a German colonial city, and a future planned Special Economic Zone. Yet, despite these destructive and repeated impositions of violence, Waco's essay speaks to the population of 12 000 residents who continue to draw on memories and possibilities of Julius Nyerere's socialist philosophy of Ujamaa, as the grounds for ongoing resistance. Waco's essay reminds us of the long histories of extractive colonialism that continue into the neo-colonial present, and simultaneously points to the importance of recognising ways of responding, and working against violent structures, often less visible and unnoticed. Here, too, memory is understood as an active and political tool of resistance.

Wanjeri Gakuru's essay offers a photographic and textual reflection of what she terms 'Bicycle Stories'. Framed by the confinements of Covid-19 and late-night cycling in Nairobi, Gakuru recalls a 2014 assignment to photograph 'unexpected Kenya', where she speaks to five women cyclists in the port city of Kisumu. Cycling is often stigmatised, and looked down on, yet it offers a sense of freedom and immense mobility to many women. The essay asks us to think through the material and spatial worlds of the bicycle, and how these are often entangled with socio-political contexts and wider narratives. As Gakuru writes, the cyclist women are 'always already embodying and performing the power to refuse'.

Rania Atef similarly highlights the importance of gendered frameworks when reading and engaging with cities, spaces and the art world more generally. Atef's art work and essay foreground the mother-artist, asking the provocative question as the title, 'Is there a bird that stops flying?' Her contribution provokes the importance of mobility and movement for artists, and what this means for those who may not be as mobile any longer, due to life changes, speaking to the economics of motherhood and feminised care-work as overlooked and often unacknowledged.

As a collection, these essays draw out and highlight questions of gender, mobility and extraction in creative practice and the wider world. Collectively, they suggest that the 'failure of memory' is always present, whether considering deep histories of slavery, familial pasts or gendered presents. The foregrounding of moments of relief, despite difficulties, draws out and expands questions that frame the *Archive of Forgetfulness*. They offer ways to think *otherwise*, feel the emotional weight of histories, remember acts of resistance and practice gestures of gratitude and care.

Maria Gabriela Carrilho Aragão

*In loving memory of my great-aunt Tia Fato,
travel companion, talisman (Fátima Mamudo)*

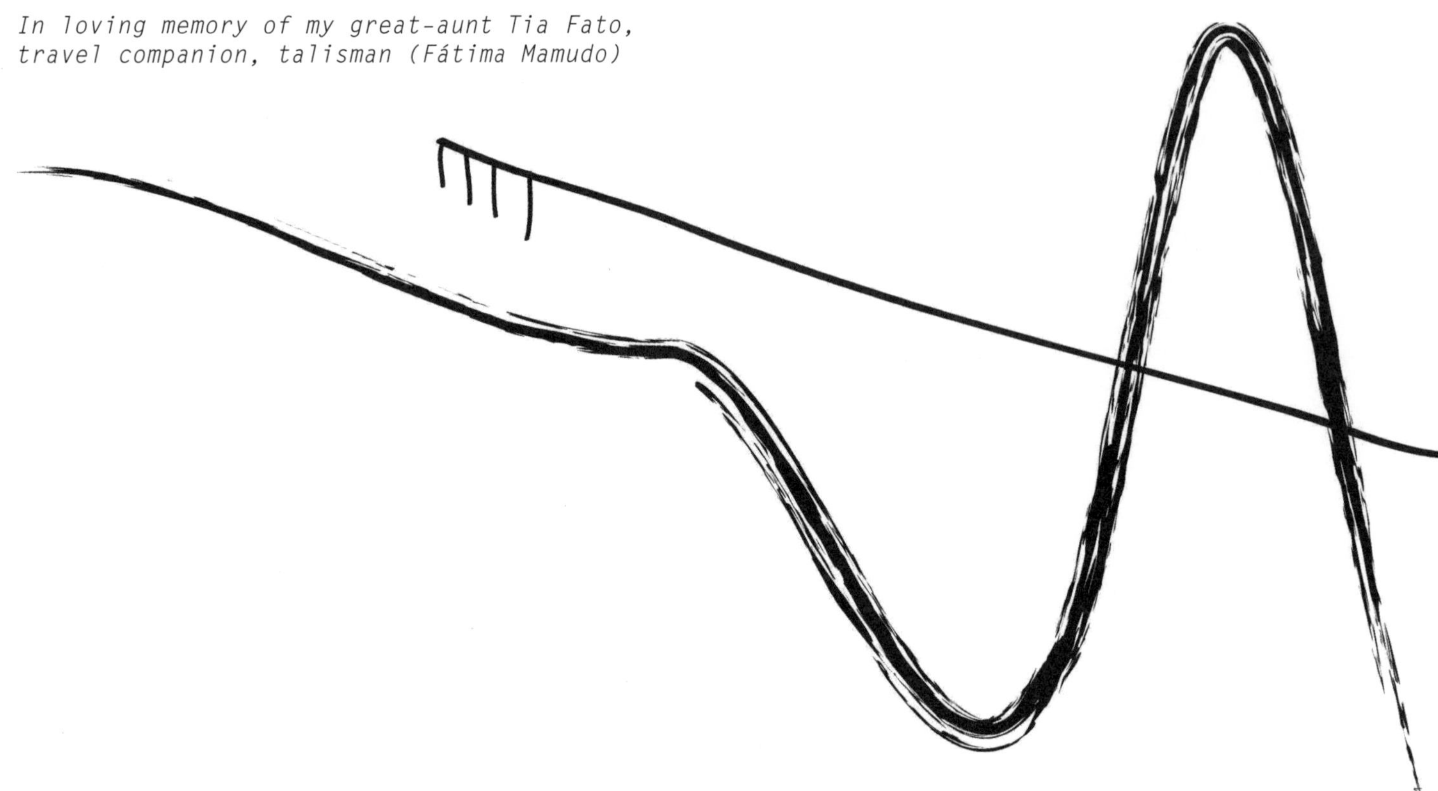

PRÓLOGO

Passaram-se quase 20 anos desde que fui pela primeira vez à Ilha do Ibo
para a estudar e visitar. Embora eu já não estudasse na Universidade
Eduardo Mondlane - Faculdade de Arquitectura e Planeamento Físico (UEM-
FAPF) na altura, a Faculdade generosamente aceitou que eu integrasse
a equipa de pesquisa do seu projecto de registo histórico do conjunto
edificado da ilha - em particular, da sua arquitectura doméstica -
posteriormente publicado como *Ibo: A Casa e o Tempo* (Júlio Carrilho,
Universidade Eduardo Mondlane - FAFP, Maputo, 2005).[13]

Na época, fiz duas viagens consecutivas: a primeira, em Dezembro
de 2001 como assistente de pesquisa, e a segunda, uns meros dois meses
depois, para resolver um assunto de família com a minha tia-avó.

É esta segunda viagem que registo nestas páginas, um diário
informal compilado por meio de fotos analógicas digitalizadas e
impressões de viagem anotadas de memória.

Na época, não me ocorreu que algures no futuro, tornar-se-ia
demasiado perigoso tomar novamente a rota Tandanhangue - Ilha do Ibo,
devido à actual situação de insegurança na região, resultante das
acções terroristas que se têm agravado desde 2017.

Eu simplesmente assumi que o Ibo seria eterno, porque os
corpos ancestrais estão no cemitério, as antigas casas de família
ainda lá estão (embora parcialmente em ruínas), e por aí fora.

Porém, ao contrário das nossas geografias emocionais, que
permanecem intactas, o tempo e o espaço não são imutáveis.

---

13   Carrilho, J., *Ibo: A Casa e o Tempo*, Universidade Eduardo Mondlane-Edições FAPF,
Maputo, 2005.

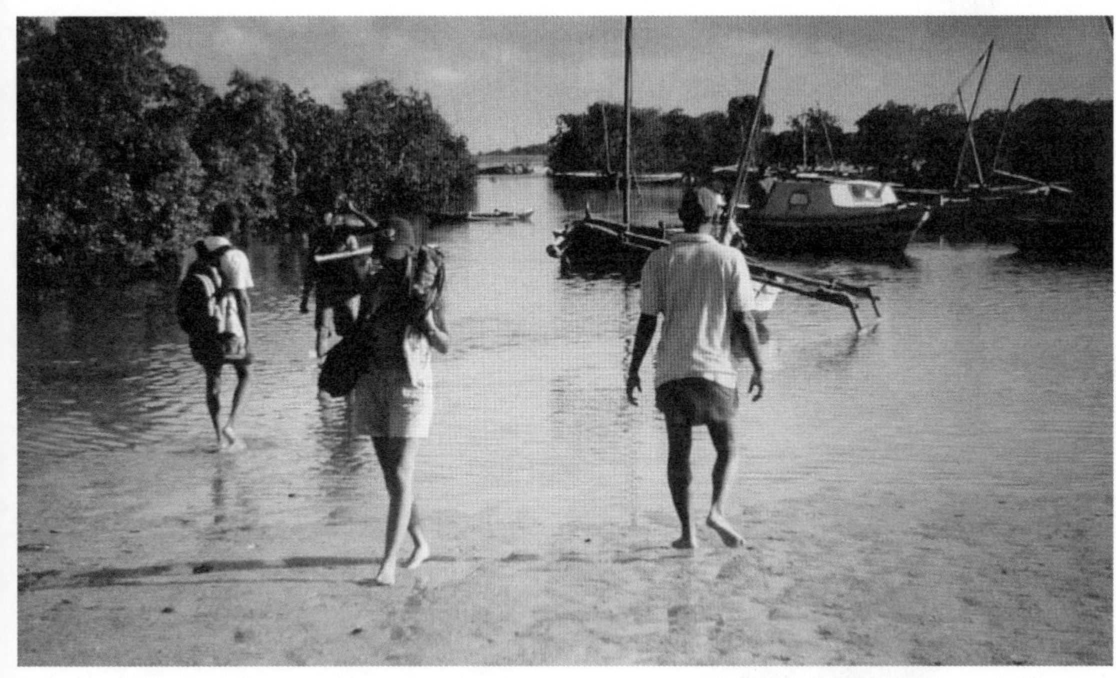

It has been nearly 20 years since I first went to Ibo Island to study and visit. Although I was no longer at Universidade Eduardo Mondlane - Faculdade de Arquitectura e Planeamento Físico (UEM-FAPF), they were kind enough to let me integrate into the research team for their archival project concerning the built environment of the island - in particular, its domestic architecture - later published as *Ibo: A Casa e o Tempo*.[13]

At the time, I made two consecutive trips: the first, in December 2001, as a student research assistant, and the second, barely two months later, to resolve a family matter with my great-aunt.

It is this second trip that is recorded in these pages, a loosely assembled travelogue of digitally scanned analogue photos and field notes jotted down from memory.

At the time, it did not occur to me that, at some point in the future, it would be too dangerous to take the Tandanhangue-Ibo Island route again, due to the current volatile terrorist action in the region since 2017. I simply assumed that Ibo would be eternal because the ancestral bodies are in the cemetery, the old family homes of various relatives still stand (albeit partly in ruins) and so on.

But unlike our emotional geographies, which may be intact, time and place are not.

<hr>

13   Carrilho, J., *Ibo: A Casa e o Tempo*, Universidade Eduardo Mondlane-Edições FAPF, Maputo, 2005.

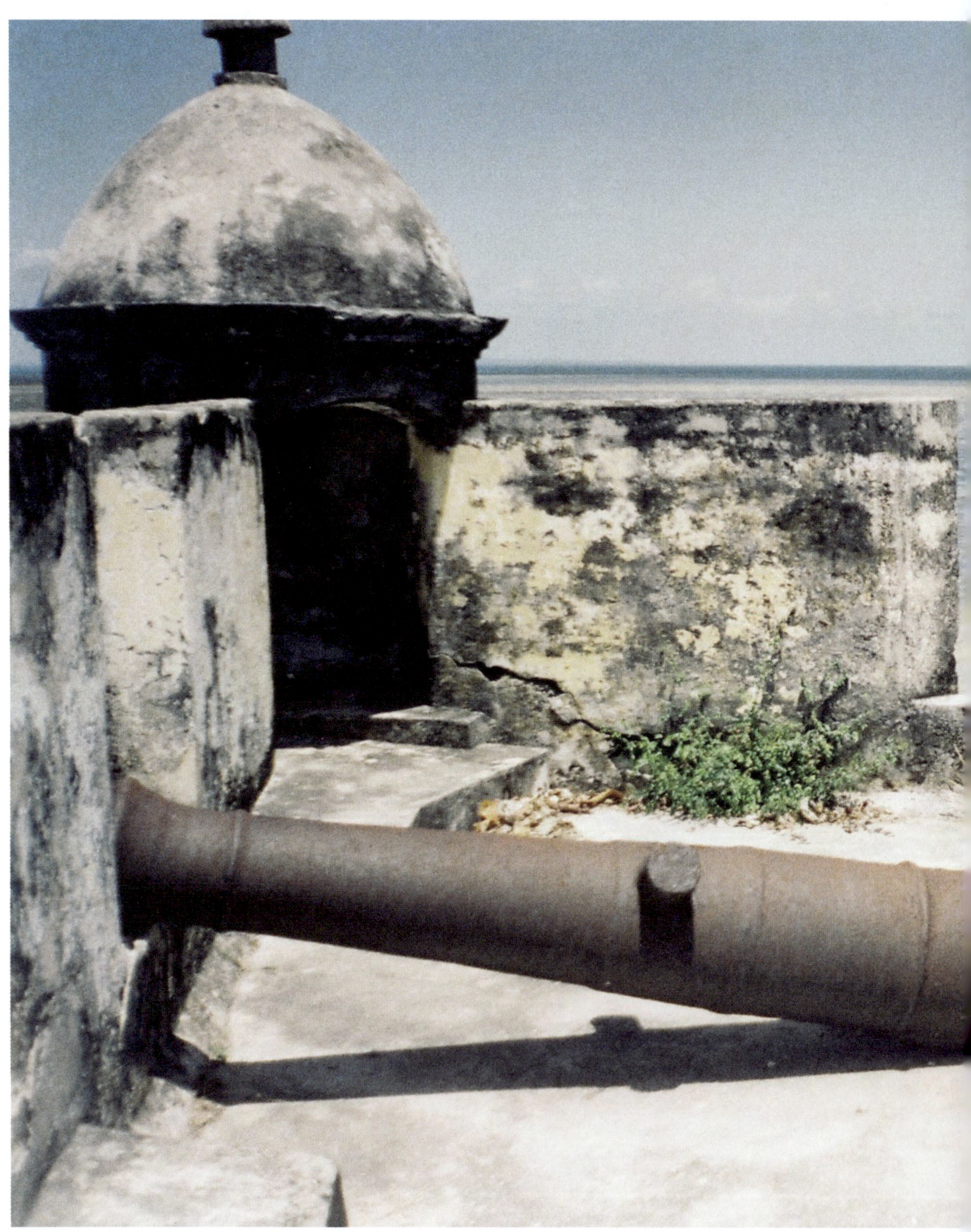

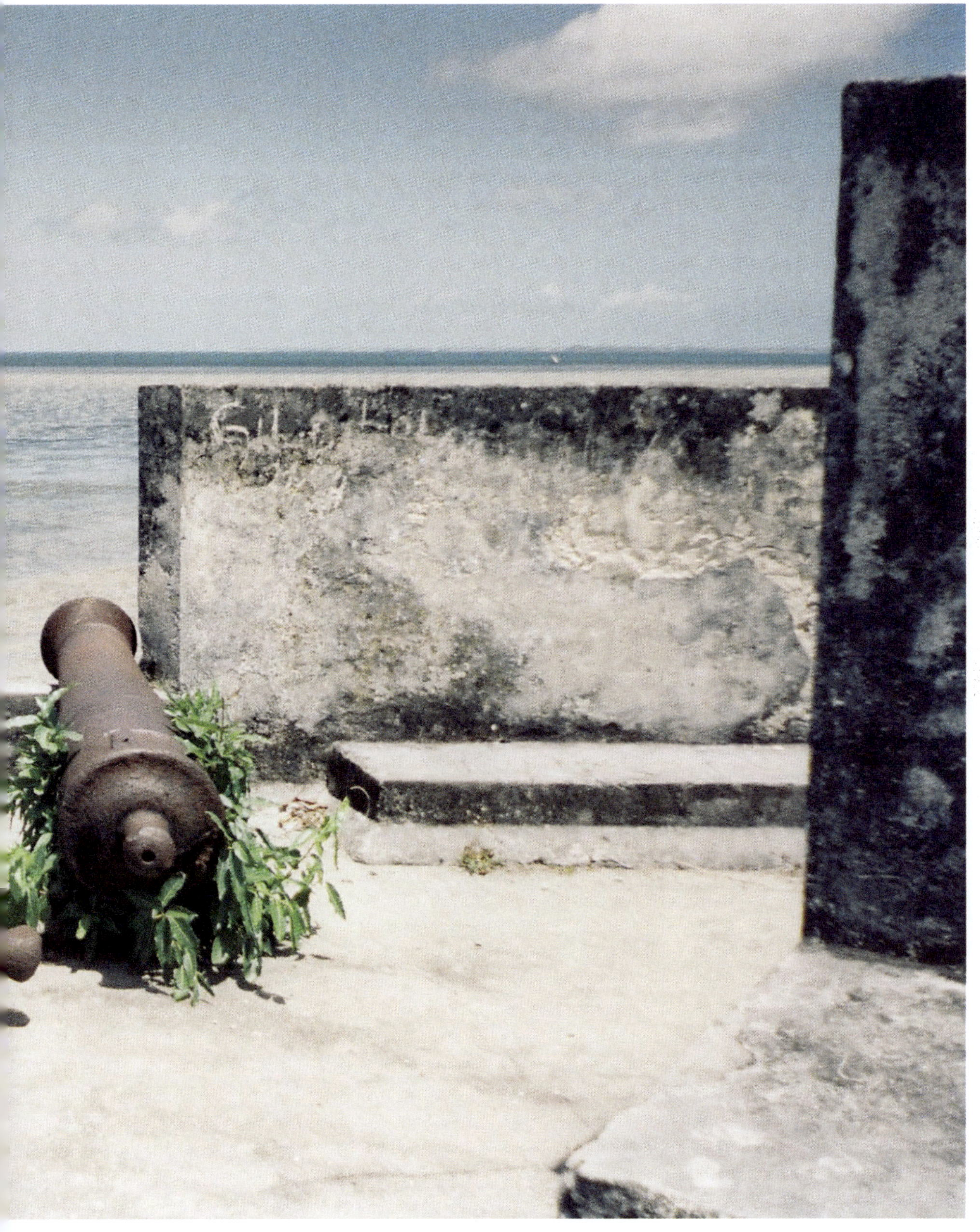

A travessia do continente para a Ilha do Ibo faz-se a partir de Tandanhangue, uma localidade costeira perto de Quissanga, no Oceano Índico. Tandanhangue situa-se a cerca de quatro horas de viagem de carro a partir de Pemba, a cidade capital da província de Cabo Delgado. Uma estrada que é principalmente de terra batida, com desníveis súbitos e troços alagados na época das chuvas.

As embarcações à vela, designadas lancha (Português) ou n'galaua (Kimwane), são táxis aquáticos que transportam cerca de 20 passageiros e carga diversa.

À mercê das marés, é preciso esperar pela altura certa, para que a embarcação possa aproximar-se da costa, cortando pelo mangal. A janela de oportunidade é pequena.

Em Tandanhangue, um embonde iro tecto serve de abrigo durante a espera. A espera pode ser longa, e a hora de partida incerta.

O antigo pontão há muito que desapareceu, engolido pelo mar, pelo que os passageiros e a carga são levados a bordo pelos tripulantes do barco, os naodas; levados a braços, literalmente.

Depois, há que manobrar a embarcação para a saída do mangal. O tempo urge.

Já no mar, uma viagem tranquila que sossega a alma, e alimenta o espírito.

Cerca de hora e meia depois, avista-se a Ilha do Ibo: o forte, o antigo pontão.

Desembarcamos num dos extremos da antiga Vila do Ibo, hoje largamente em ruínas. Habitada de memórias e de espíritos, rodeada pela vida dos novos bairros.

Por eles viemos, os espíritos.

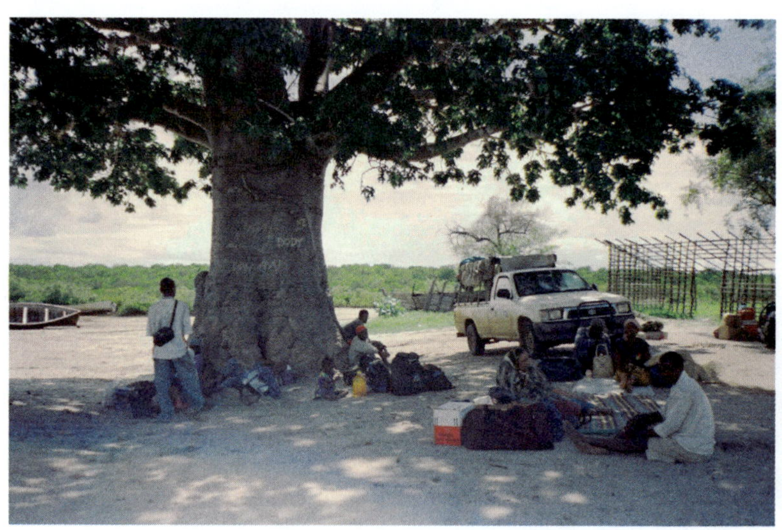

A ÁRVORE-TECTO
Janeiro, calor

Que tal seria, contemplar o embondeiro como elemento arquitectónico? Os componentes estão lá: as raízes, fundações. O tronco, pilar-mestre. Os ramos e folhas, cobertura. A árvore como abrigo ideal, providenciando sombra e frescura durante a espera indeterminada pela chegada do barco. Ao redor, o comércio de essenciais: chá e bebidas frescas, fruta, bolachas.

The crossing from the continent to Ilha do Ibo is done from Tandanhangue, a coastal village outside Quissanga, on the Indian Ocean. Tandanhangue is about four hours away by car from Pemba, the capital city of Cabo Delgado Province, in the north of the country. The road is primarily of compacted read earth, with sudden dips and rises and the occasional flooded stretches during the rainy season.

The transport boats, named lancha (Portuguese) or n'galaua (Kimwani), operate as sailing water taxis that transport an average of 20 people and diverse cargo. At the mercy of the tides, it is necessary to wait for the right time for the boats to approach the land, cutting through the mangrove. The window of opportunity is small.

In Tandanhangue, a baobab tree shelters the travellers during the wait, which can be long, the departure time uncertain. The old wooden pontoon is long gone, swallowed by the sea, and so both passengers and cargo are carried onboard literally in the arms of the ship's crew, the naodas.

Once all onboard, the manoeuvring begins, to steer the boat towards the mangrove exit and out to sea. The timing is urgent and precise. Once out into the open sea, tranquillity soothes the soul, feeds the spirit.

About an hour and a half later, we can suddenly see the island in the distance: the fort, the old pontoon. We disembark on the southern end of the old Ibo Village, today mostly in ruins. Inhabited by memories and spirits, surrounded by the life of the new neighbourhoods.

It is they we've come here to meet, the spirits.

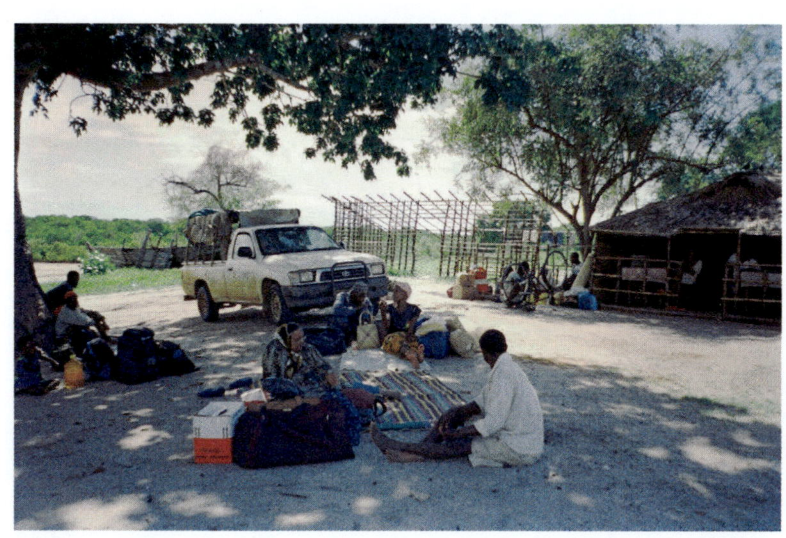

THE TREE-ROOF
That January heat

What if one regarded the baobab tree as an architectural element? The constituent parts are there: the roots as foundation, the trunk as master-column, the branches and leaves as roof cover. The tree is the ideal shelter, providing a cool shade during the uncertain wait for the arrival of the boats. Around us, essential goods for sale: tea and cool drinks, fruit, biscuits.

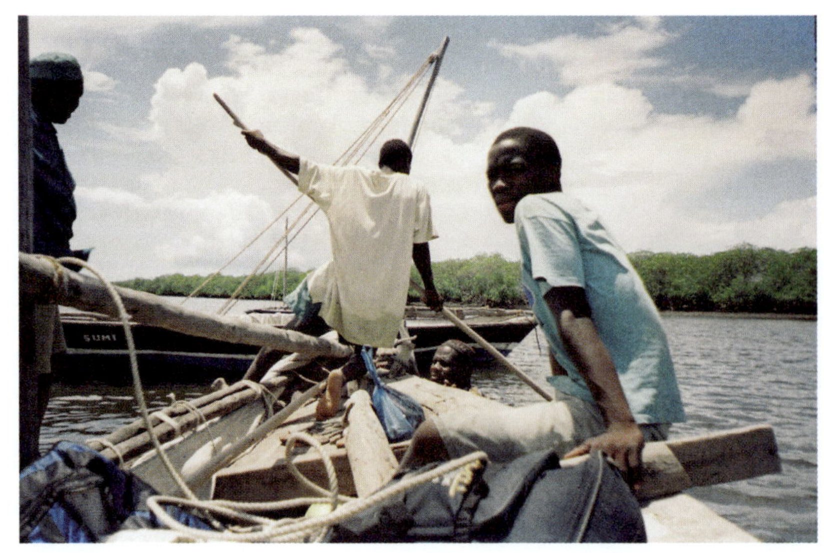

NAODAS
Marinheiros, bagageiros, guias

Por eles somos carregados para aceder à n'galaua (embarcação), devido à ausência do pontão desaparecido pelo mar. Com a sua perícia se manobra a saída do mangal, e mais à frente, à chegada do Ibo, se negoceia a passagem por entre bancos de areia. Navegantes, as suas roupas confundem-se com o azul e o branco-céu, numa harmonização cromática, talvez acidental, com o ambiente do ganha-pão.
      Dia-sim, dia-sim.

AZUL

No azul irreal do céu-mar, a linha do horizonte ancora a realidade. Aqui e ali, uma outra n'galaua de pescadores e ilhéus, memórias da terra firme. No marulhar das ondas, um universo sonoro que é também espaço físico.

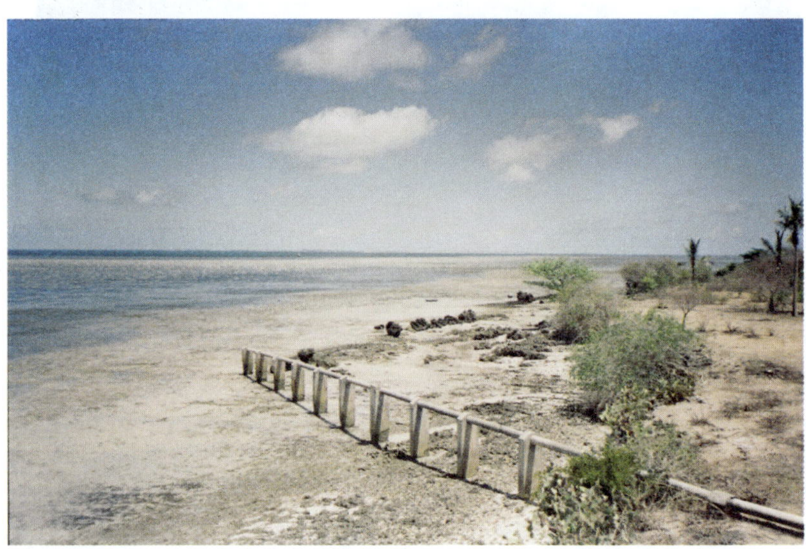

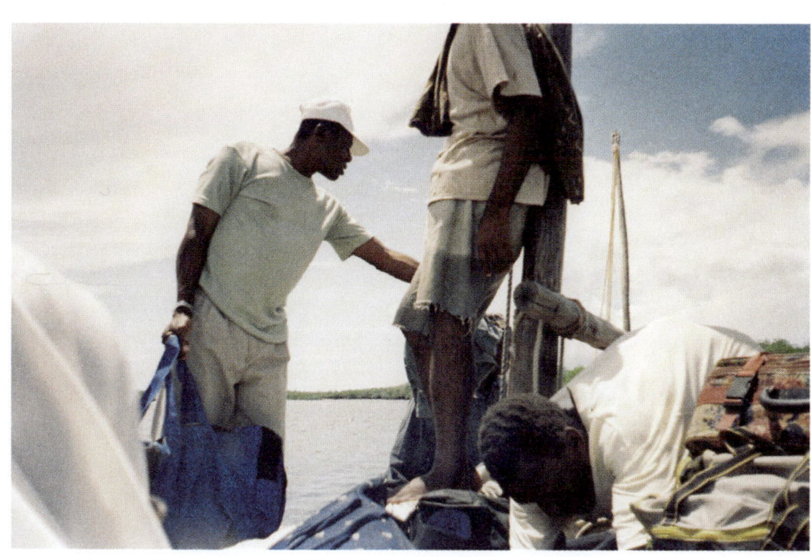

NAODAS
Sailors, porters, guides

It is they who carry us in their arms to board the n'galaua (boat) since the sea has long disappeared the wooden pontoon. It is their skill that manoeuvres the boat towards the mangrove exit and later negotiates a path through the sandbanks upon arrival in Ibo. Seafarers, their clothes match the blue-white sky, an accidental chromatic harmony with the environment which earns them their daily bread.

Day in, day in.

BLUE

Amidst the unreal blue of the water-sky continuum, the horizon anchors reality. Here and there, other fishing n'galaua and islets, memories of *terra firma*. In the soft splashing of the waves, a sonorous universe that is also a place.

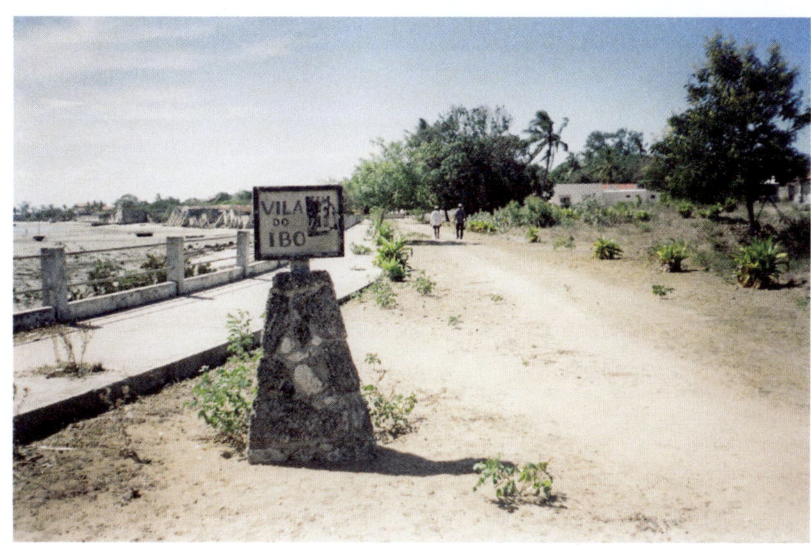

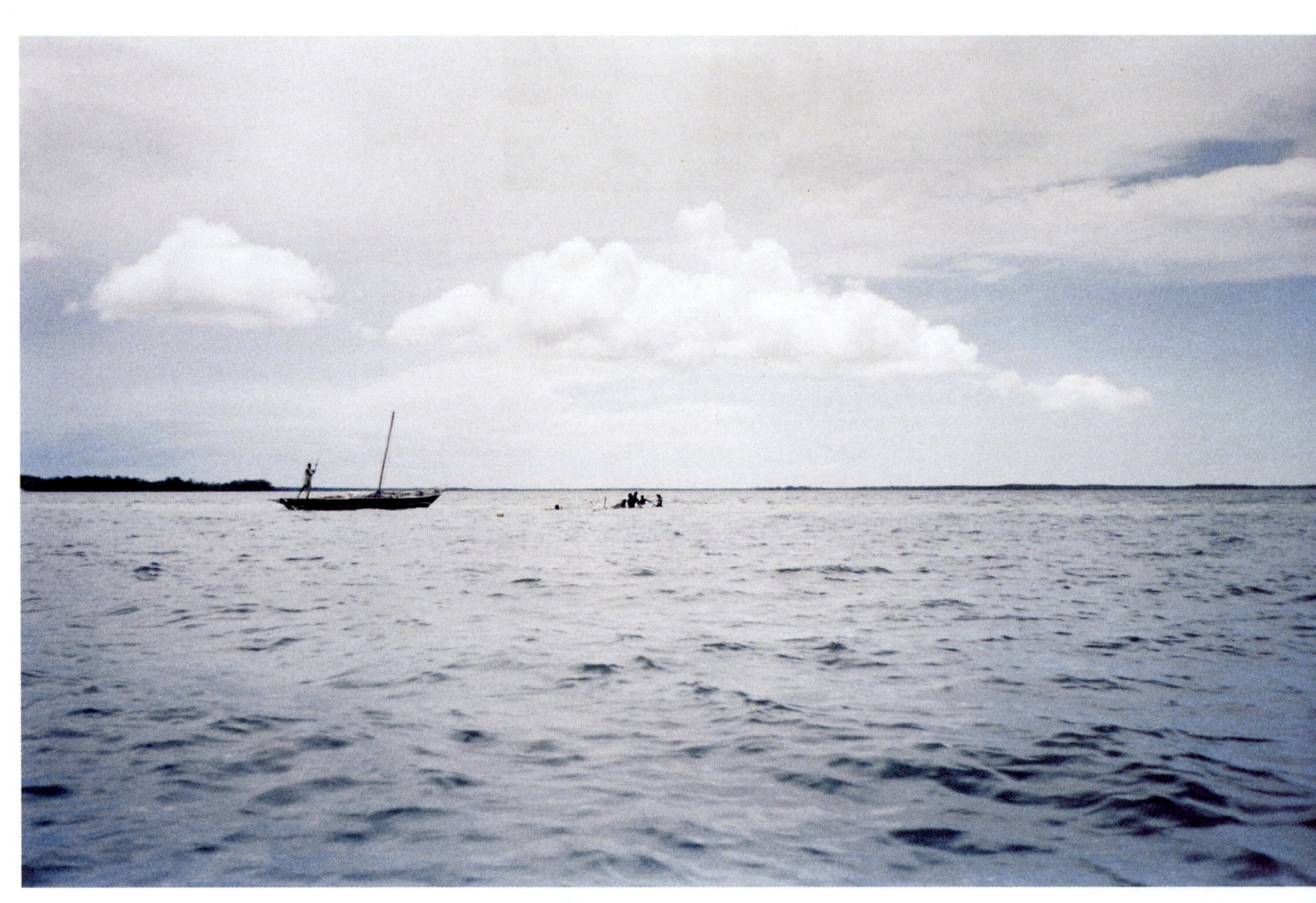

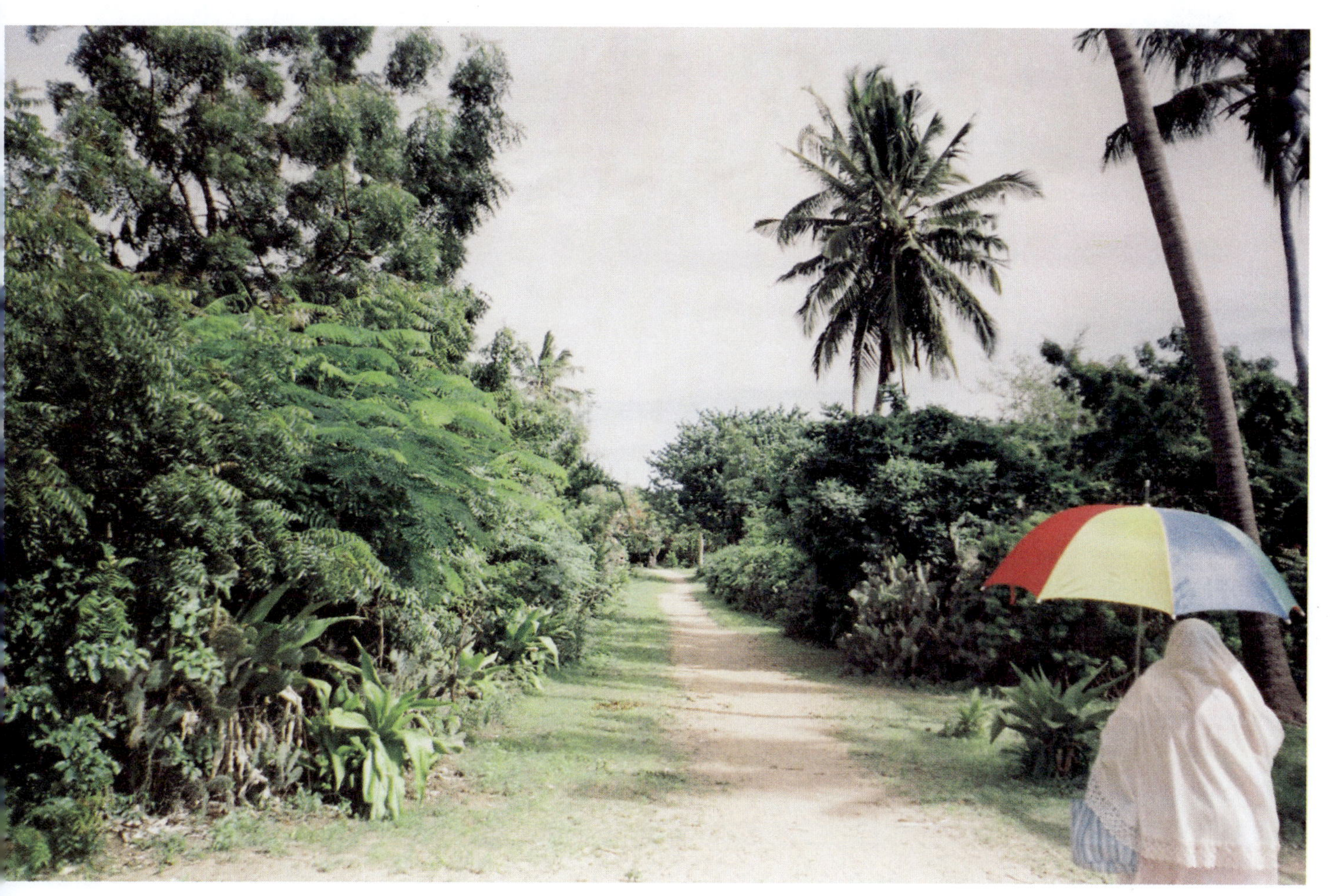

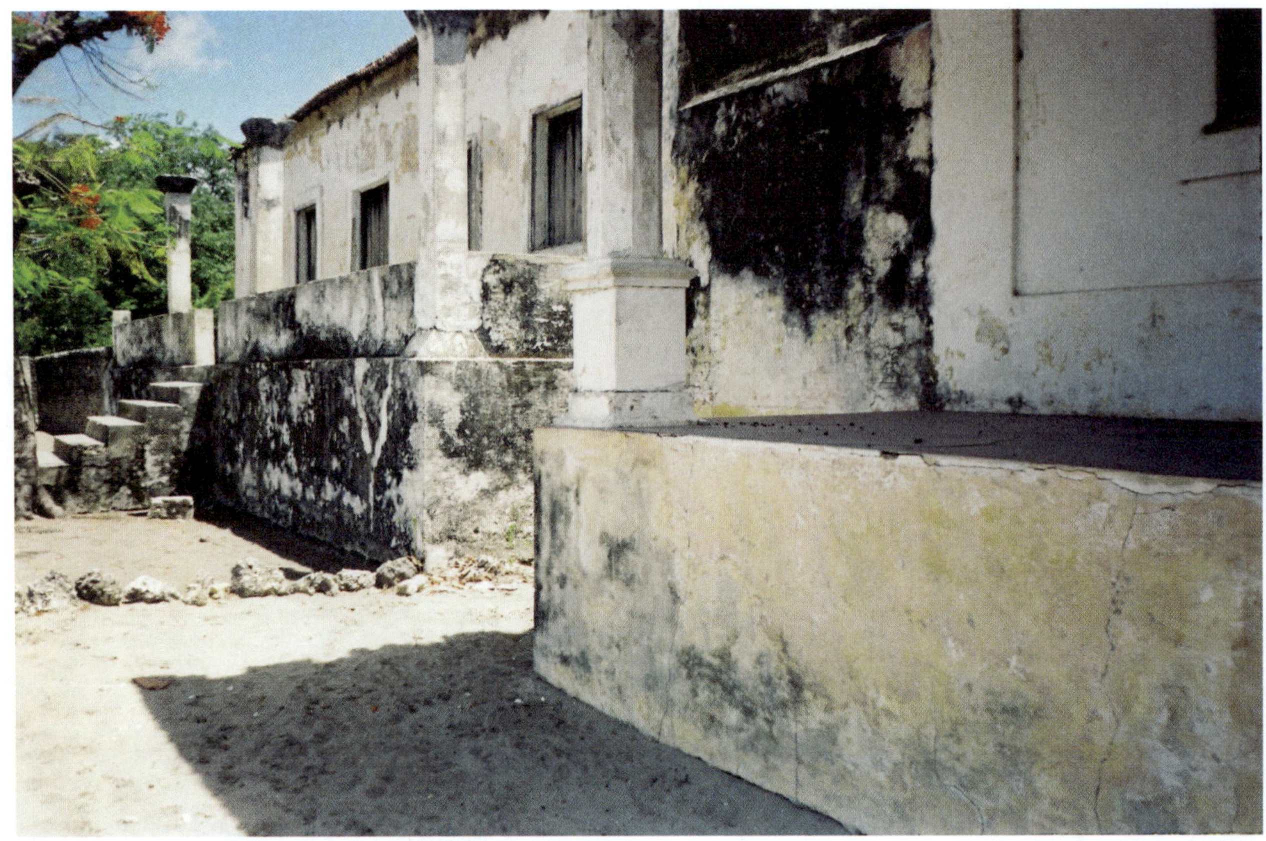

DESEMBARQUE

Devido à presença de bancos de areia, a embarcação aproxima-se da Ilha desenhando um suave ziguezague, como se a cortejasse. Pouco depois, chega-se a um dos extremos da Vila do Ibo.

Desembarcamos, novamente sem pontão, carregados a braços pelos naodas. No ar, o silêncio insular, porém não desconfortável: há vida, só que não se vê. Porque chegamos no pico do calor (11h-15h00), durante o qual os habitantes se mantêm ao abrigo das casas. Para nós visitantes, uma chegada que é um começo.

ANTIGA VILA DO IBO

A antiga Vila está praticamente deserta, e em ruínas. Casas de dono, fechadas e abandonadas. Todavia, estranhamente expectantes. Talvez pelos bons ossos que têm, ou talvez, pelos degraus intactos, a convidar o acesso às varandas elevadas, platéias domésticas para o palco outrora quotidiano das ruas principais. Ruínas habitadas de memórias e espíritos, onde até a vegetação aguarda deferimento para crescer, de tão escassa.

CAMINHOS

Saíndo dos limites da antiga Vila, há caminhos bem frequentados, com vegetação luxuriante e variada, convidativos.

Um dos caminhos passa pelo cemitério muçulmano, e mais além, termina no cemitério cristão. Nos cemitérios, uma prece e uma invocação, entre campas antigas.

Um regresso, que anunciará a partida.

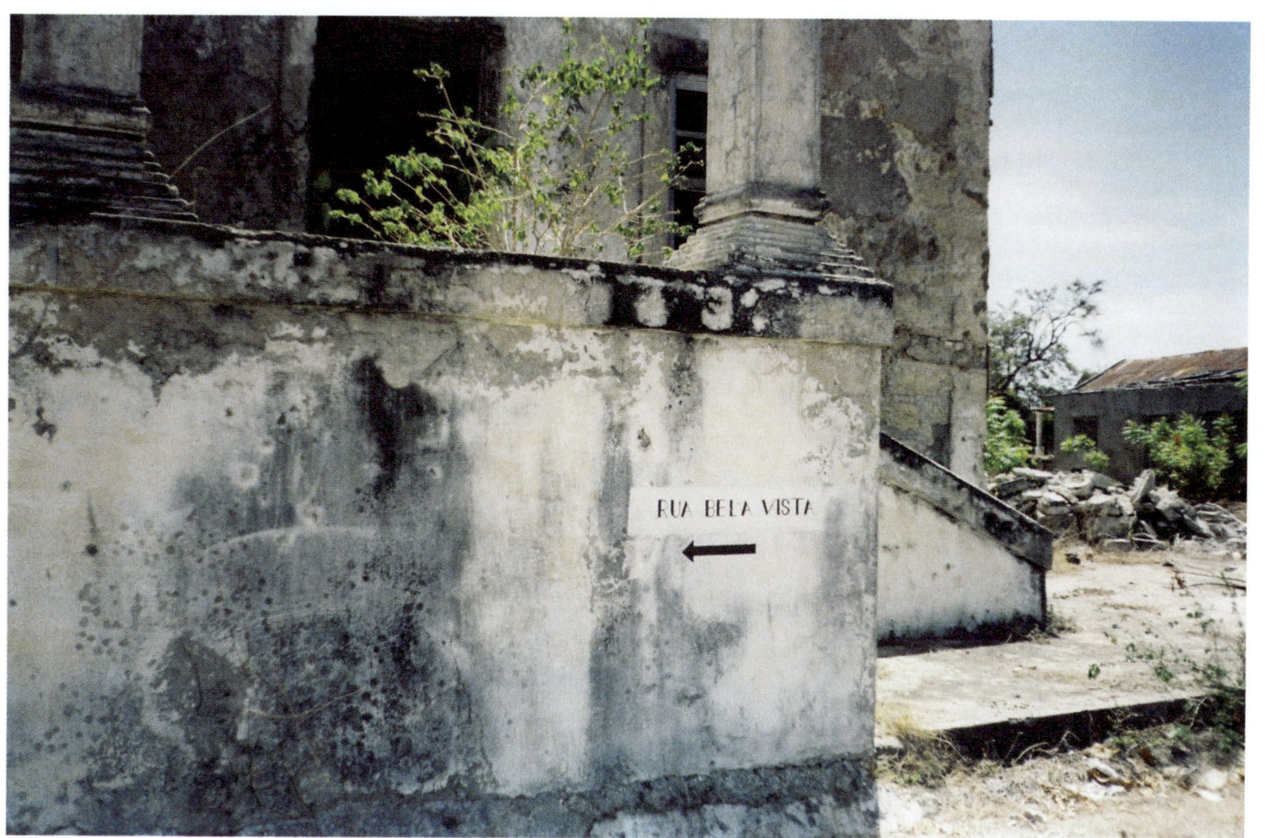

DISEMBARKATION

Due to the presence of sandbanks, the boat approaches the island slowly, in a soft zigzag, as if courting her. A little while later, we arrive at the southern end of the old Vila do Ibo.
We disembark, again without a pontoon, carried by the naodas. In the air, that insular silence, albeit not uncomfortable: one senses that there is life close by, albeit unseen. Because we arrived during the peak heat hours (11am-3pm), a time when the island residents remain indoors, resting. For us visitors, the arrival heralds a beginning.

THE OLD VILA DO IBO

The old village is practically deserted, and in ruins. Houses that have owners, and yet are closed and seemingly abandoned. Nevertheless, strangely expectant too. Perhaps because of their good bones, or their intact front steps, inviting access to the raised verandas, domestic viewing stands to the once quotidian stage of the main streets. Ruins inhabited by memories and spirits, where even the vegetation awaits deferral to grow, so sparse it is.

PATHWAYS

Outside the limits of the old village, there are well-trodden paths, beckoning us with lush and varied vegetation.
One of the paths goes past the Muslim cemetery and ends further along on the Christian cemetery. In the cemeteries, a prayer and an invocation, among the ancient graves.

A return that will signal our departure.

É sobretudo da serenidade que me recordo, de uma certa qualidade de som. Sem gritos ou chamamentos, sem música alta ou cânticos. Apenas aquela qualidade difusa de lá estar e pouco ouvir. Porque há uma prioridade de som quando nos encontramos numa ilha pequena: primeiro o rítmico marulhar das ondas, e de seguida tudo o resto, amortecido.

Na primeira viagem, essa serenidade fora quebrada pelo canto vulgar de um galo ao amanhecer. Assustou-me, o galo, pois mal dormira com as histórias de djinn que o guarda tinha contado depois do jantar. E se me viessem cumprimentar, os ancestrais? Na época, a ilha funcionava com geradores a diesel, que eram desligados prontamente às 22h. Eu tinha não-dormido apertando uma lanterna contra o peito, depois de a vela se extinguir.

Esta segunda viagem foi diferente. Desta vez, estava com minha tia-avó e dormia como um bebé ao seu lado. Sem sonhos, nem pesadelos. Apenas com o som distante do mar e as suas orações matinais, embora delas não me recorde com precisão. Ela era como um talismã, uma presença calma e serena. A irmã mais nova da minha avó. Nascida na ilha, ela não precisava de falar muito para se comunicar, nem mesmo comigo. Talvez já pressentisse que esta viria a ser a sua última viagem em vida à ilha e, embora não fosse essa a intenção original, terá aproveitado para se despedir, comunicando silenciosamente com o local. Rezando, e ouvindo.

Alguns de nós têm a sorte de conhecer a nossa ancestralidade, de poder traçar a nossa história através dos corpos que nos trouxeram ao mundo e daqueles que nos criaram, que deram e criaram espaço para nós. Esta tia-avó era especialmente querida porque foi tudo isso. Por vezes ficávamos com ela em sua casa, quando éramos pequeninos, nos anos pré-escolares. Até hoje, as suas filhas têm alcunhas especiais para mim. Daquela época, recordo-me sobretudo do cheiro dos retalhos de tecido com os quais às vezes brincava, empilhados no chão ao lado da sua velha máquina de costura de pedal. Vinte anos depois, era ela quem olhava por mim nesta viagem, e outros quinze se passariam antes dela ficar muito doente e deixar-nos durante o sono, não sem antes me dizer, algum tempo antes, *'Quem me dera ainda aqui estar para conhecer os teus filhos, quando vierem.'*

Maria Gabriela Carrilho Aragão nasceu, vive e trabalha em Maputo. É licenciada em Arquitectura pela Universidade do Cabo, onde foi também Tutora e Examinadora Externa. Exerce como arquitecta desde 2007 e ainda, ocasionalmente, como escritora, artista e curadora independente, usando os seus dons para habilitar outros, ajudando-os a clarificar e traduzir a sua própria visão criativa.

It is the serenity that I recall best, a certain quality of sound. No shouts or callings, no loud music or chanting. Just that aural quality of being there and hearing little. For there's a priority of sound when you are on a small island: the rhythmic sea first, then everything else, buffered, subdued.

On the first trip, it had been broken by the ordinary sound of a rooster at dawn. It had startled me; I had barely slept because the guard's post-supper djinn stories had kept me up. What if they wanted to greet me, the ancestry? At the time, the island ran on diesel generators, which were switched-off at 10 pm without fail. I had slept-not clasping a flashlight to my chest after the candle went out.

But on this second trip, it was different. This time, I was with my great-aunt and slept like a baby, next to her. No dreams, no nightmares. Just the buffered sound of the sea and her morning prayers, although I don't distinctly recall those. She was like a talisman, a calm, serene presence. My grandmother's youngest sister. Born on the island, she didn't have to say much to communicate, not even to me. Perhaps she had already sensed that it would be her last living trip to the island, and, although that wasn't the original intention, took the opportunity to say her goodbyes in advance, silently communicating with the place. Praying, and listening.

Some of us are lucky enough to know our ancestry, trace our history back to the bodies that carried us and those that raised us, who held space for us. This great-aunt was especially dear because she did just that. We used to stay at hers sometimes as young children, pre-nursery school. Her daughters have special nicknames for me to this day. Of that time, what I recall best is the scent of fabric scraps on the heap I sometimes played with, next to her old pedal-action sewing machine. Twenty years later, she was still looking after me on this trip, and another fifteen would go past before she would get very ill and pass away in her sleep, not before telling me, sometime before that, 'I wish I could still be here to witness the birth of your children, when they come.'

Maria Gabriela Carrilho Aragão was born, lives and works in Maputo. She has a degree in Architecture from the University of Cape Town, a profession she has practised since 2007, and has also been a tutor and external examiner at that same institution. Occasionally, she also writes, makes art, and designs functional objects, and uses her skills to enable others, helping them to clarify and translate their own creative vision.

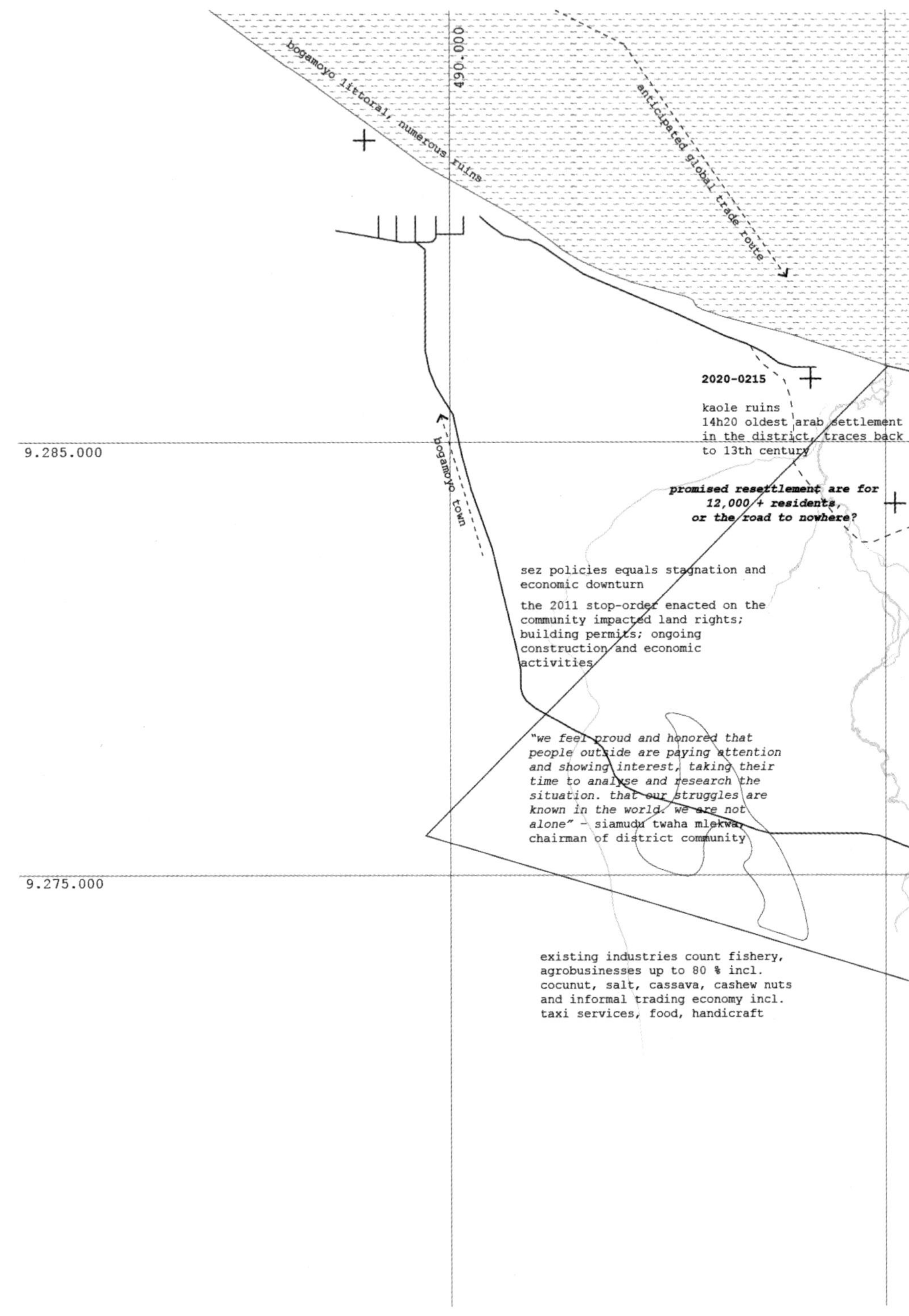

Field Notes 02-2020, Bagamoyo,
Tanzania, Margarida Waco

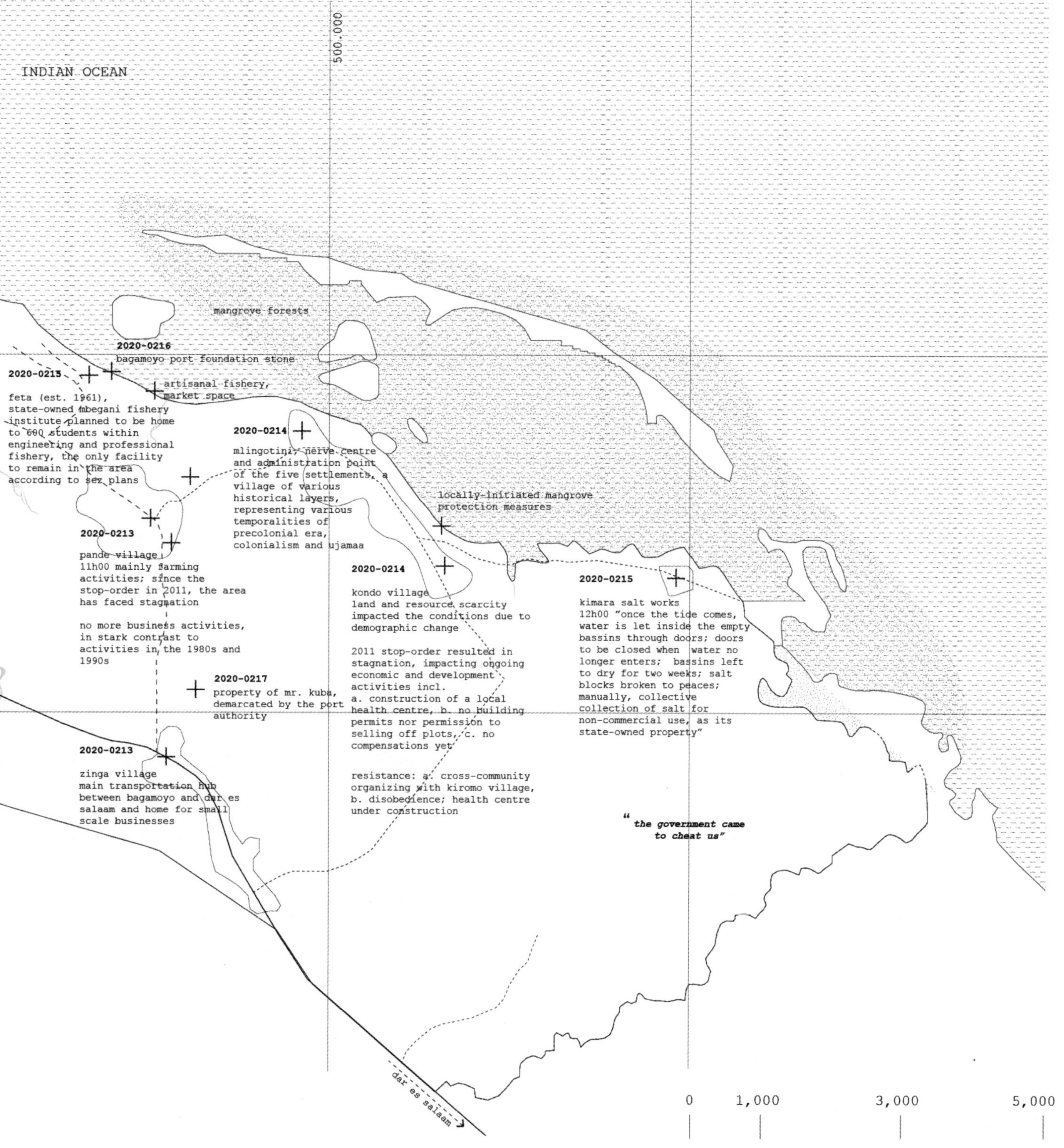

INDIAN OCEAN
500,000
mangrove forests
2020-0216
bagamoyo port foundation stone
2020-0213
feta (est. 1961),
state-owned mbegani fishery
institute planned to be home
to 690 students within
engineering and professional
fishery, the only facility
to remain in the area
according to sez plans
artisanal fishery,
market space
2020-0214
mlingotini, nerve centre
and administration point
of the five settlements, a
village of various
historical layers,
representing various
temporalities of
precolonial era,
colonialism and ujamaa
locally-initiated mangrove
protection measures
2020-0213
pande village
11h00 mainly farming
activities; since the
stop-order in 2011, the area
has faced stagnation
no more business activities,
in stark contrast to
activities in the 1980s and
1990s
2020-0214
kondo village
land and resource scarcity
impacted the conditions due to
demographic change
2011 stop-order resulted in
stagnation, impacting ongoing
economic and development
activities incl.
a. construction of a local
health centre, b. no building
permits nor permission to
selling off plots, c. no
compensations yet
resistance: a. cross-community
organizing with kiromo village,
b. disobedience; health centre
under construction
2020-0217
property of mr. kuba,
demarcated by the port
authority
2020-0215
kimara salt works
12h00 "once the tide comes,
water is let inside the empty
bassins through doors; doors
to be closed when water no
longer enters; bassins left
to dry for two weeks; salt
blocks broken to peaces;
manually, collective
collection of salt for
non-commercial use, as its
state-owned property"
2020-0213
zinga village
main transportation hub
between bagamoyo and dar es
salaam and home for small
scale businesses
" the government came
to cheat us"
dar es salaam
0   1,000   3,000   5,000

At the threshold of the Indian Ocean, in the north-eastern corner of Tanzania, lies Bagamoyo. Once the town served as an administrative capital during the brief moment of German colonial rule and as a notorious slave-trading outpost in the 19th century, weaving African bodies into a system that built modern capitalism. Some kilometers southwards its tropical littoral are located five self-built villages borne out of Nyerere's socialist philosophy of Ujamaa,[14] that make home to a population of about 12 000 living off small-scale farming and artisanal fishing.

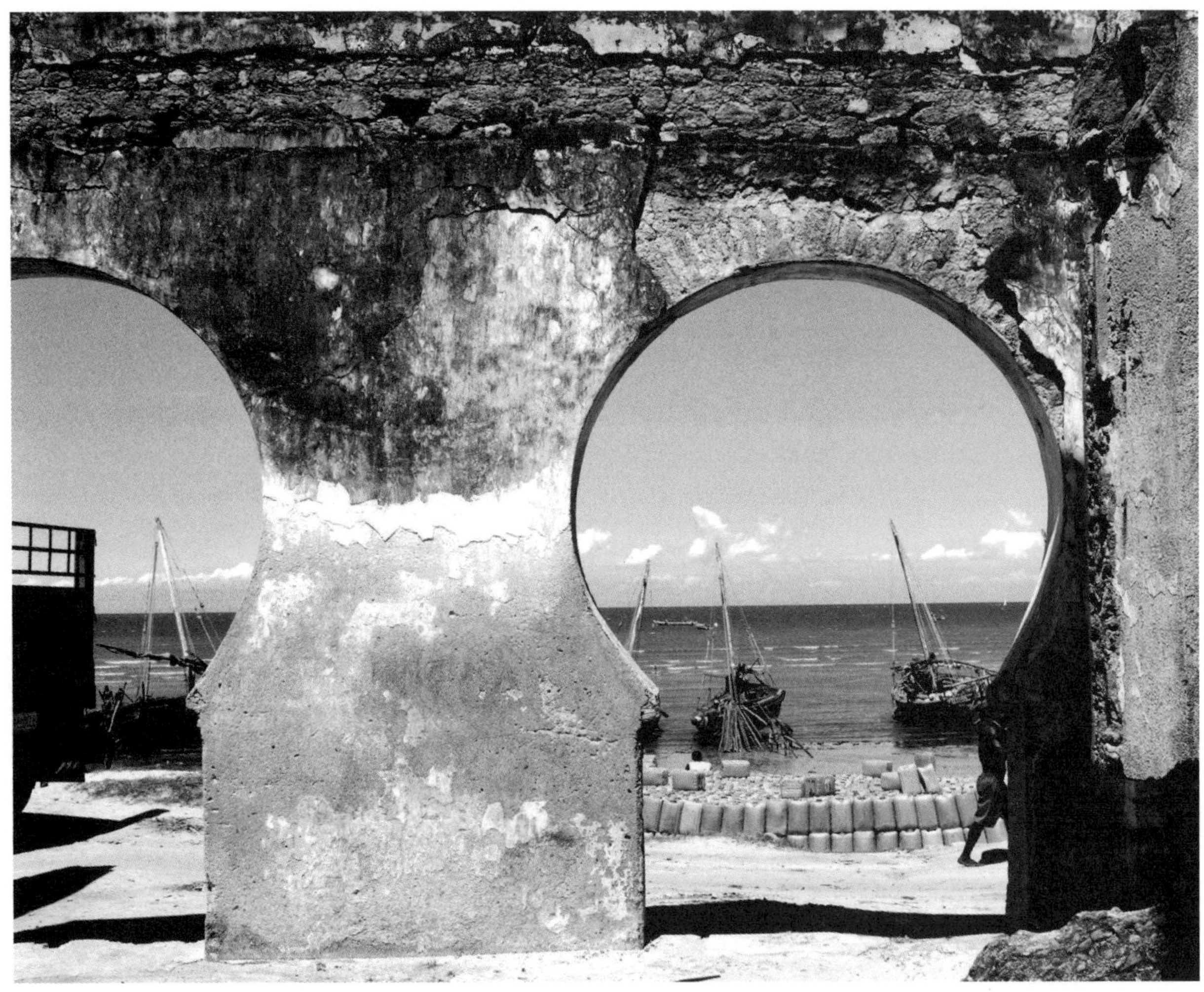

14   A Swahili word usually translated as 'family hood', Ujamaa was also the name given to the social and economic policy developed and implemented by the late president of the Republic of Tanzania, Julius Nyerere, after the country gained independence from Britain in 1961. See also Calitz, Serah-Ingrid, *Sino-African Counterpoints*, Master's Thesis, TU Delft (2018).

Soon, however, 9 800 hectares of this rich and fertile soil will be woven into a planetary network of multi-directional trade. Conceptualised under the framework of a Special Economic Zone, the site is about to endure a radical spatial transformation that will benefit a global population and place locals at the margins.

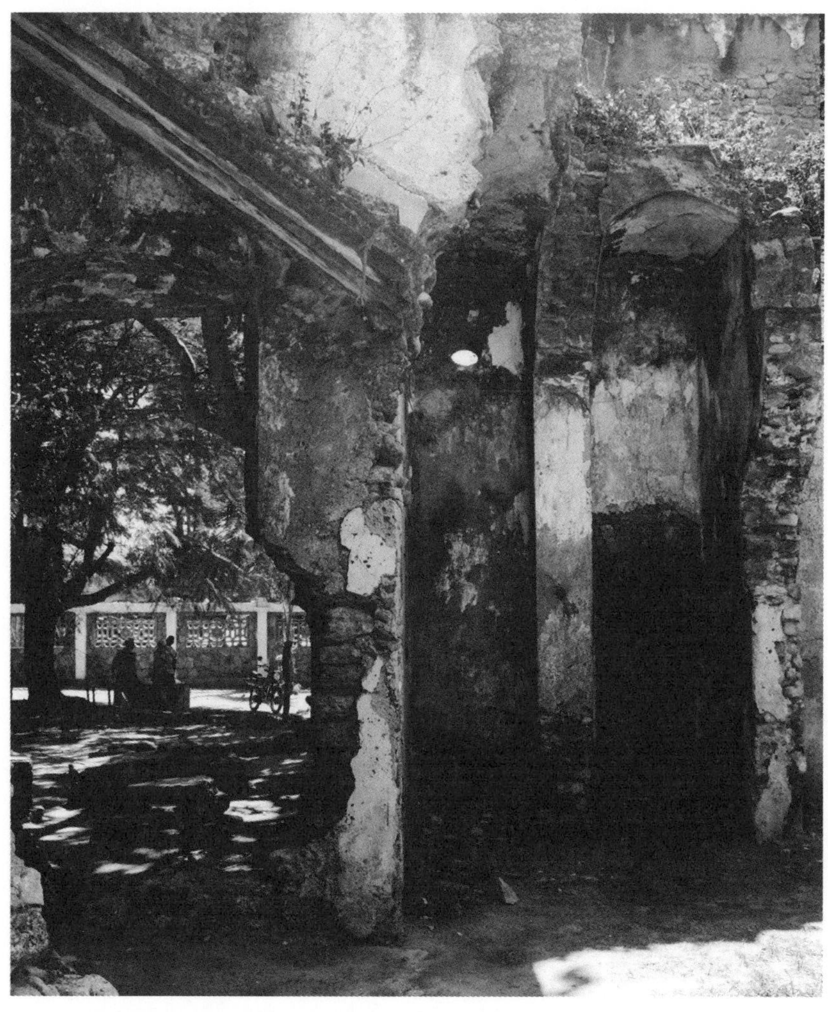

Ruins located at the Bagamoyan
littoral perpetuate legacies of
slavery and colonial praxes, such as
the former Customs House built by
Omani sultans, Margarida Waco, 2020

In his essay 'Africa in the New Century'; Achille Mbembe writes that the African continent is the last frontier of capitalism, a key laboratory of the world in the making, and a place where the future of life itself, of the Earth, the human and other species might be played out.[15] Echoing Mbembe, history repeats itself as contemporary African landscapes are once again converted into fertile grounds for global capitalism that is fuelled by the proliferation of extractive industries that profit from plundering the earth, weaving people, money, natural resources and commodities into a network of global exchange. This set of geopolitical arrangements has led to vast spatial reconfigurations in places across the continent and have become foundational to new forms of financial speculation. Moreover, such spatial practices create a loophole, allowing for new economic ventures that are largely driven by the interests of global powers, national and private enterprises. Invariably, these interests incline towards a capitalist production of space that relies on spatial interventions guaranteed to generate more capital - in the short term.

To this end, architectures of logistics - from the construction of railways, roads, ports and, most notably, free zones - play an important part in enabling such endeavours and advancing ideas of anticipated (economic) futures. These architectures of logistics set the invisible rules that govern spaces of everyday lives and are transforming African cities into sites of power negotiations on the one hand, and sites of resistance on the other. Two of such spaces where these intricate relationships crystallise are the Free Trade Zones (FTZs) and Special Economic Zones (SEZs) that have emerged at an unprecedented rate across the continent. These zones, governed by a certain kind of techno-rationalism, are designed to operate and perform in a very particular way.

These infrastructure spaces, however, seem to return to their historical foundations as they continue to act as agents for urban-spatial transformations in the realm of racial capitalism. If colonialism and the transcontinental slave trade established the circulations foundational to modernity[16] with waves of logistical infrastructures designed to serve colonial economies, in particular, the European and colonial free ports, such historical ties and spatial logics continue to live on, only this time hiding under the mask of neoliberalism and globalisation.

ARCHITECTURES OF
EXTRACTION

FTZs and SEZs are often located at the margins of the city, occupying existing ports. As stated, these zones are not new to the continent and have historical precedents in European and colonial free ports.[17] As a phenomenon originating in Western colonial praxes, they claim a colonial continuity that entangles the history of free trade enclaves, territorial regimes and racialised land dispossession. They are designed to increase exports, bypass government restrictions and outsource investment in infrastructure development by informing global

15   Mbembe, A., 'Africa in the new century', *The Massachusetts Review*, 57, 1 (2016), pp. 91-104.

16   A phrase coined by Adeyemo, Camp and Randulfe in a programme brief for the Royal College of Art ADS2 Studio exploring the realm of the demonic (2020).

17   See Meghan Maruschke's authorship on the subject of ports and zones, in particular, 'Are there connections between previous free port practices and Special Economic Zones? The case of Mumbai's ports', TRAFO - Blog for Transregional Research, April 2015. The full blog post is available at: https://trafo.hypotheses.org/2112.

urbanism.[18] These zones - some in operation, some in the making - across multiple geographies in Bagamoyo, Chambishi, Djibouti, Lekki, Lusaka, Mombasa, Ogun,[19] to name a few, are demarcated territories of exclusions that embody multiple paradoxes. While the modalities of new infrastructure spaces on the continent primarily serve as spatial apparatuses for economic performance, they also conflict with the everyday spaces of those individuals who cannot relate to abstract networks of global capital flows.

Moreover, these zones act as spaces for anticipated futures and financial speculations.[20] They materialise as arenas for dreams of industrial modernity and boundless growth - in which goods, resources, money and people travel through spatial and temporal borders in their ceaseless chase of a neoliberal dream, relying on transnational flirtations. Consequently, they are multi-layered sites: extra-territorial spaces for incentivised urbanism and subject to legal regimes different from domestic ones, with no consideration for the historical legacies nor the regional identities they form part of. Yet, these zones may also come to symbolise new spheres of action and laboratories for radical imaginations of African futurities through which Blackness can be negotiated.

BLACK RESISTANCE

Returning to Bagamoyo, a town layered with multiple temporalities and entangling conflicting narratives, its shores embody the crumbling remains of racialised violence, where the legacies of colonialism, regional genealogies and present-day artisanal praxes exist side by side, and where spaces and buildings that historically produced various forms of violence enacted on Black bodies have undergone processes of reappropriation, only to become new territories of which Blacks and the descendants of former enslaved Africans are now custodians. The site is currently in the midst of a political standoff in connection with the planned SEZ. The future anticipated by this zone is expected to be carried through a pro-industrial spatial policy that aspires to transform 9 800 hectares of sacred, ancestral land into an industrial urban fabric financially backed by China and Oman in an 80:20 per cent split.[21] The SEZ will displace an indigenous community and rid existing infrastructure in the name of welcoming 30 000 new residents of Chinese and Omani origin, and more to come. In other words, an entire community will be displaced in lieu of a labour force that will engage in a variety of extractive businesses that straddle multiple sectors - i.e., salt mining, agro and cement processing to name a few - but which are linked to systems of environmental degradation and capitalist exploitation. To this end, the indigenous population will be reduced to objects among other objects rather than act as agents within their ancestral landscape.[22] In a quest to call this process

18   See Easterling, K., *Extrastatecraft: The Power of Infrastructure Space*, Verso Books, London, 2014.

19   Bräutigam, D. and Xiaoyang, T., 'African Shenzhen: China's special economic zones in Africa', *Journal of Modern African Studies*, 49, 1 (March 2011), pp. 27-54.

20   Cross, J., 'The economy of anticipation: Speculations and Special Economic Zones', *Comparative Studies of South Asia, Africa and the Middle East*, 35, 3 (December 2015), pp. 424-437.

21   Mchome, E., Ngamesha, I., Richelsen, A. et al., 'COWI - Bagamoyo SEZ Master Plan', Final Report (January 2013), developed for Export Processing Zones Authority EPZA. The full report is available at: https://tdu.or.tz/app/uploads/2018/01/Bagamoyo-Master-Plan-Final-Report.pdf.

22   A view that was historically formed by settler colonialism. The concept is borrowed from a conversation between Mpho Matsipa and Léopold Lambert titled 'Post-apartheid spatial futurities' as part of *The Funambulist* podcast series 'A True Moment of Decolonization'. The podcast is available at:

into question, it would be productive to reassess the postcolonial legacies upon which the country was built.

In rejection of the spatial politics deployed during the German and British colonial regimes, designed to meet the needs of a colonial economy which articulated the productiveness of urban spaces by positioning people, territories and resources in myriad specially designed ensembles, in 1964 Julius Nyerere, the founding father of a newly independent Tanzania, launched Ujamaa - a nation-wide philosophy with a spatial component: Villagisation. Rejecting the successive colonial experiments Tanzanians had been subjected to prior to independence, Ujamaa was implemented in a quest to rethink space, territory and landscapes in new ways to ultimately escape the logic of colonialism. As a result, Black subjectivity was put at the centre to articulate a radically different future. With Ujamaa's restorative and transformative ideological positioning, Nyerere intended to undo the incipient class-formation of the colonial empire and recreate traditions inherent to the pre-colonial institution of the extended family in Tanzania. Ujamaa, therefore, sought to dismantle the idea of urban life and the urbanisation processes that accompanied it. It did so by attempting to re-establish a traditional level of mutual respect, of collectivisation and 'returning the people to settled, moral ways of life'. In short, it came to signify the rejection of capitalism and colonial logic, only to be disrupted by the Structural Adjustments imposed on the country, forcing Tanzania to adopt neoliberal policies.

Against the backdrop of this legacy, Ujamaa's uncompromising ideas, however, continue to live on in current tactics and acts of resistance deployed by the community in Bagamoyo. Insisting on their rights to remain custodians of their land, on their ways of being, they continually oppose the global regime of mobility. Through organised micro-tactics deployed at multiple scales, and under the leadership of five village representatives, new languages are continuously developed to vocalise their struggles and disparities. These include spatial interventions such as the construction of new spaces of necessity as a health care centre and new homes to meet the needs of a growing population (without permits); the strengthening of local micro-trading networks by collectively investing in new commercial spaces and modes of transportation allowing for ease of interconnectivity; and through a series of gatherings, conversations and community organising - all of which are designed to oppose the stop-order policy enacted on them, leaving the community in stagnation for a decade.

In the optics of these tactical arrangements, the acts of insurrection may allow us to think beyond the ways we conceive of infrastructure as being 'reticulated systems of highways, pipes, wires or cables' or as spatial networks that allow us to move through time and space, but rather as AbdouMaliq Simone so eloquently put it, we may also consider *people as infrastructure*.[23] The efforts of the community have not only come to emphasise both the economic collaboration and the spirit of collectivisation as forms of resistance amongst residents seemingly marginalised by a global trade regime. They have first and foremost come to symbolise examples of resisting a system of racial capitalism that plays out on African soil by centring Black subjectivity.

23   Simone, A., 'People as infrastructure: Intersecting fragments in Johannesburg', *Public Culture*, 16, 3 (2004), pp. 407-439.

Margarida Waco
originally hails from
Angola, having lived
between geographies
spanning from Democratic
Republic of the Congo,
the Republic of the
Congo, France and
Denmark. She holds a
degree in architecture
from the Royal Danish
Academy (KADK) and
the Aarhus School of
Architecture. Her work
lies at the intersection
of architecture,
research, publishing
and curating. In
addition, she heads
the Strategic Outreach
at *The Funambulist*, a
bimestrial magazine
dedicated to the
politics of space and
bodies. This essay is an
extension of her Masters
thesis work titled *Sino-
African Flirtations*
(2020) which explores
Special Economic Zones
in Africa, with a
particular focus on
Bagamoyo, Tanzania.

'I know I can't change the future, but I can change the past. It is the past, not the future, which is infinite. Our past was appropriated. I am one of the people who has to reappropriate it.' – Toni Morrison[24]

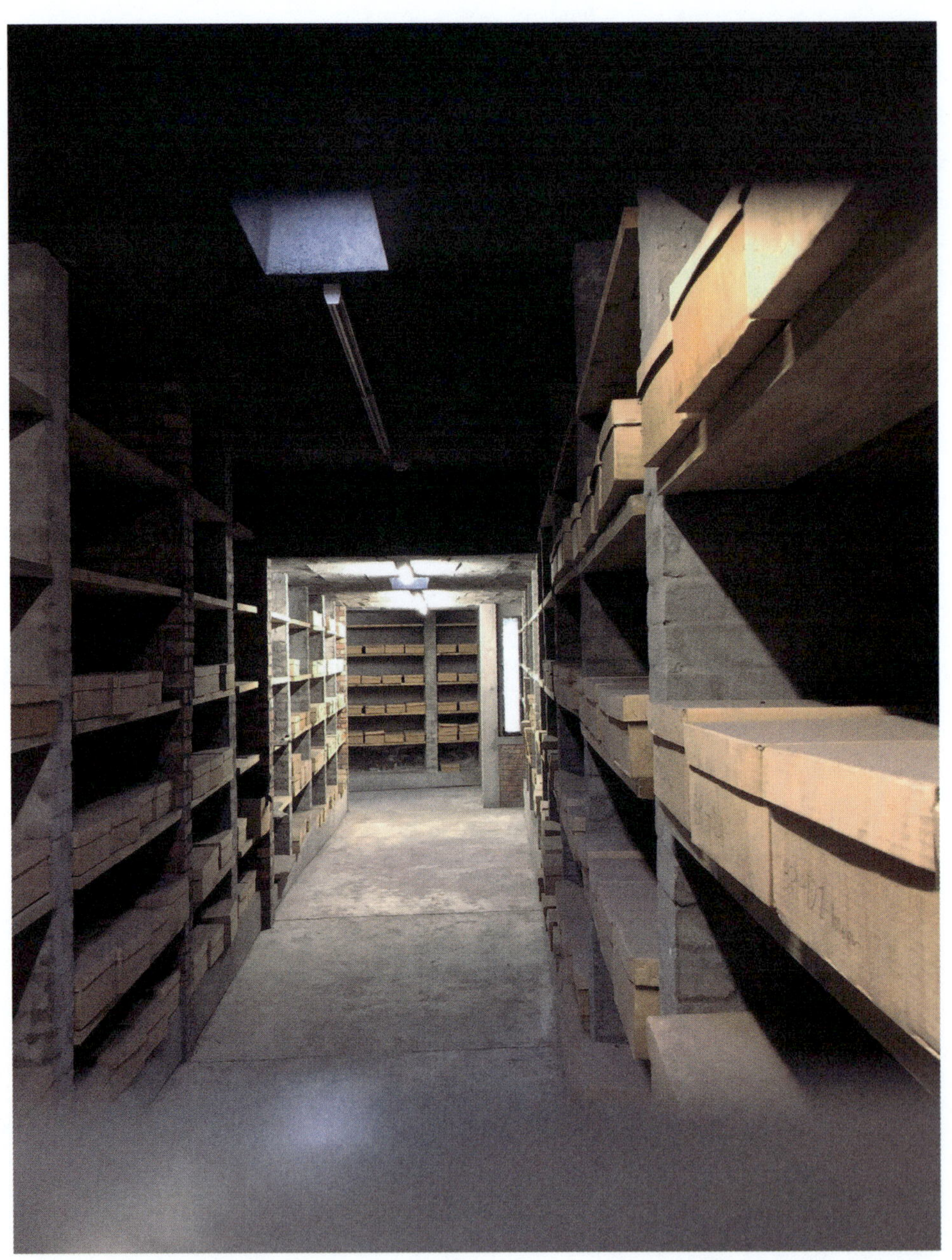

Prestwich Memorial Ossuary,
Stacey Vorster 2020

24   Morrison, T., *Conversations with Toni Morrison* (edited by Danille Kathleen Taylor-Guthrie), University Press of Mississippi, Jackson, 1994, pp. 14-15.

I first met Groote Catrijn in the Western Cape Archives and Records, housed on Roeland Street in Cape Town. I was on a research trip attempting to map out slave histories — visiting the Iziko Slave Lodge, Prestwich Memorial, The Company's Gardens, excavation sites near Gallows Hill and Museum van de Caab in Franschhoek. All these sites were key points in my journey to understanding the city's haunting colonial past. I wanted to understand how the present is constituted through histories of slavery.

Later, when I relocated to Cape Town, I interacted regularly with these sites of memory and my relationship with them evoked a strong sense of connection. The great injustices that had been committed against enslaved men, women and children loomed over my head and the more I thought about these histories, the more gratitude I felt towards my ancestors. My continual return to Groote Catrijn was not because of a direct lineal connection but rather something in her story drew me to her. I wanted to know how she came to be a washerwoman at the Cape Fort during Jan Riebeeck's commandership and how her life unfolded within the oppressive walls of the Fort. As with many enslaved people, details of Groote Catrijn's life are few and far between and fail to account for periods of her life before and after enslavement.

Born c.1631 in what is currently known as Pulicat, India, Catharina (last name unknown), sometimes referred to as Catharina van Paliacatta, Catharina van Bengal and Groote Catrijn, was brought to South Africa through Batavia (present-day Jakarta, Indonesia). According to formal records situated at the Museum van de Caab in Franschhoek, Catharina was brought to the Cape Colony at the age of 26 as a prisoner, to serve out a life sentence for the murder of her lover, Claes van Malabar. Claes was also a slave in Batavia. Defending herself from Claes's abuse, Catharina is said to have hit him with a ladder across his stomach. Claes died four days after the incident, due to complications resulting from a burst bladder, and, in the aftermath, Catrijn was convicted and banished to the Cape Colony. This act of defending herself, I thought, might point to a wider pattern of resistance against oppression in Catrijn's life.

Catharina, believed to be the first recorded female convict, arrived at the Cape on 21 February 1657, working as a washerwoman for Cape Fort commanders. Her journey from Pulicat to Batavia is not well documented. (The ship would have stopped in Batavia presumably because the Dutch East India Company (VOC) dominated the textile trade between Pulicat and Batavia.) In 1669, Catrijn, then working as a washerwoman at the Cape Fort, had a child with a German soldier, Hans Christoffel Snijman. The child took his father's name, and his lineage can be traced to a family of winemakers owning the Solms Delta Wine Estate in Franschhoek. Groote Catrijn mothered another child, Petronella Everardsz. Petronella's father is believed to be Pieter Everaerts, who served in The Council of Policy, which was the highest authority of the VOC in the Cape at the time. Catrijn mothered two more children; Susan and Anthoni (who were possibly born before Christoffel) but these children either died early or were not formally recorded. Eventually, she married Anthonij Jansz van Bengale, an enslaved man from India, in 1671. Her life after this marriage is largely unknown. Records place her death between December 1682 and February 1683 in the Cape.

Groote Catrijn's life story makes visible the complexities of surviving conditions of enslavement and points to tangled relationships of genealogy and heritage between European sailors and soldiers and enslaved women. Survival within states of precarity and fragility necessitated fluid and negotiable ways of being. It is difficult to fully grasp and articulate moments of agency within oppressive conditions, but from the little that we know it seems obvious that they existed. Groote Catrijn makes it possible for us to think through loopholes that are possible within states of terror as well as the possibility of survival outside of what we might think of as 'an escape'.

In thinking about Groote Catrijn's life, I invoke gratitude as a mode of attunement. My gestures include reflecting, imagining, dreaming and communing. The inclination towards gratitude as a gesture in the recollection of slave narratives is premised on the belief that if we are unable to let the dead rest, then our recollection of their lives should at least, in part, be in their service.

In the *Anthropocene Unseen*, social anthropologist Iza Kavedžija describes gratitude as that which combines generosity and humility, noting, 'it [gratitude] encourages us to recognise the importance of others in making our lives liveable'.[25] The extent to which our lives are liveable is linked to those for whom the terror of living was incalculable - slaves who were stolen from their homelands, transported and transplanted into foreign territory and forced to survive in horrifying conditions of violence. By remembering their lives, we are reappropriating the past as a way of understanding our current states of being. Reappropriation - read through Morrison's quote above - is an essential tactic towards collapsing linear readings of time. It allows one to reach into the infinite past and reorient oneself towards it. Through Morrison's methods, one can sense one's connection to the past. For Kavedžija, this connection can be experienced and made visible through practices of gratitude. She writes: 'it could be said that gratitude makes acting in the world possible, by making us aware of the interconnected nature of life.' We are connected to our histories, and contemporary life is inextricably linked to the realities and effects of slavery. Pumla Dineo Gqola asserts this interconnection in her 2010 book, *What is Slavery to Me?*. Gqola examines South Africa's construction of itself during a time of transition and how slavery is evoked and remembered as part of negotiating ways of being. For Gqola, history is a continuation in space and time (and not always in a linear trajectory), where she notes, 'uncovering memory and history demands a critical attentiveness to the uses of the past to negotiate positions in the present'.[26]

25   Kavedžija, I., 'Gratitude', in Howe, C. and Pandian, A. (eds), *Anthropocene Unseen: A Lexicon*, Punctum Books, Santa Barbara, 2020, pp. 221-225.

26   Gqola, P.D., 'Introduction: Tracing (re)memory, thinking through echoes of colonial slavery in contemporary South Africa', *What is Slavery to Me? Postcolonial/Slave Memory in Post-apartheid South Africa*, Wits University Press, Johannesburg, 2010, pp. 1-22.

In remembering Groote Catrijn, I imagine possibilities of understanding while also leaving room for opacity where certain moments of illegibility and evasiveness can be respected. I accept the impossibility (and necessity) of ever fully understanding Groote Catrijn but, taking instruction from Michel-Rolph Trouillot's *Silencing the Past*, I will continue in the unceasing labour of thinking through historical narratives outside of the structuring principles of erasure and trivialisation. Erasure follows from a denial of enslaved people's sense of interiority. The inner characters of the enslaved are often rendered unimaginable and therefore denied. This form of erasure lacks the imagination to conceive of ways in which enslaved people were able to create meaningful lives despite their oppression. Similarly, trivialisation underplays what a great feat it is for enslaved people to have survived. Trivialisation sees no terror, but it also sees no beauty in the lives of the enslaved. In a conversation recorded in 2016 as part of a series at the Duke Divinity School, 'Black outdoors: Humanities futures after property and possession', Fred Moten alludes to this relationship between terror and beauty, noting, 'anybody who thinks they can come even close to understanding how terrible the terror has been without understanding how beautiful the beauty has been against the grain of that terror is wrong. There is no calculus of the terror that can make a proper calculation without reference to that which resists it. It's just not possible.'[27] Similarly, it is impossible to think about the traumatic conditions that made up Groote Catrijn's life without thinking of her life as what Saidiya Hartman refers to as a beautiful experiment.

Going back to the question of letting our dead rest, thinking through why we feel compelled to go back to the grave, and why we feel the need to dredge up the lives of enslaved people, Saidiya Hartman recognises the set of oppositions inherent in 'placing yet another demand upon the [dead] girl, by requiring that her life be made useful or instructive'[28] and proposes a reading of the work of memory as a labour of care that works against silencing and neglect. I believe this labour of care can be practised through small but important gestures of gratitude.

Gestures of gratitude are sounded out through unbounded relationality; they perform a labour of care and expression. This type of labour works against the violence of forgetting and offers a kind of communion—thinking of each other and thinking with each other through time, because we owe each other everything. It is a dedication to those often forgotten, whose lives are encountered in ledgers, court records and inventories.

Nkgopoleng Moloi is a writer and an MA student in contemporary curatorial practices at Wits University. Using archives and exhibition histories, her research explores womxn's mobility, attempting to understand and draw attention to factors that enhance or inhibit womxn's freedom of movement. Her interests are in history, art, language and architecture.

27   Moten, F. 'The Black outdoors: Humanities futures after property and possession', Duke University Divinity School, 2016. Available at: https://humanitiesfutures.org/papers/the-black-outdoors-humanities-futures-after-property-and-possession.

28   Saidiya Hartman. 'Venus in Two Acts', *Small Axe*, 26 (June 2008), pp. 1–14.

Rania Atef

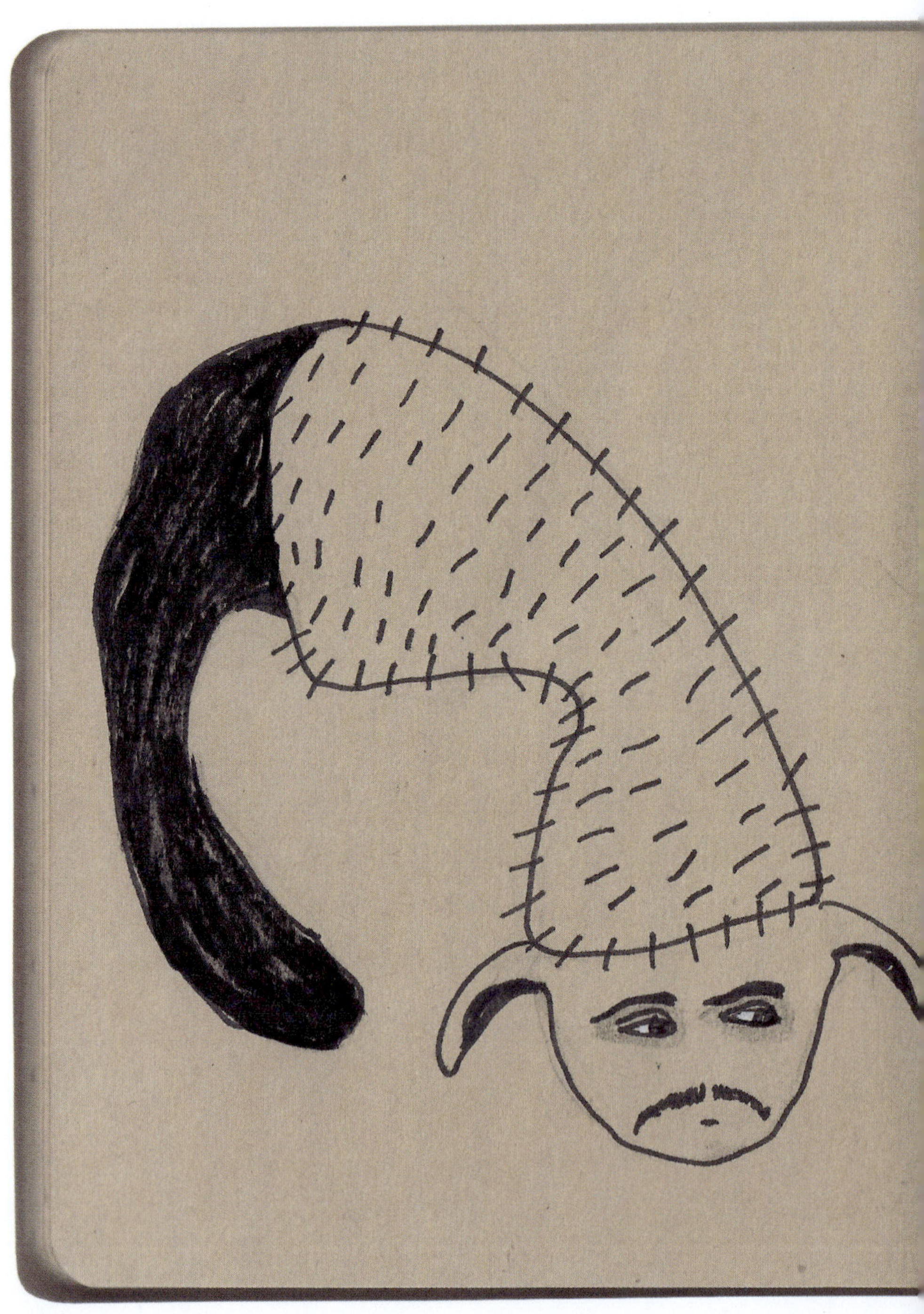

Despite the severity of the times and the troubles this has caused for
me as a mother-artist, I cannot deny that there is a hidden relief at
the demise of mobility for artists. Although movement is a necessity
for artistic work and its development, it becomes a burden for mother-
artists. I do not mean to generalise here, but I think there are many
who share these same feelings with me and are also questioning how the
art scene will move on from this moment. Will the means of operation
change or will we return to the status quo?

This image is part of the project
'Conversations in a Beehive', 2020

- أنا عندى معرض فى يونيو
- هتسافرى؟
- لا. صعبت الشغل
- طلب كويس، هتاخدى فلوس؟
- لأ، دس هيدفعوا الانتاج.
- يعنى ايه؟
- رتشامات وكده، انا لشغل بطلع يعنى يا ماما
- امال امتى هتبقى تباخدى فلوس؟
- معرفش، قدام ان شاء الله..
- هاهاها - هاهاها
- يلا ربنا يوفقك..

The train has stopped. There is no one gasping to catch up. Everyone is seated and the state of 'staying' has become compulsory and not optional. My feelings of anxiety, tension and constant thinking have abated (temporarily) since I am no longer required to answer any more questions, or think of more planning.

As soon as I receive an invitation or acceptance letter for a residency, exhibition or artist talk, a barrage of the following questions usually springs to mind:

> Should I take my daughter or not?
> Will she feel disappointed?
> Will she feel disappointed if I left her?
> Should I feel guilty?
> How many days can I leave her with her my dad and my mom?
> How much can I compress my schedule in order to return earlier?
> Who will fetch her from school while her father is at work?
> What if I take her with me?
> Will I be able to work while she is present?
> Will she be bored?
> How shall I entertain her?
> How can I instal and prepare the work?
> (I can work continuously for hours, subsisting on snacks, but she is only a child, and she shouldn't be in this situation!)
> Who will pay for her airline ticket?
> Can the host or the institution bear the price of her ticket?
> The answer is most often no!
> Can I use my artist fees to pay for her ticket?
> Will it be enough?
> What will be left?

Speaking of institutions, I feel that for them being a mother-artist is almost invisible across all levels. They do not support flight tickets for children, nor are most residency programmes prepared or ready to receive mothers with children. And most funds and grants do not accept childcare as an item in a budget.

I was talking once with the director of a cultural institution and he said that they are about to set up a residency programme and they are currently in the stage of organising housing. I asked him, 'Do you accept mother-artists with their children?' He answered, 'Ooooh, it did not cross my mind that mother-artists will apply, but now we can consider this!'

Another time I received a travel grant that covered the cost of transportation, living and accommodation, but then something popped up and I had to take my daughter with me. I then had to find a way to pay for her flight ticket, which was the highest and most difficult item for me, cost-wise. I contacted the grant donor and they agreed to replace the housing item with my daughter's ticket. I then contacted the host - who had sent the invitation - and they offered to provide me with accommodation from their side. It took a lot of organisation and correspondence, but there was a glimpse of hope for the beginning of a vision and understanding of institutions towards the situation of the mother-artist.

No one wants to be unseen or to be denied the opportunity to exhibit and participate in discussions, and thus develop in her art practice. We are not in a situation of choosing to travel. We travel to exhibit, develop, discuss and meet with a wide spectrum of audiences. However, mother-artists face bureaucratic and logistical barriers, along with institutional infrastructures that do not accommodate them. This additional burden makes opportunities that seem like a dream to everyone turn out to be real difficulties that are not easy to deal with or escape from.

When I started writing this text, I did not want to seem to be complaining or nagging or asking the world to take responsibility for my decisions and choices. I wanted to share my thoughts, and that might count, to some who share similar circumstances, and this way we will not be possessed by the feeling of loneliness and Isolation. Maybe you will read this text and feel reassured.

Rania Atef is a visual artist who is interested in investigating reproductive and labour discourse on individual and collective levels, focusing on the infrastructure of social and cultural institutions. Enrolled in TASAWAR curatorial studies (TN), Rania also attended the MASS Alexandria programme 2018/19 (EG) and holds a BA Degree in Product design in 2011 (EG). She is part of the 'K-OH-llective' artists group.

Through a thicket, you see four women perched on bicycles, laughing and high fiving each other. Their *lessos* are colour coordinated, and woven baskets laden with produce dangle off the handlebars. It is a produced moment, warm and bright, perfect for inclusion into a calendar and a coffee table book. But away from the camera's gaze, the women speak of less joyful things, of being anomalies, the subject of jeers and insults. It is 2014 and I am out on assignment to capture 'unexpected Kenya'. The high-fiving women are cyclists from the port city of Kisumu, selected from an eclectic group of eight. They are in their early 30s to late 50s, a mix of entrepreneurs and homemakers alike. Although cycling increases their mobility, not everyone sees it that way. The women all speak of being accused of 'spoiling men's food' by cycling.

This is our time,
Sebastian Wanzalla,
2017

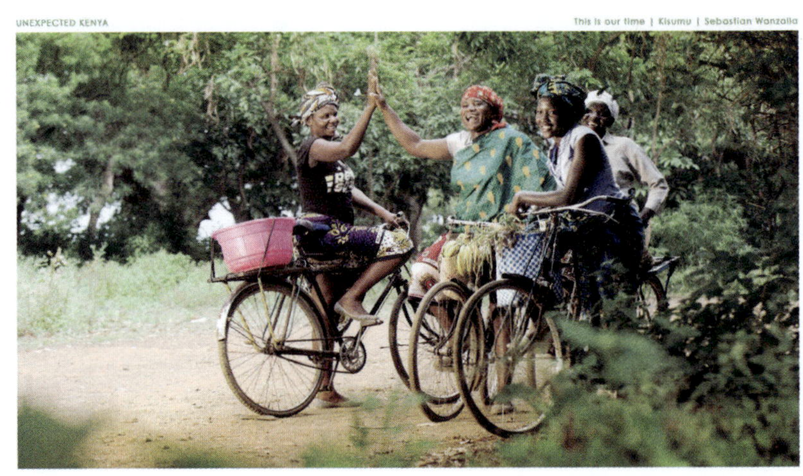

      Kenyan scholar, Professor Wambui Mwangi, prefaces her *New Inquiry* essay, 'Silence is a woman' with a quote from Gikuyu architecture: 'The general term for a woman is 'mutumia', meaning 'one whose lips are sealed'.[29] In East Africa, like everywhere else, the female body is often a target for male domination and censorship. Yet, throughout history, Professor Mwangi points out, women have always found ways of turning their bodies into weapons of subversion. 'Women's power deployed in this way can only be oppositional, always a challenge, always-already embodying and performing the power to refuse.'[30]

      To cycle is to be highly visible. It is to be vulnerable to the elements. Yet to cycle is also to trust in oneself and be propelled forward by muscle and sheer willpower. In this context, the image of a woman cycling is oppositional, always a challenge, always-already embodying and performing the power to refuse.

29   Mwangi, W., 'Silence is a woman', *The New Inquiry*, 4 June 2013. The full text of the essay is available at: https://thenewinquiry.com/silence-is-a-woman/.

30   Ibid.

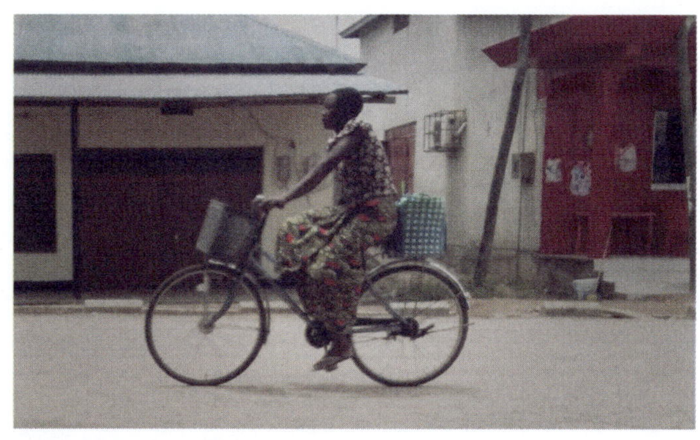

Shopping basket and chill. A woman rides a bicycle in Nzega, Tanzania
Doin' work. A woman in Nzega, Tanzania, rides her bicycle as she goes about her business, Wanjeri Gakuru. 2017.

It is 2013. Kisumu county assembly member Caroline Owen tries to pass a by-law banning women from riding bicycles and motorcycles sideways. Absurd as it sounds, she gains support. The act of sitting with legs astride on two-wheeled transport is 'demeaning', she says, 'uncultural'.[31] 'Legs Together: Law to Uphold Culture for Kenya's Female Bike Riders', reads one headline.[32] Scrolling through the comments section beneath the news clip on YouTube, a commenter writes: 'And how are they supposed to ride the motorcycle again? Or are they always just going to be passengers?'[33]

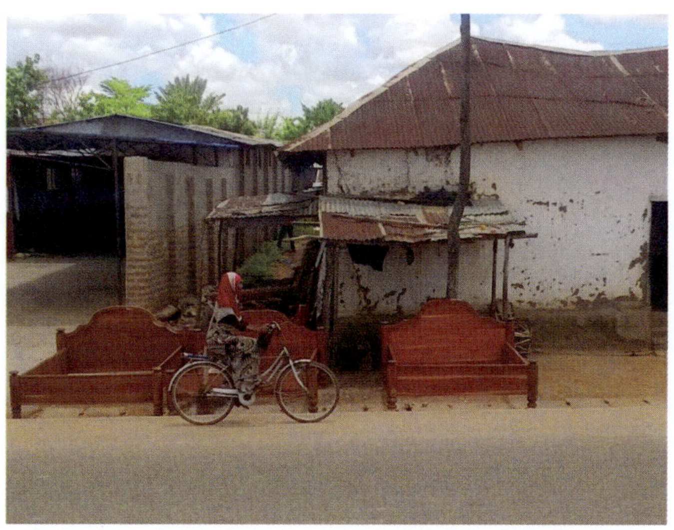

Lady red. A young headscarfed woman cycles past a furniture seller in Nzega, Tanzania, Wanjeri Gakuru, 2017.

31   The KTN News Kenya insert featuring Kisumu county assembly member Caroline Owen is available on YouTube as 'Kisumu Boda Boda Motion targeting women riders', 10 August 2013, and can be viewed at: https://www.youtube.com/watch?v=ZI8D4HCfsVA.

32   Wale-Olaitan, K., 'Legs together: Law to uphold culture for Kenya's female bike riders', *African Rubiz*, 22 August 2013. Available at: https://africanrubiz.org/2013/08/22/legs-together-law-to-uphold-culture-for-kenyas-female-bike-riders/.

33   'Kisumu Boda Boda Motion targeting women riders', 10 August 2013, KTN News Kenya.

In recent years, bicycle access programmes have donated two-wheelers in their thousands to communities across Africa with marked increases not just in education quality but employment opportunities, reproductive health and property rights. 'Wheels of Change', a 2017-2018 report on the impact of bicycle access in rural Zambia, found that giving girls access to bicycles reduced their absence from school by 28 per cent: 'The program also improved measures of empowerment, including girls' sense of control over the decisions affecting their lives i.e., their "locus of control" increased.'[34]

'The earliest bicycles in Kenya were used by the unholy tripartite of colonial conquest: administrators, missionaries, and settlers',[35] writes Kenyan journalist and archivist, Owaahh in his essay, 'Nita Ride Boda Boda' for *The Elephant*. By 1930, bicycles had grown in popularity, but they remained accessible only to working-class men. The women who managed to ride bicycles did so because they came from families that already owned one. Reliant on their patriarch's benevolence, Owaahh notes that a good number of stories of the first women to get an education involved a bicycle, often of a father carrying his daughter to school.

2017. I am travelling across the Greater East Africa, with a mobile literary and arts festival, when I notice something peculiar, a rural town in Tanzania where women cyclists abound. The numbers are astonishing. The place is called Nzega, and the women wear dresses and *lessos* and *buibuis* as they ride. Some have water jerricans strapped to their bicycles and others have babies on their backs. It is the casualness that strikes me, and I feel an immediate kinship with these women, a kinship that stretches back to a similar encounter in Kisumu three years earlier.

The women of Nzega inspire me to purchase my first-ever bicycle. I track down a seller in the town and out of rows and rows and rows of beautiful second-hand Japanese imports I find my stunning beauty and name her after the town. And years later, when a global pandemic narrows our lives, I will take to cycling in the estate parking lot in the small hours of the morning. Lanes then emptied of children and their anxious guardians, music blasting in my ears and the night sky up above, I will feel freedom.

All oppression is connected. All freedom is connected.
— Staceyann Chin[36]

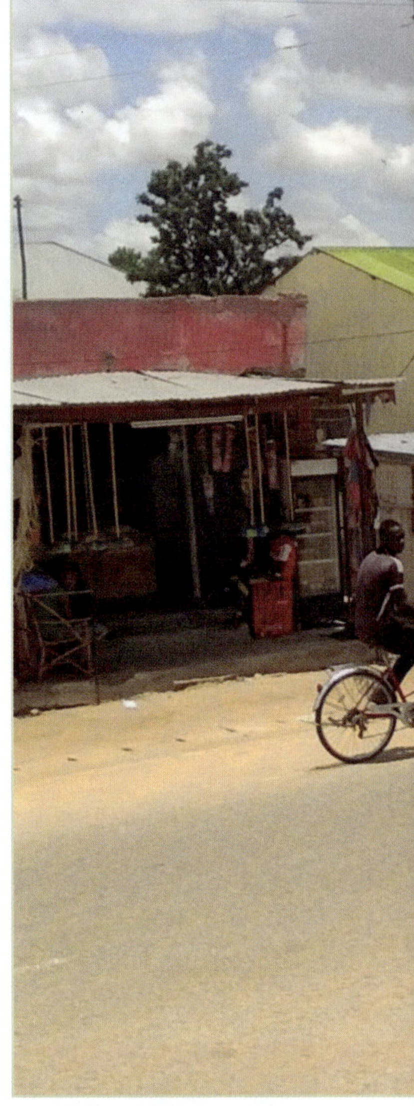

Catch me if you can. A woman adorned in a lesso powers down the streets of Nzega, Tanzania, Wanjeri Gakuru, 2017.

34   In rural Zambia, researchers partnered with World Bicycle Relief to evaluate the impact of bicycle access on girls' educational and empowerment outcomes. The findings of that study, 'Wheels of Change: The Impact of Bicycle Access on Girls' Education and Empowerment Outcomes in Rural Zambia', are available at: https://www.poverty-action.org/study/wheels-change-impact-bicycle-access-girls%E2%80%99-education-and-empowerment-outcomes-rural-zambia.

35   Owaahh, 'Nita ride Boda Boda': How the bicycle shaped Kenya', *The Elephant*, 28 March 2019. The full text of the article is available at: https://www.theelephant.info/culture/2019/03/28/nita-ride-boda-boda-how-the-bicycle-shaped-kenya/.

36   Chin, S., 'All oppression is connected', 25 July 2014, Available at: http://whyaminotsurprised.blogspot.com/2014/07/staceyann-chin-all-oppression-is.html.

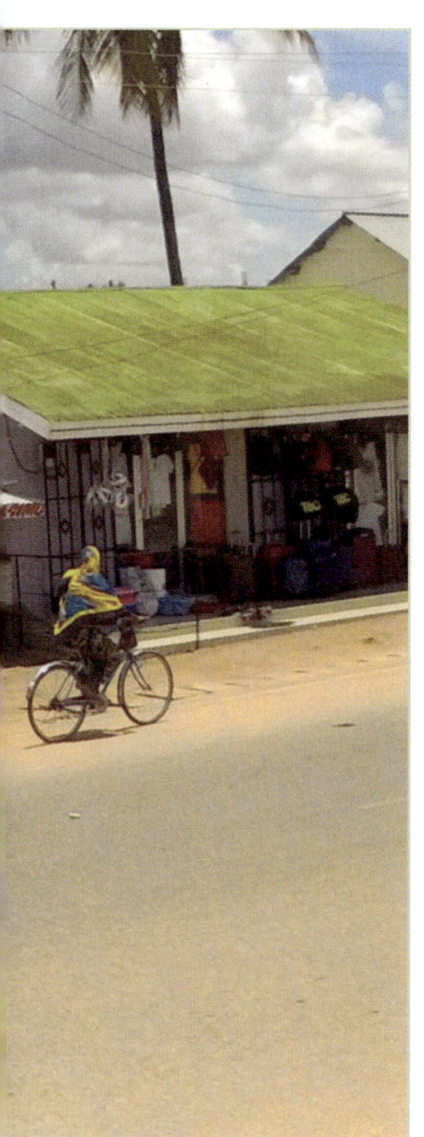

In his essay, Owaahh references a newspaper advert in *Mambo Leo*, a local language daily, placed by the British bicycle manufacturer, Raleigh, in June 1930. The Raleigh bicycles were known colloquially as 'Black Mambas' or 'Blackies'. To this day, Raleigh remains popular among blue-collar workers and is a staple in lower-income households across East Africa. It is what the women in Kisumu rode. And yet, when high-level conversations regarding road infrastructure, alternative modes of transport or green energy take place, the dominant image in the heads of town planners is that of an elite cyclist - here it could be male or female - who owns a roadster worth tens of thousands and can be seen whizzing past in the 'appropriate' apparel, cycling shorts and glasses, reflector jackets and helmets. There is a hierarchy regarding whose cycling body matters.

Despite my *Nzega*'s history, I am an urban cyclist myself, part of a troubling narrative that ought to change. Professor Mwangi writes of 'Wanjiku', an iconic representation of the ordinary Kenyan citizen whose name never appears in news broadcasts or newspaper pages. And as I scroll through the websites with smiling faces of happy bicycle recipients and urban planning panels stuffed with engineers and architects, I think of Professor Mwangi's description of Wanjiku as 'the voice of those who are subject to the actions of the powerful but never powerful themselves'.[37]

I write about the everyday cyclists and the beauty I see in them because they matter. There is a great measure of speculation involved in all this, I know. I didn't interview the Nzega women, for instance, and my desire to ascribe special meaning to their lives perhaps unfairly demands that they tell some larger story than simply being who they are. What I know for sure, however, is that everything I saw and felt in Nzega and Kisumu mirrors how friends in Amsterdam and Berlin interact with their bicycles. I can see clearly that a bicycle can and does represent everything I want for myself and women everywhere: freedom, autonomy and fluidity.

Wanjeri Gakuru is a freelance journalist, essayist and filmmaker. A cross-section of her writing has appeared in Transition Magazine, The Elephant, CNN, The Sunday Times, LA Times Magazine and The Africa Report among others. She is an alumna of the 2014 Farafina Creative Writing Workshop. She was selected as the 2018 Literary Ambassador for Nairobi by Panorama: The Journal of Intelligent Travel and is a 2021 Baraza Media-Fringe Graph Fellow. Between 2018 and 2020, Wanjeri served as Managing Editor of Pan-African writers' collective, Jalada Africa and in 2021, she was appointed Jalada Africa's Board Secretary. Wanjeri has contributed variously to curatorial projects and publications including: *Just A Book* (Goethe-Institut Kenya, 2016), Jalada Mobile Literary and Arts Festival (Jalada Africa, 2017), #RafikiZetu: Kenyan *LGBTIQ Stories, as told by Allies* (Denis Nzioka, 2019), *Family Matters* (Goethe-Institut Namibia, 2021) and Archive of Forgetfulness (2021). Read her work at www.wanjeri.com.

37   Mwangi, W., 'Silence is a woman', *The New Inquiry*, 4 June 2013.

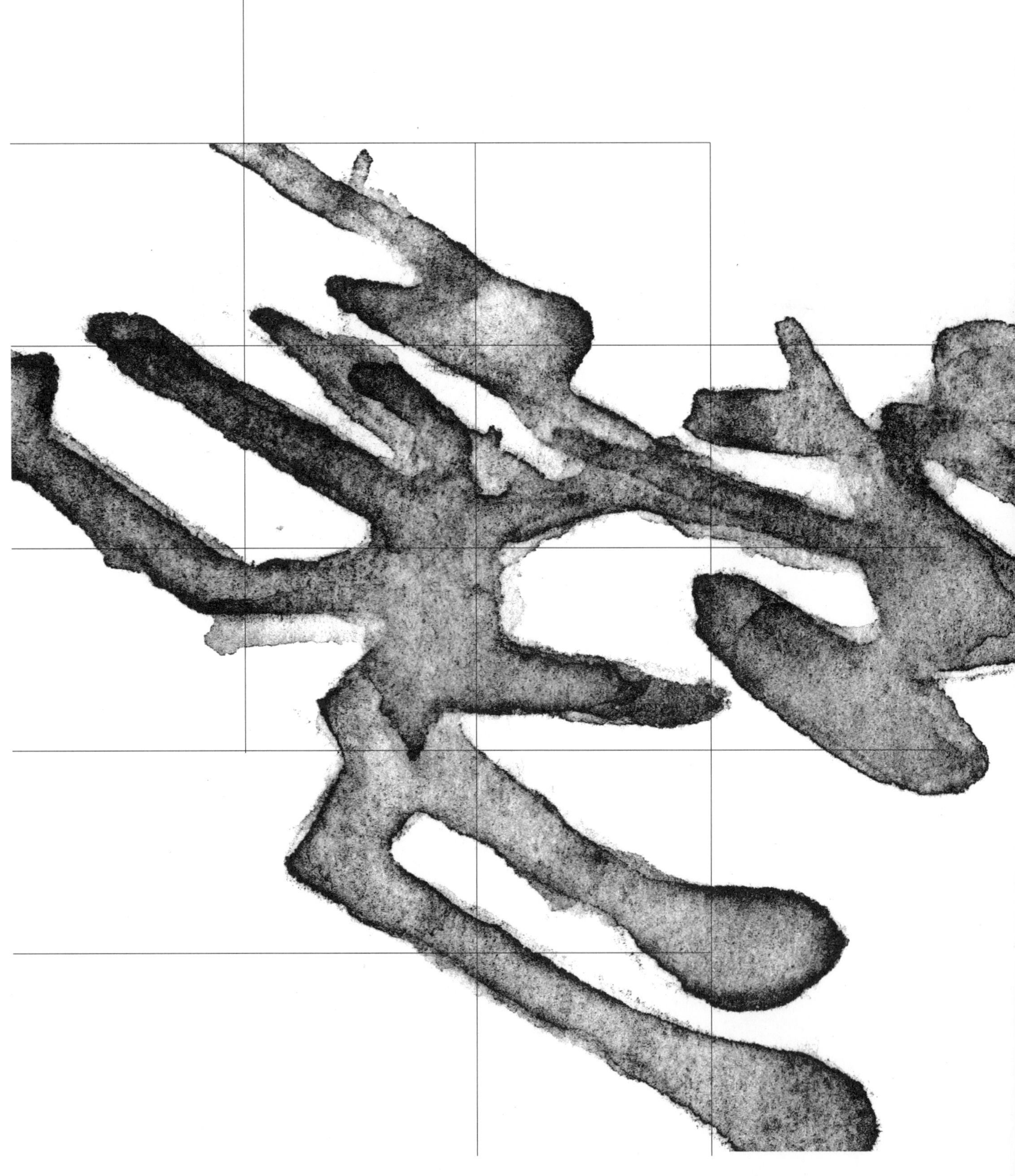

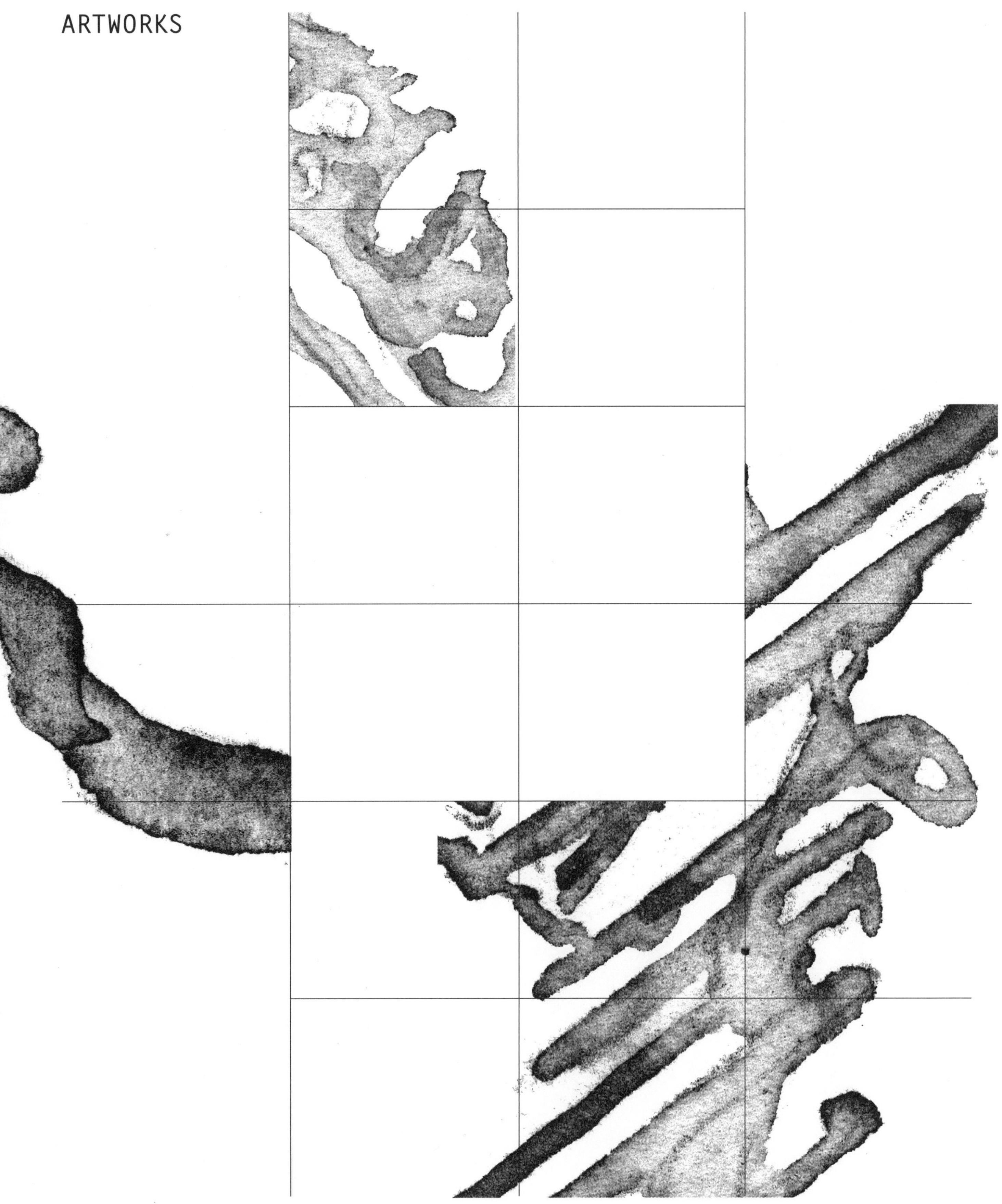

The *Archive of Forgetfulness* received an immense response to the open call from across the African continent and diaspora.[38] The final selection launched in April 2021 responds to questions in the call, yet also provokes a sense of wonder, possibility, immense beauty, care and radical praxis. The works operate at the unstable border between binaries, suggesting an ecology of mutual interdependence: remembering and forgetting, individual and collective memory, human and more-than-human, past and future. While territorial borders are spoken to, borders in the works also become metaphoric devices as a means to ask new questions, test out mixed methods and tell different stories. The various projects weave together questions around liberatory processes and engage with deep pasts and deep futures. They offer threads for dreaming and imagining alternative realities, forge political allegiances and suggest alternative knowledge frameworks in the face of consistent, extractivist, anti-black and anti-poor violence. The works range from poetry to drawing and virtual reality, to audio playlists, spoken-word, film and more, often occupying multiple forms at once.

The website design for the *Archive of Forgetfulness* has been a means to hold together the varied and wide-ranging voices who speak through the platform. The graphics map the wide range of geographies and contexts of the projects, utilising distance, time and scale as the constituent elements to create an ordering device. Each work is ascribed an object and a shadow.

---

38   Twenty-two projects and five essays were selected from over 300 submissions received.

The inclusion of the shadow as present, textured and visible is a means to elicit an engagement with that which is displaced or untranslatable. The shadow complicates the act of indexing through objects, by speaking to that which is often seen but unnoticed or overlooked. Yet, as the landing graphic on the home page of archiveofforgetfulness.com illustrates, this is also a map which folds and bends in on itself. It recognises the longitude and latitude of geographical coordinates, and simultaneously offers a series of multiple readings of the submissions. Building on this moving metaphor, the website invites an audience to read the archive backwards, forwards and in-between.

The immense range and extent of the works included in thematics, approaches and geographies is not intended as exhaustive or encyclopaedic. These are not easy nor straight-forward projects, and the questions they ask require a certain labour from their audience; they demand an engagement with the opacity of time and space. Following Antillean philosopher Édouard Glissant, opacity is not a lack of clarity or obscurity. It is instead, 'that which cannot be reduced'.[39] The linear nature of a printed catalogue cannot do the same work as the website. It offers instead yet another means of reading and engaging with the artworks, here, through the slowness of the turned page.

39   Glissant, É., *Poetics of Relation* (translated by Betsy Wing), University of Michigan Press, Ann Arbor, 1990, pp. 191.

FOR WANGARI MAATHAI
AT UHURU PARK
Aleya Kassam (Kenya)

In 1989, the Kenyan government wanted to destroy Uhuru Park to build a 60-storey business complex. Wangari Maathai led the protests that saved Uhuru Park so millions of people in Nairobi could enjoy a green space to gather, walk and breathe in. Thirty years later the Kenyan government thought people had forgotten. In 2019, in another attempt at dispossession, the Kenyan government wanted to steal Nairobi's breath again, this time to build an expressway to the airport. Wangari Maathai's spirit was with the protests to save Uhuru Park. On that day, Aleya Kassam wrote this memory poem, as a warning. The soil always remembers.

Aleya Kassam is a Kenyan feminist, storyteller, writer and performer. Her work explores the spaces between imagination and memory, often using ritual as a way to access those realms. She is a co-founder of the award-winning content studio, The LAM Sisterhood, which fills the world with stories for African women to feel seen, heard and beloved.

In this series, Arafa Cynthia Hamadi explores their culture with an intent to find themself within it. They are from Dar-es-Salaam and have found themself actively and in-actively living in other towns along this Swahili coast. This has led them to a process of relearning about her home, the cultures and the people who live there. The Kujiona Series is born from this process and includes the conversations and creations they accumulated in the last three months of 2020. The artwork is created using a scavenged Swahili dhow that acts as a metaphorical connection to their coastal cultural history. Care and restoration of the dhow becomes a means to have wider conversations around the work.

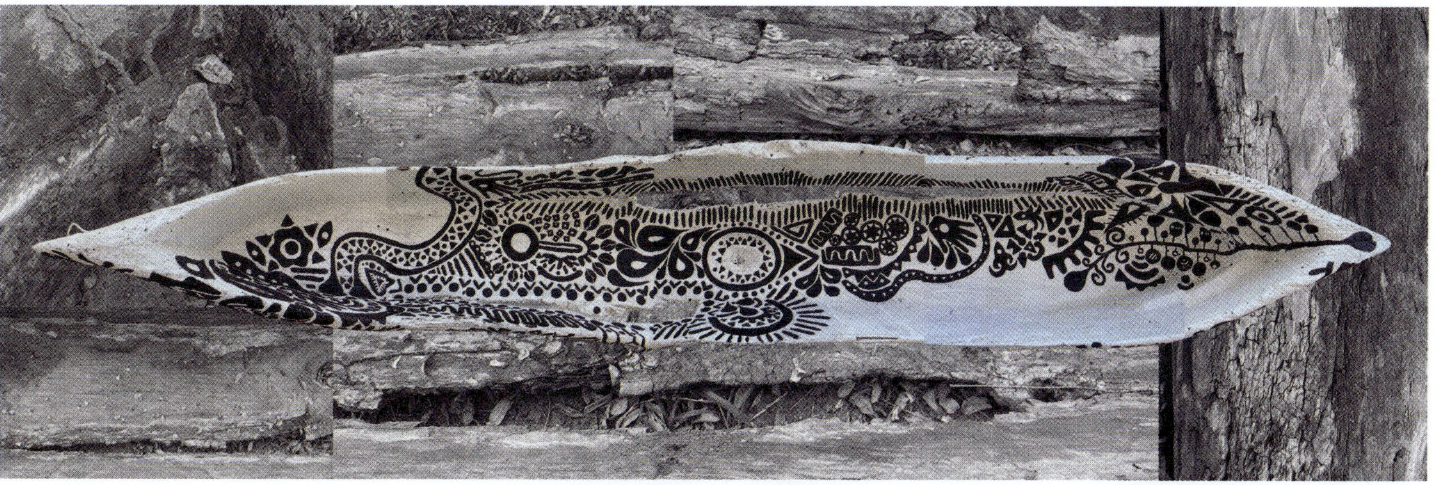

Arafa Cynthia Hamadi
is a non-binary, multidisciplinary artist working in Tanzania and Kenya. They create artwork in various mediums that address the intersections of the conceptual and the physical, as well as the ephemeral and the permanent, in hopes of provoking their visitors into considering their daily realities. Arafa's work also explores their queerness in relation to space and occupancy. They work in the realms of 3D design, graphic design, sculpture and architecture.

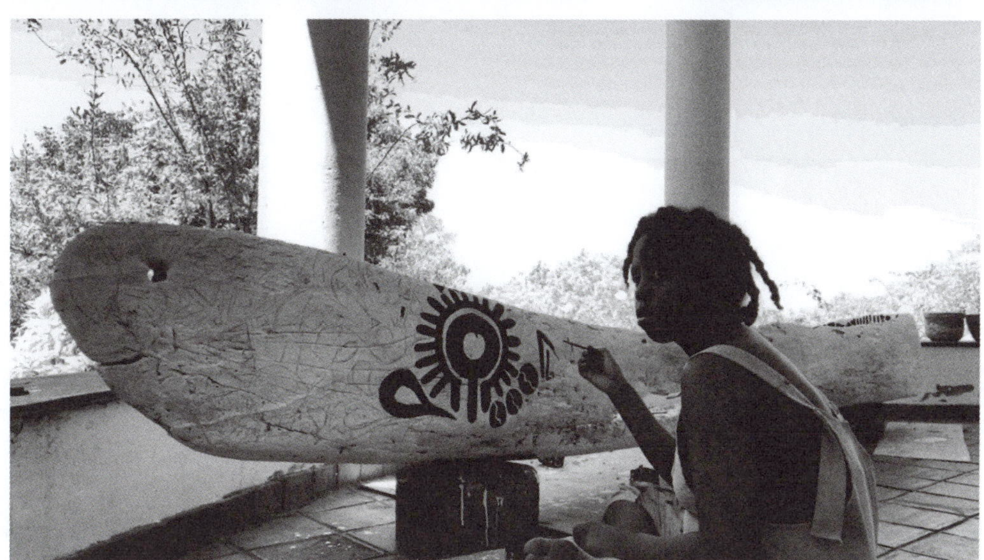

THE BRIDGE
Caio Simões de Araújo (South Africa)

Inaugurated on 10 November 2018, the bridge connecting Maputo to the fishing village of Katembe, on the other side of the Maputo bay, is paradigmatic of Chinese-led infrastructural megaprojects in the global South, in general, and in Africa, in particular. The bridge is not, however, merely a monumental engineering project. It also involved great economic change and restructuring of public finances and carried with it the promises of urban renewal and the development of Southern Mozambique broadly. While the bridge carries with it the 'promise of infrastructure' - the promise of modernity and economic development - it also points to the dangers of neocolonialism under neoliberal globalisation and Chinese financing in the global South. This visual essay, 'The Bridge', assembles an immersive, experiential and memorialist register of the instances of public performance surrounding the Maputo-Katembe Bridge in its moment of inauguration in November 2018. All images and sounds were collected during the weekend in which the infrastructural project achieved its triumphal conclusion: from excerpts of public speeches by members of the Frelimo party and the Chinese engineering firm in charge of the project - the China Road and Bridge Corporation - to the various criticisms voiced by members of civil society. The camera is in constant movement, facing the bridge from various vantage points in the city of Maputo; while the viewer is invited to come aboard, to cross the bridge as the camera moves across too. The various positions of the camera - located inside a car, a bus, a tuk-tuk, the ferry boat, or placed in front of various landmarks of the city - is representative of the multiplicity of conflicting vantage points, affects, memories and experiences surrounding the bridge as an 'omnipresent infrastructure' making its mark in the cityscape.

Caio Simões de Araújo is an anthropologist and historian based in Johannesburg, South Africa. He is currently a postdoctoral researcher at the Wits Institute for Social and Economic Research (WiSER), at Wits University, where he works in the Project 'Regions 2050', headed by Achille Mbembe. His research explores the relationship between memory, history and infrastructure in Southern Mozambique, especially by looking at the social and cultural lives of infrastructural projects and the political imaginaries revolving around them.

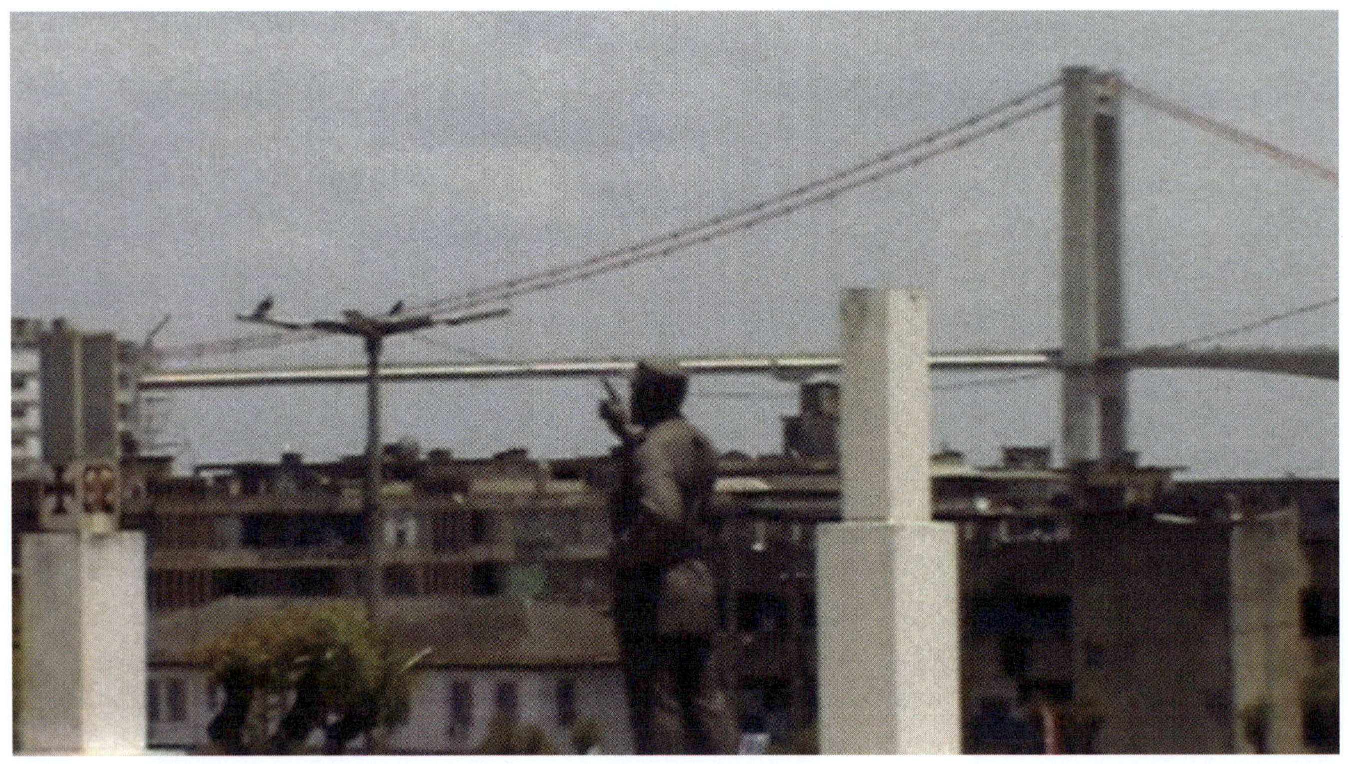

The legacies of colonialism, settler-colonialism and neocolonialism, apartheid and the Group Areas Act live on in the present as many are forcibly removed from their land, and are dehumanised, killed or criminalised for this occupation while the South African Defense Force, South African Police and the Anti-Land Invasion Unit have committed mass crimes and operate outside of the law. This is a struggle South Africa is not alone in, as similar atrocities are/were committed by armies elsewhere in Africa and by the Israeli Defense Force against Palestinians who have been killed, dispossessed of their lands and whose homes have been demolished. The film asserts that people are occupying, not invading the land, as they can't be invaders in something that belongs to them. The act of existing becomes an occupation.

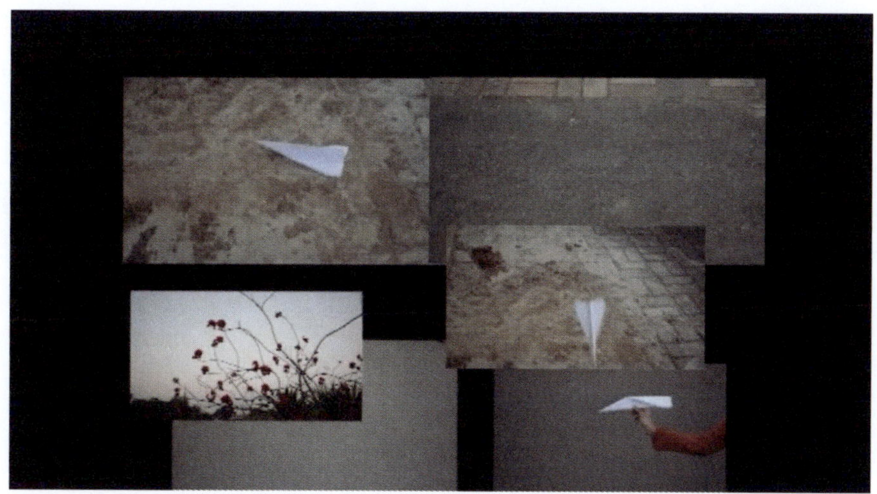

Cheriese Dilrajh was born in Durban and has a BA in Fine Arts from the University of the Witwatersrand, though her more legitimate knowledge comes from the streets. Her areas of interest include (but are not limited to) migration, indentured labour, complexity of meaning and the making of new meanings by radically dreaming, conversation and knowledge production. She experiments with sampling fragments of the worlds she encounters through sensory, audio, visual, written, multitudinal forms, social practice and cultural work (as well as occupation and disruption, where necessary). Often these worlds are birthed by inheritance and are a becoming of her story.

GQOM WAVES
DORMANTYOUTH/Thelma Ndebele (South Africa)

Gqom Waves is a short mix composed of music that was made from sampling Gqom sounds, a music genre born and cultivated in the rural hills of KwaZulu-Natal, South Africa. This genre came out of the minds of experimental club kids using pirated music production software. The mix speaks of the transgressive power of musical innovation, where economic, social and physical borders have not stopped the world from moving their bodies to its frequency. The voices heard overlayed in this mix are from those beyond the African continent who have embraced the sound and have added samples of their own country's familiarity in tone and cadence to make new borderless, hybrid genres such as UK Gqom.

DORMANTYOUTH is the DJ alias of Johannesburg-based, non-binary architect **Thelma Ndebele.** Their interest in the intersection of music and architecture led to them using DJing as a research method for their Master's dissertation (GSA, UJ) on mixing music as an act of temporal place-making within the night club space.

'Casablanca Run the Covid' is a techno-poem for the eyes and the ears. A lonely scooter travels through the deserted streets of Casablanca during a Covid-19 lockdown in 2020. Filmed vertically by a 360° cam, this piece takes us through an anamorphic crossing of a ghost town, emptied of life. Casablanca becomes an empty planet, bristling with moving protuberances and dancing architecture, moving to the rhythm of the race. Casablanca, an urban virus, is crowned with palm trees, candelabras, towers, bell towers and minarets. The city unrolls and curves, tattooed with flowing graphics and is bathed in an iridescent amniotic space of obscure light.

Zouhair Laalam is a Moroccan photographer and videographer from Casablanca, and **Kamel Ghabte** is a digital artist and consultant from Cenon. In addition, Ghabte is a consultant and composer of electronic music, and an instructor in digital audio and digital interactivity. Magnetised by their shared passion for moving images, dancing sounds and digital interactivity in real-time, they now mix their talents and skills in 'My digital food', their creation and research lab.

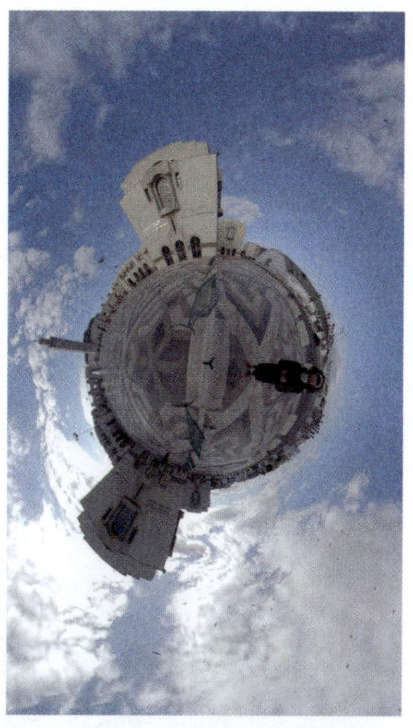

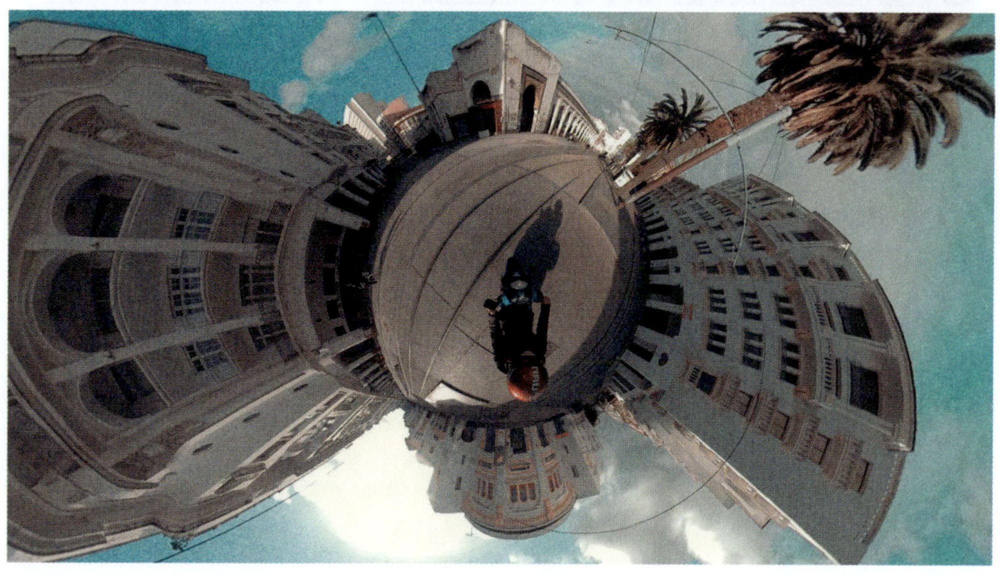

Digital Beings comments on our growing and deepening relationship with the digital realm, and the corresponding changing nature of our interactions with the natural world. Looking at the massive wave of digitisation, which has accelerated due to the global pandemic, the work asks how far the digital realm might be an extension of the human in this new future. And is science and technology the next inevitable step of evolution, extending the human's current physical and mental limitations? The work explores the physical products of this rapid digitisation, focusing on aeroplanes and the internet, and the profound effect they have on our relationship with the self, others and the wider environment.

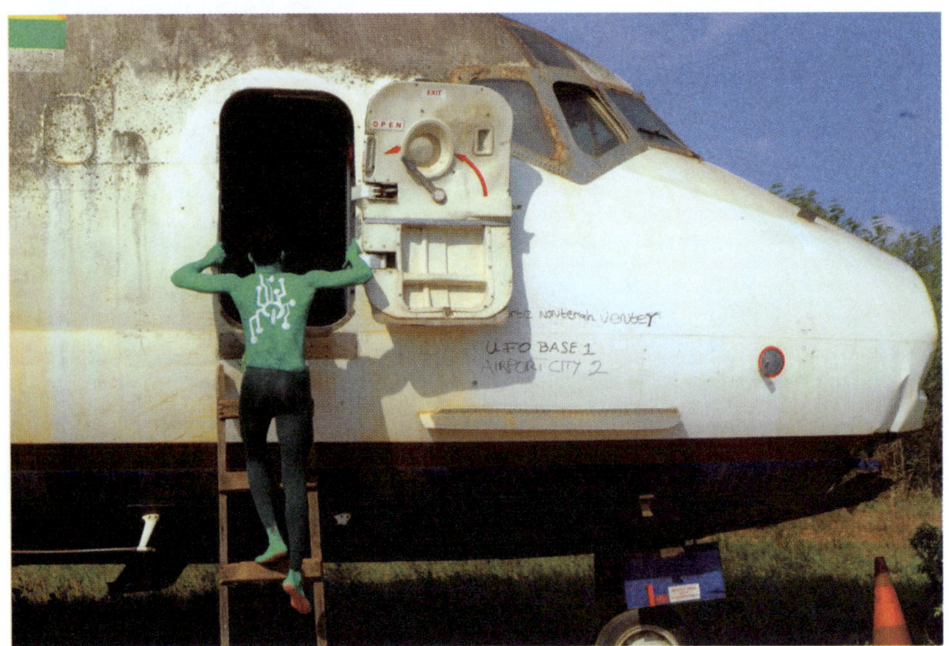

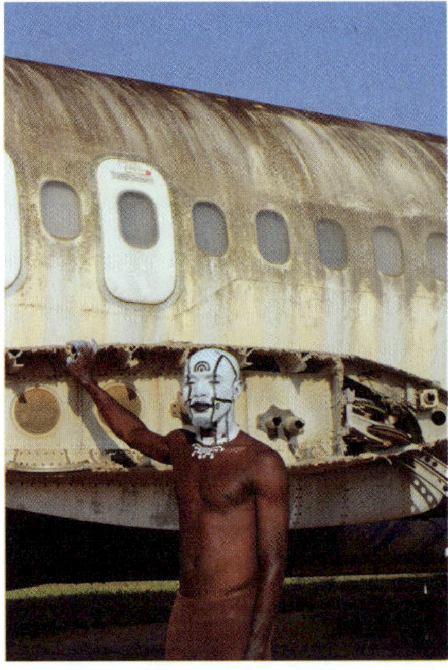

Kwasi Darko is a new media artist living and working in Ghana. His work uses visual artistry and performance art to explore his ideas. He became recently interested in investigating ideas such as transhumanism and our renewed relationship with digital realms and technology, stemming from recent global events.

Integrate v. [ˈˈin-tə-ˌgrāt]
1. combine (one thing) with another to form a whole.
2. bring into equal participation in a social group or institution.
Refuge n. [ˈref. juːdʒ]
(A place that gives) protection or shelter from danger, trouble, unhappiness.

These films are part of a series of documentary shorts on LGBTQ+ migration and refuge. They tell the story of a protagonist who was forced to leave Nigeria to save himself and his love. *Part I: Refuge* tells the journey of an African gay refugee seeking asylum in Germany. In *Part II: The Kiss*, an African refugee visits the Gay Holocaust Memorial in Berlin. The film is a performance exploring the romance and terror of a simple kiss.

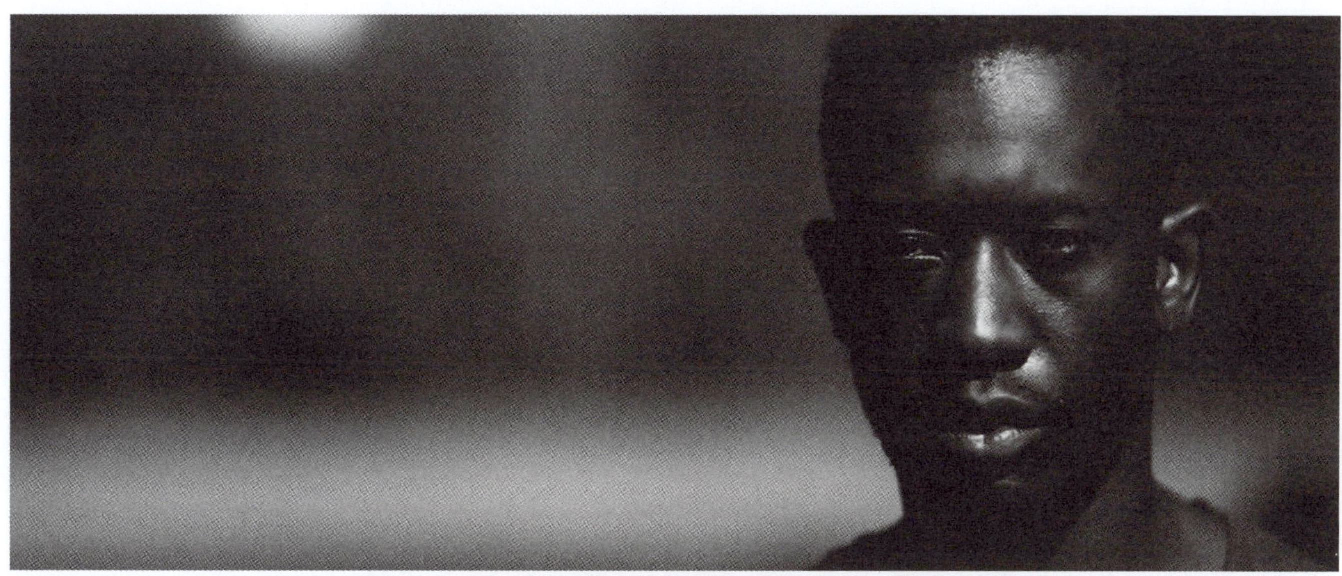

Leandro Goddinho is an award-winning Brazilian filmmaker dedicated to LGBTQ+ issues. In 2015, he was selected by the German Chancellor Fellowship for Prospective Leaders sponsored by Alexander von Humboldt Foundation to research and develop a documentary project on LGBTQ+ Diaspora, called *The world is round so that nobody can hide in the corners.*

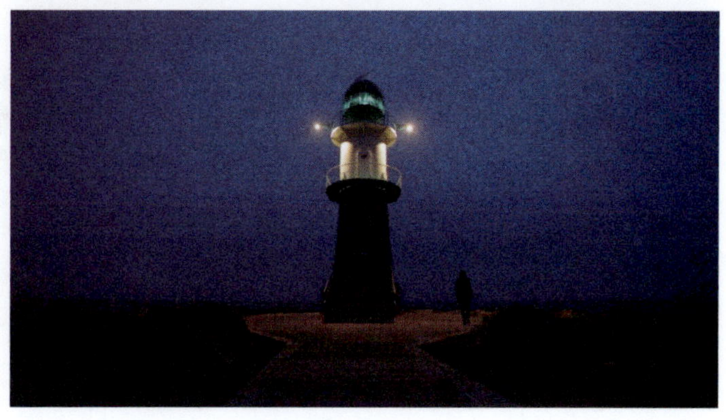

For over a year Lo-Def Film Factory have been engaged in a research project looking at archives, mapping and physical resources in central and southern Africa. Geo-Quiz is an old '80s geography board game they happened across. It did not have instructions so they could not figure out how to play it and instead decided to experiment with it. This video forms part of a broader project looking at uranium in the DRC and South Africa - a mineral that has been at the root of great conflict. The work looks at the relationship between raw materials, technology and movement. This builds on an interest in the ways colonial practices have continued into this century, and how technological infrastructures trace the routes of former empires.

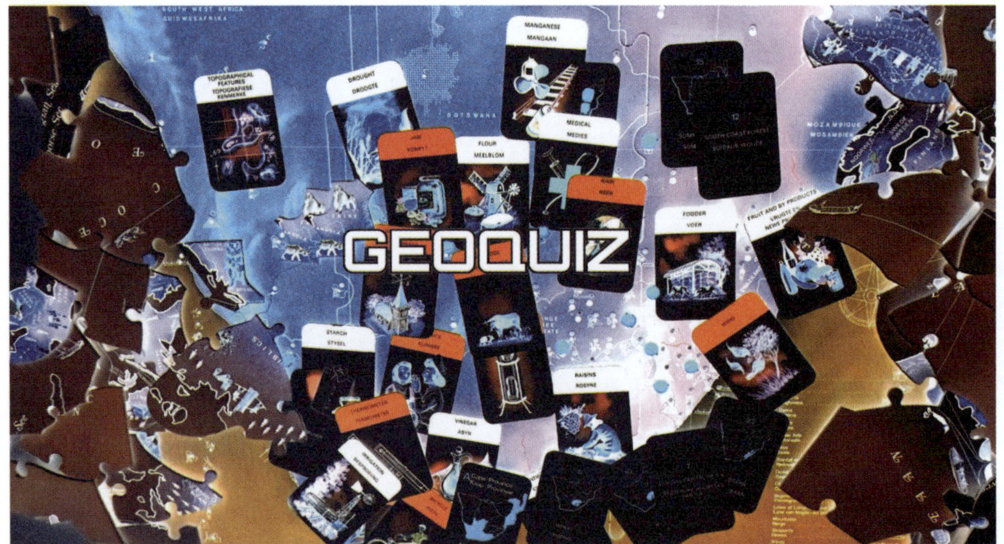

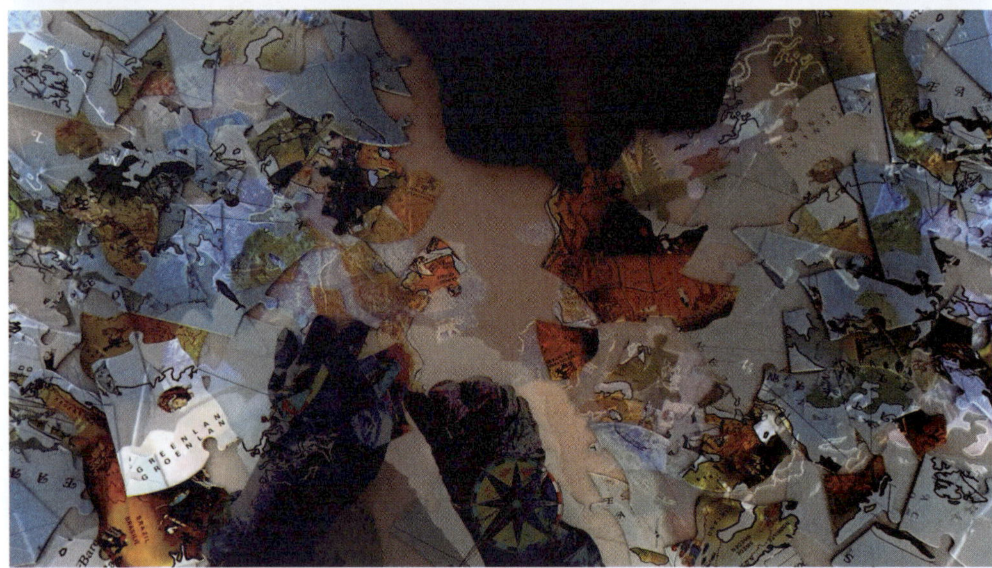

Lo-Def Film Factory is a participatory community cinema initiative created by Francois Knoetze and Amy Louise Wilson. Employing an experimental praxis that emphasises co-creation and mistake-making, it aims to create space for video storytelling. The initiative places value on the transmission of ideas and experience over high production value.

Emergence: Afri Viola is a performance art piece that merges the traditions and conceptual visual language of art and technology of Virtual Realities. *Emergence Afri' Viola* is immersed with visual cues retelling forgotten and omitted histories of African people and the landscape through the re-imaged colourful, comical and animated world of pop-culture. It is inspired by a fresco from the 1400s by Masolino da Panicale, in which a dead 'Westernised' Christ is shown at the moment of Resurrection. This art work aims to overturn this convention of the white messiah, while exposing the long-term effects of the colonial project through religion on the Black African identity and the plundering of land and mineral resources - stripped and stolen, only to be re-appropriated into a mouthpiece of Western colonial propaganda. VR and video enable the viewers to have a sense of being there - of living in the moment happening, captured. This can teach us how to see deeply, which is the essence of all spiritual practices. Technology is ultimately a spiritual force and a part of our inner beings.

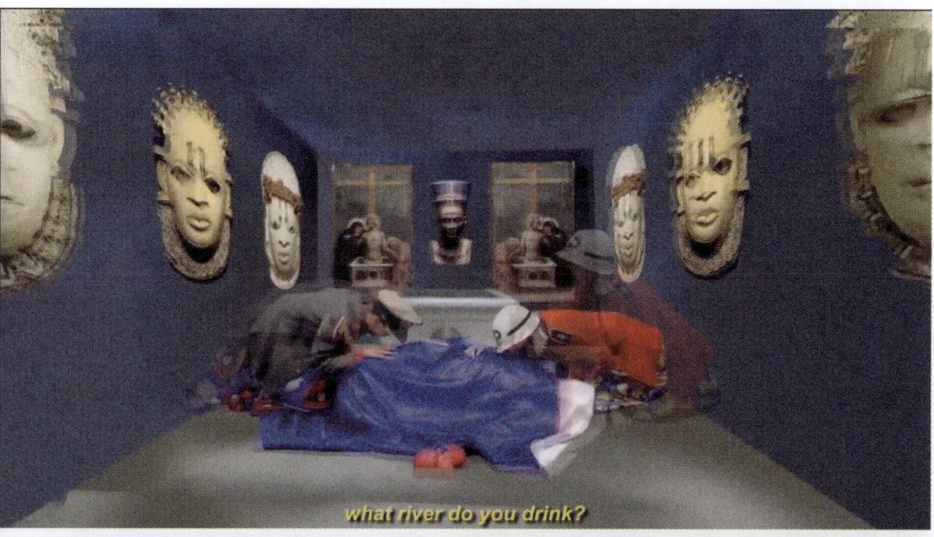

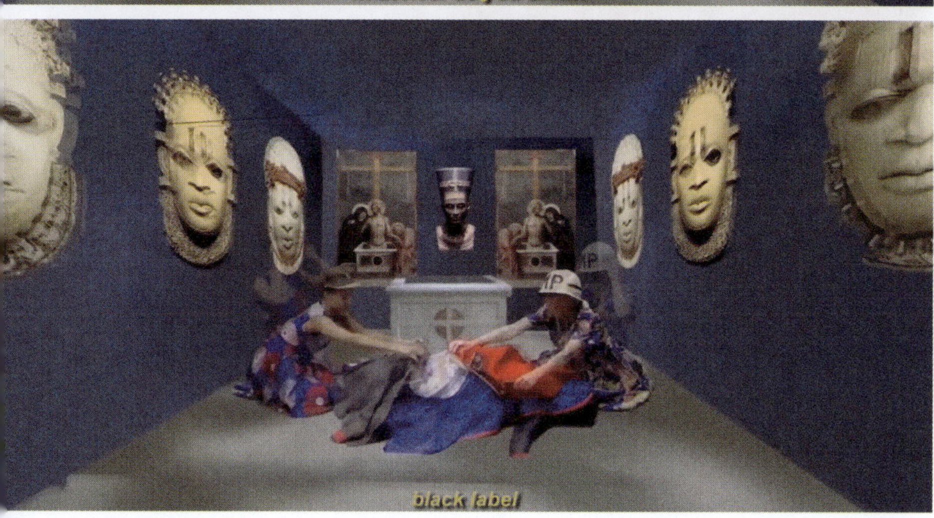

Magolide Collective was formed in 2019 by Adilson De Oliveira and Mzoxolo 'X' Mayongo, the multi-mix media duo, who names this act 'visual alchemy', a notion related to their moniker. 'Magolide' is a colloquial Xhosa term describing someone with gold (teeth, chains, watches) and references the socio-political histories of Johannesburg, a city literally built on gold - and on the labour of black migrant workers. They also draw from the ancient philosophical/scientific practice of alchemy. The collaborative nature of the artistic duo is based on radical acts of decolonial theory, thinking through their practice in both academic framing and cultural working in the production of knowledge as much as the creation of artistic expression. Their work has been shown at a number of international exhibitions and events, including the Kampala Biennale (Uganda, 2021), *i-D* Magazine's Global Design Graduate Show (UK, 2020), P-OST Contemporary in the Netherlands (2021) and at the Arts Council of the African Studies Association Triennial (ACASA) (2021).

'Siyagoduka' means we are leaving or are on our way. It speaks to the nature of departure; whether it be in the physical sense or spiritual sense through death and ritual ascendance. While witnessing the forced and now declared illegal inhumane removals in Hangberg, Ocean View and Khayelitsha in Cape Town during the Covid-19 lockdowns, the author was reminded of the long history of forced removals in South Africa, and beyond, from the 1913 Land Act to the Tulsa Oklahoma Massacre. History has a cyclic recurrence that has a way of reminding us of the cracks in our systems of governance and existence. This prompted a consideration of the process of coerced, forced or 'voluntary' black migration due to unfavourable circumstance and living conditions, to find new life and prosperity. Siyagoduka is about being on the move and the journey that lies ahead. The work takes on science fiction and dystopian aesthetics to speak to the extraordinary nature of the times we live in as outer-worldly expressions of travel through painting, and a 3D-augmented-reality interactive digital experience.

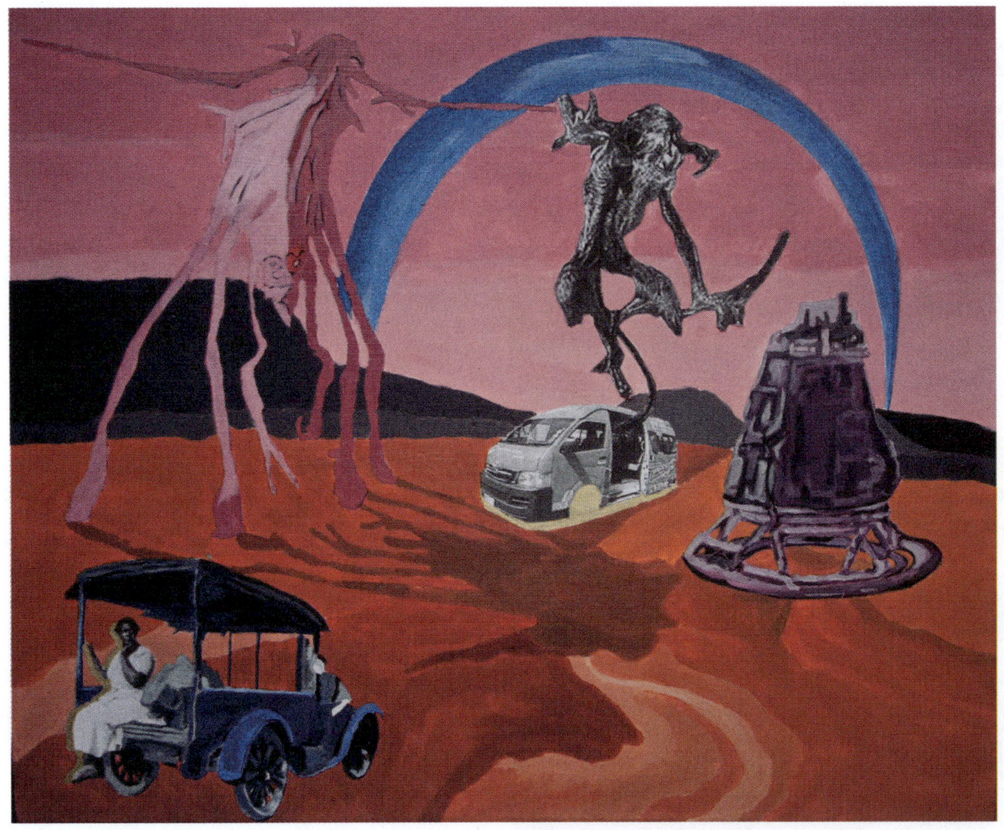

Malebona Maphutse is a Johannesburg-based multidisciplinary artist with a BA (Fine Art) degree from the University of the Witwatersrand. A recent Institute of Creative Arts fellow, her work has existed in/at several exhibitions, spaces, and happenings including the Bergen Triennial 2019 (*The Dead Are Not Dead*), and the Stellenbosch Triennial 2020 (*Tomorrow There Will Be More of Us*).

Red Earth is an ongoing research project which aims to capture, analyse and reimagine personal West African ancestry, language and geological movement within virtual afterlife, the accelerated 'posthuman' state now upon us. As is often witnessed in flora, displacement and relocation can affect the well-being of biological entities. Red Earth explores the metaphysical dissonance that occurs from living in non-linear virtual space and time across hemispheres, by distilling, partly through code, what occurs when translating thought between language forms. These distillations take the form of geological totems, data topography as manifestations of the missing earth as it were. These processes attempt to engage with metaphysical discord within re-routed and excavated cultural identity, led by Yoruba continuity of spirit (beyond the body). The data extracted from these experiments have then been moulded into sculptures that take their lead from, and reimagine, Yoruba totemic and geological items.

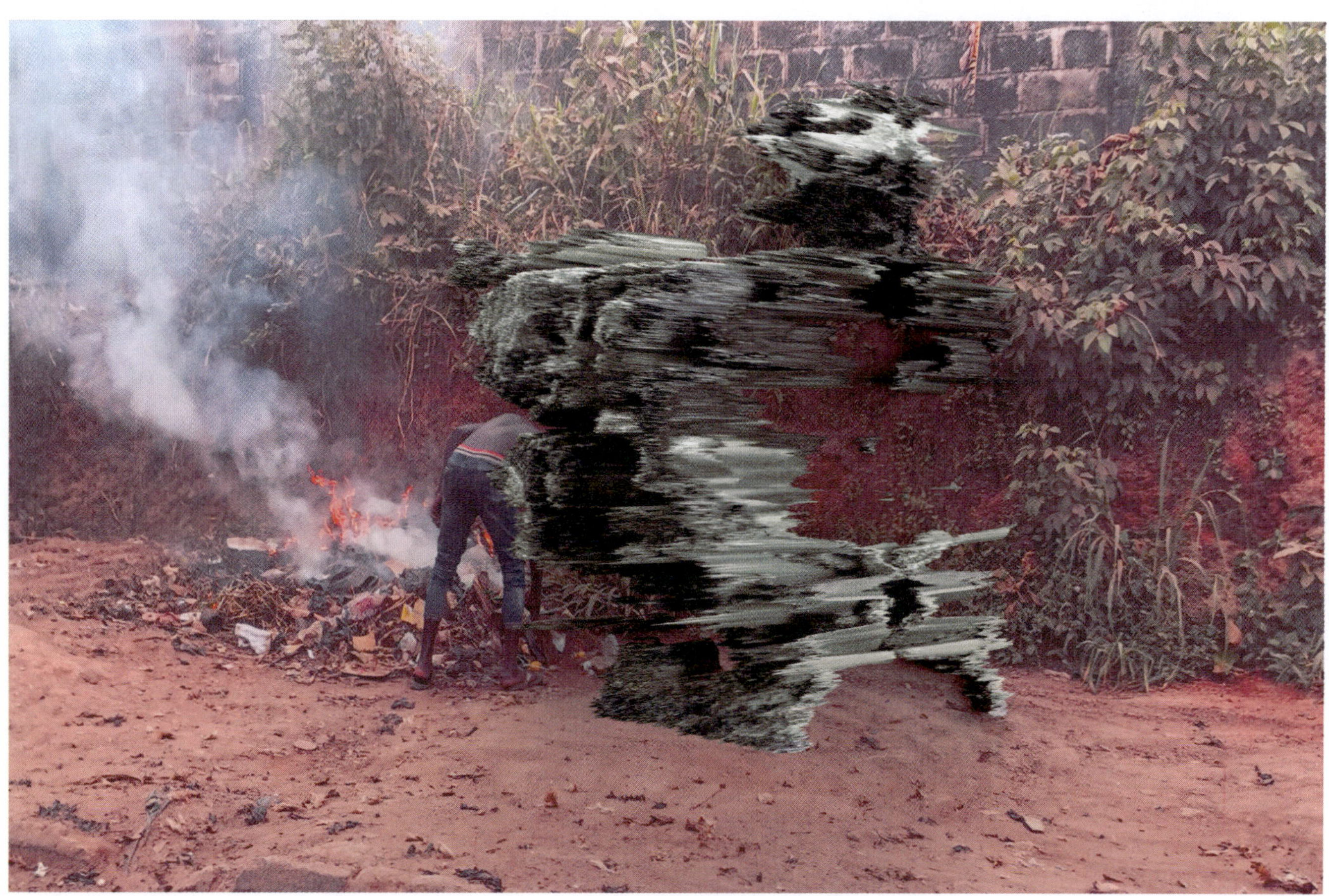

Michael Salu is a British-born Nigerian writer, artist and critic, whose work and ideas find a place in a multidisciplinary practice. His written work has appeared in several literary journals, magazines and art publications and he has exhibited visual work internationally. He runs House of Thought, a creative research practice and consultancy and is the former creative director of *Granta*. He currently lives between Berlin and Lagos.

To arrive at a place is an event that indicates a host of prior things; the awareness of the destination and the correct journey to take, the bodily ability for the movement and the implications for this movement. This latter aspect is both physical, in the biological capacity to take on the strain that distance will inflict, and spiritual, in the ritual consequences that accompany travel. From these interdependencies, a gestural and architectural tradition can be witnessed, one that has developed a rich set of tools and strategies for remembrance. This work is a mnemonic tactic that privileges the geometry of the corner, the anatomy of the joint and the place of the dead as three parts of a geographic archive that resists erasure, that denies forgetfulness. 'Arriving at the Corner' is a piece that seeks to locate what haunts and remains between the fibres of each muscular contraction, upon every moment of arrival.

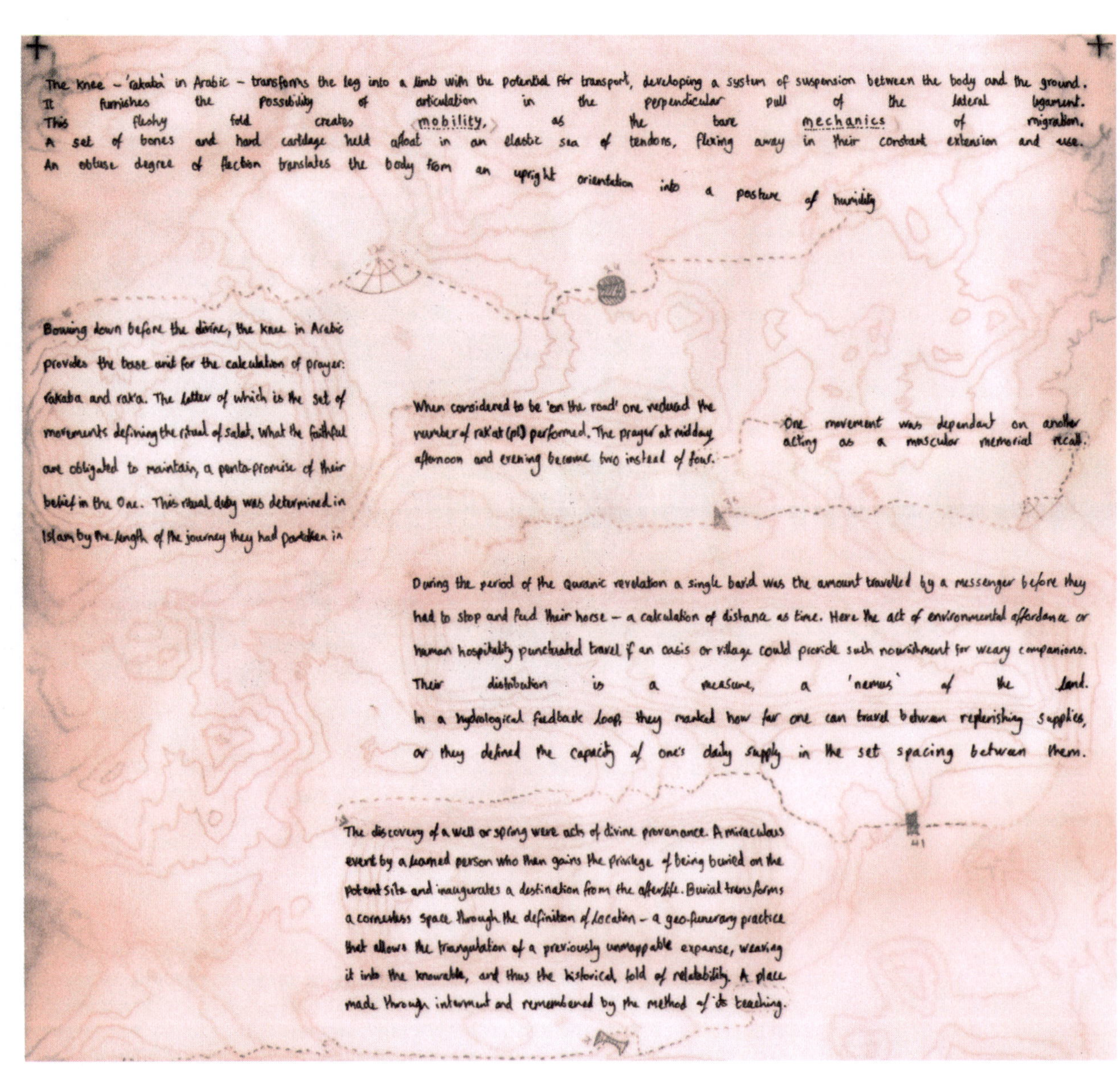

The past, as remembered by those that had passed, and their resting place, is a passage made legible through its demarcation. The tomb, in the inscription upon it, creates an utterance, a sonic space of instruction.

An enunciated prayer as a phonological form of teaching, in which the oral exercise, the learning inherited from and directed by the dead, animates the place in which they rest. The 'zawiya' (lit. translated as 'corner'), is a school-tomb typology. An architectural junction as edifice that augments this pedagogical practice.

The moment of epitaphic delivery generates notes to aid memory for future recall, recital and mobility—to enable finding future destinations. A visit is made possible by the hospitality provided in the endowment of the dead and the knowledge of their location. The Zawiya ultimately distinguishes what constitutes the sacred in an area bounded by a set of corners, giving scale and reference to this complex geography. A visitation for such a pious purpose is known as a ziyara. Many ziyarat (pl.) define the itinerant pilgrim's pedagogical circuit.

At its most essential, the building is reduced to a line with enough kinks to delimit the inside from the outside.

Through this difference, both from others and from the realm of the profane, the pious body becomes consecrated. A theological formulation which is taken a step further, for the deads' remains also gain the power of blessing the living, the ability to bestow 'baraka'. It is only in the physical proximity with the material remains that one is able to gain access to this provision.

An adjacency that is claimed by the request for asylum.

A complex furnishes and surrounds the tomb, operating as an extended echoic chamber and an elongated stage for live audition the relation of the body of knowledge, as signified by the subterranean corpse, and the body of the migrant student, as foreign arrival, is tied to the necessary proximity and adjacency to the spoken vibrations resonating between them. The zawiyas - as an astute corner amplifies what was taught, raises it above the threshold of perceptible audibility, allows it to be heard anew. In this space, sound becomes a corporeal method of navigation, and genealogical legibility An architecture that creates an elegy - as an instructive series of signals that are fated to fade away

The bent leg is the focal point in the tactile act of prayer in the sacred rite of supplication, as pleading for forgiveness, or in the appeal for shelter. A supplication is the ancient ritual of touching the knee (or altar) for the suppliant in Greek Tragedy, lowers their stature, crouches down, in a place of debasement, an alien arrival that places them 'on the limit'. The knee returns the figure back to the earth. The final ritual of death is evoked by prostration, through bending the leg into an anatomical corner to enter a chthonic state of near-death. A liminal position made possible by the knee.

A muscular hinge that shares its root with the word for 'generation'.

The heralding procession through birth after death connects to the understanding of supplication in Arabic. Translated as both 'dua' - the act of asking for mercy and gaining baraka - and tawsila word that designates the moment (as both time and place) of getting to know a previously unknown person. To learn of the corner, through the knee, creates an architecture that is transnational and intergenerational in the utmost sense, as historic destination, and future resource

The zawiya and its anatomical corollary define an urge to gather and retain out.

Moad Musbahi is an artist and curator. Together with the Harun Farocki Institut, he is currently co-curating the research and exhibition project 'Taught to Travel' investigating migration as a method for cultural production and political expression, focusing on the pedagogical practices and forms of knowledge that movement engenders. He was recently a resident at the Singapore Art Museum.

'Let Me Come & Be Going' uses modes of transportation as a conduit to investigate class, culture and citizenship. It offers a reflection on the individual and collective experience of being on a journey for a 'better life', constantly grappling with what we are dealt, and aggressively trying to move towards arriving at the material markers of 'success', which are constructed and powered by inhumane conditions. It is an affirmation that, for us, despite disruptions to our psyche and societies, we have created powerful movements and practices rooted in the simplicity, beauty and celebration of life. In other words, We Move.

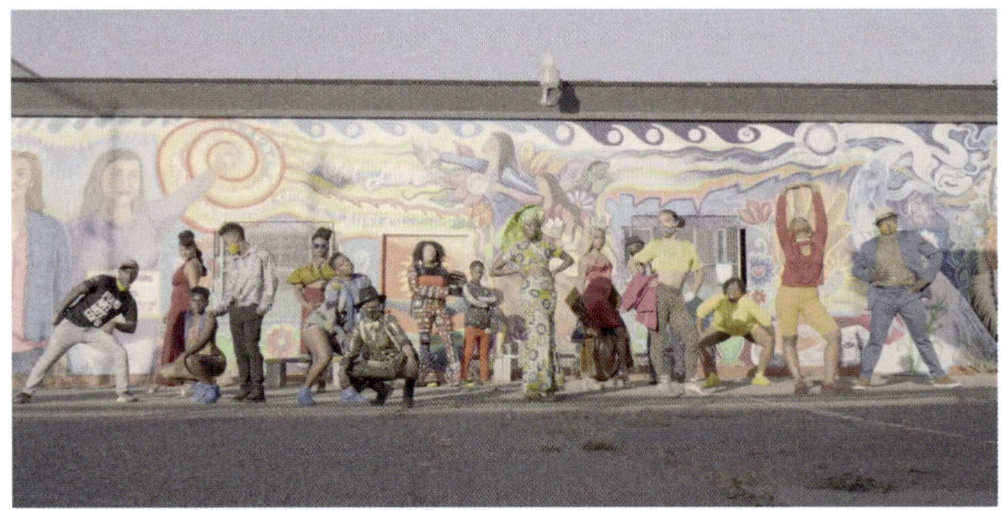

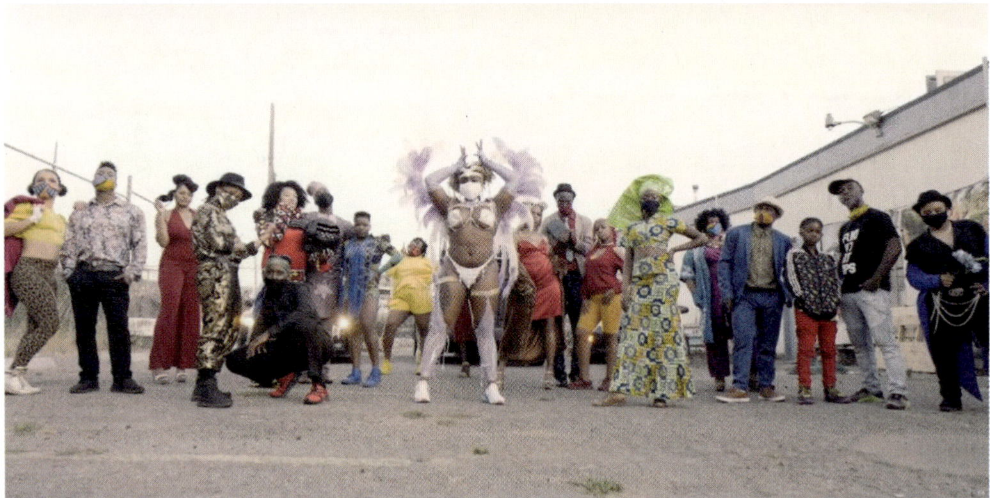

Nkeiruka Oruche is a cultural organiser, multimedia creative and performer of Igbo descent, who specialises in Afro-urban cultural intersections with identity, public wealth and sociopolitical action. She is a co-founder of BoomShake, a liberatory musical community of oppressed peoples, and director of Afro Urban Society, a hub for global Black creatives.

'Flight time letters and songs' engages with what it feels like to sit through a pandemic with the company of sound and words. The act of sitting down and writing letters is one way of moving through the punishing silence of this time. Using this slow-food form of expression has helped the artist to eat every feeling that has made a home in this body; to respond to isolation and loneliness; to return to sentimentality and detail; to hear the travelling sounds and forms of escape that I dearly miss.

Nombuso Mathibela is a Johannesburg-based feminist educator, writer, vinyl collector and selector. Her sonic research interests span across folk, anti-colonial, nationalist and feminist music histories and political aesthetics. She is part of an African ecofeminist collective that works on anti-capitalist ecological justice, political education and histories.

'Nouveaux Memoire Vieux Pagne' navigates through complex inheritances and histories, tearing them apart, unravelling, questioning, deconstructing and reconstructing an identity, therefore making new memories out of old clothes. Our clothes bear witness, they carry a pure, undiluted essence of who we are and hold stories of the places we have been in memory. These African print materials, African lace, and the linings from my mother's clothing are no different. Language is particularly important, and present, as it plays a primal role in shaping and constructing identity. Language is interchangeable and the work engages with how one perceives and comprehends that which is not translatable into their language of primary comprehension.

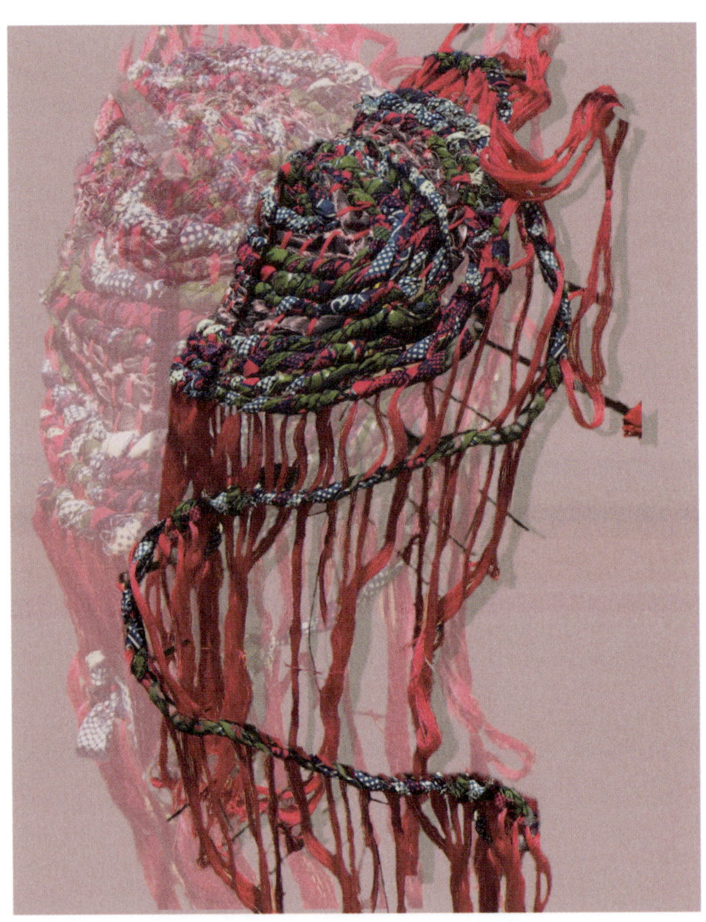
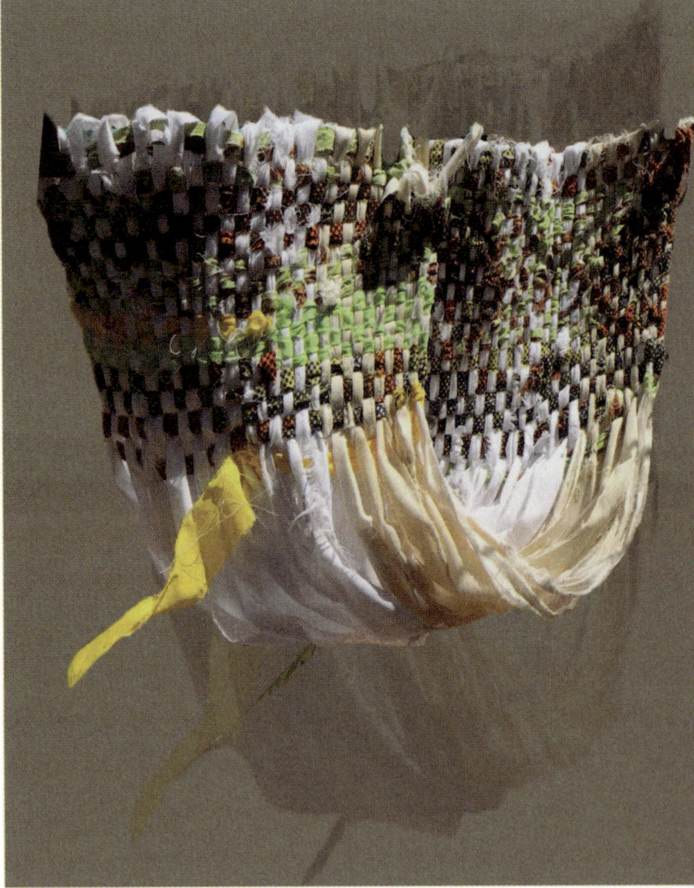

Princia Matungulu is a Congolese artist, currently studying towards a degree in Fine Arts at the University of the Witwatersrand. With the only ties to her birthplace being oral histories and African cloths passed down by her mother, Matungulu's practice engages with these histories and materiality through the intricacy of the weaving process. The resulting sculptures bear records of a personal and imagined history.

'Unmapping: Contaminated Representations' is a project that began in 2020. Lockdown forced the world to a halt, and the work began as an exploration of the continent through Google Earth. It also draws on a book compiled by UNESCO in 1963 that houses a map locating a large number of resources and minerals across the African continent. The preface for this collection is a mapping for 'when the rest of the world runs out of minerals - it was necessary to know where to find them'. Drawing on this UNESCO publication, the artist set out to locate each of these resources from above on Google Earth - all of which became marked through a mine. Each collage houses a collection of the same type of mine across Africa, layered on top of each other to the point that one is unable to tell where one ends, and another begins. The combined maps point to the historical process of erasure along with the destruction of memory and the environment inherent to mining. What is the landscape without its minerals - and what is brought to the surface as a result of extraction?

Shayna Rosendorff
is a Johannesburg-based artist and art commentator. Working in photography, sculpture and drawing, her conceptual focus is the mined landscape and the politics of the representation of land and landscape in South Africa. She has participated in numerous exhibitions, runs Overheard in the Gallery, and in 2021 she was one of the winners of the BMW x WITS Art Project.

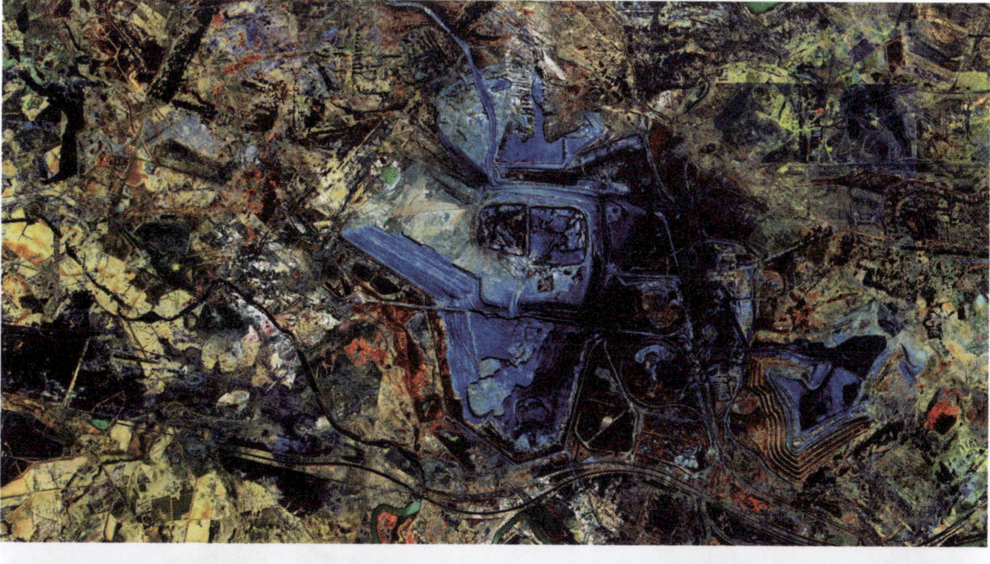

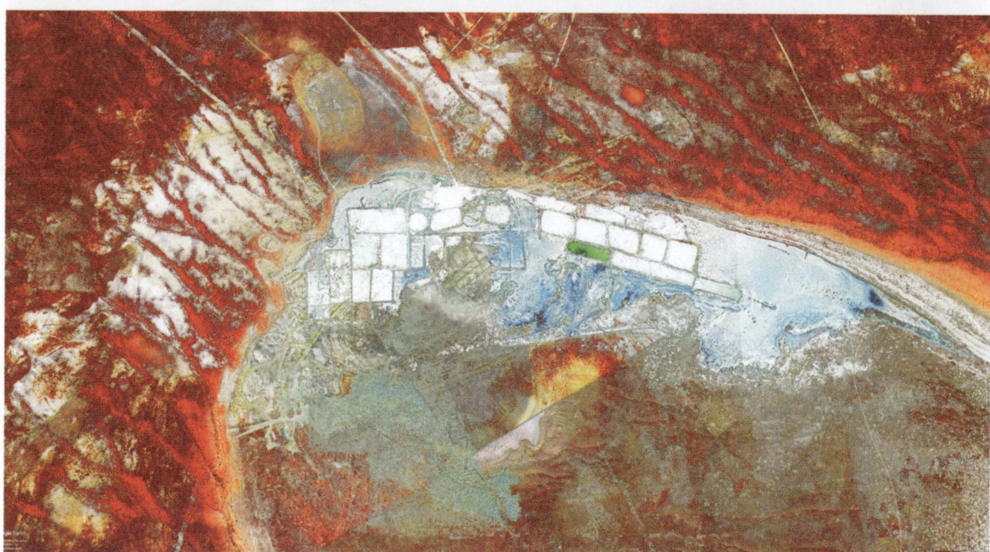

In modern standard Arabic, the pandemic is translated as Al-Ga'hah, which is pronounced Al-Gayhah in Egyptian Arabic; the colloquial Egyptian pronunciation tends to smooth the characteristic and specific bumpy sound for daily conversations. Yet, during the Covid-19 lockdown, this phonetic trick became useless and the whole metaphor was jammed with Al-Waleed among others. Facing the sudden loss of his smell and taste senses, he tries to maintain his sanity by analysing this new situation and speculating on the consequences of being infected.

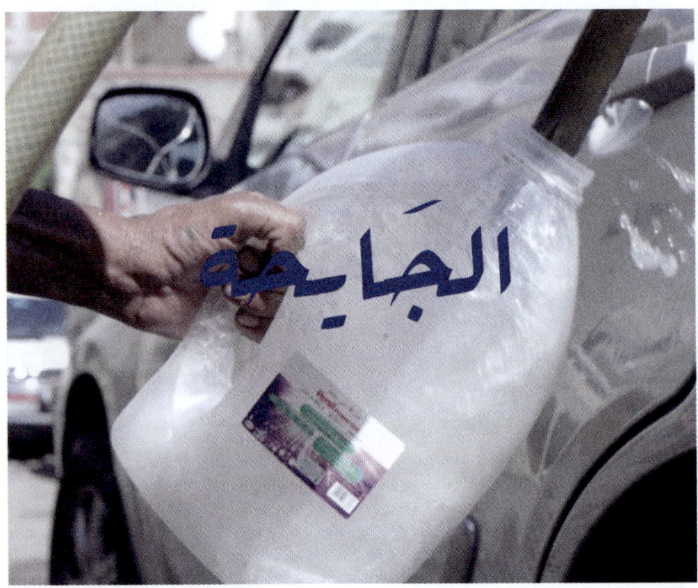

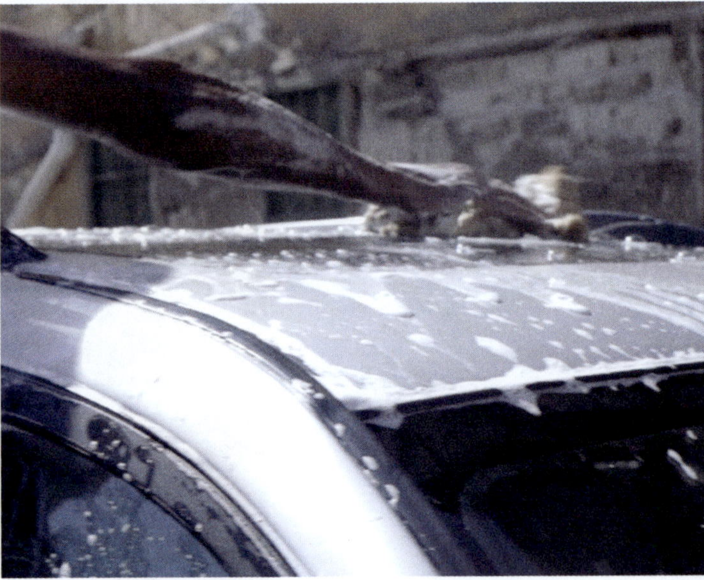

Sharief Zohairy is an independent director, screenwriter and producer based in Alexandria. After graduating from the Faculty of Medicine, then in 2006, he directed his first short fiction film. Several other films followed. Since 2013 he has focused on writing screenplays, two of which have received awards.

Banange! is a short experimental film shot on 16mm that follows a mother as she teaches her daughter how to speak Lugisu in an attempt to reconnect her to the motherland, a memory long fragmented by the echoes of time and abstracted by the blur of distance. Learning a mother tongue is the practice of re-learning a history. The film adopts techniques of overlay and distortion as a means to speak to the doubling and distance of a diasporic experience.

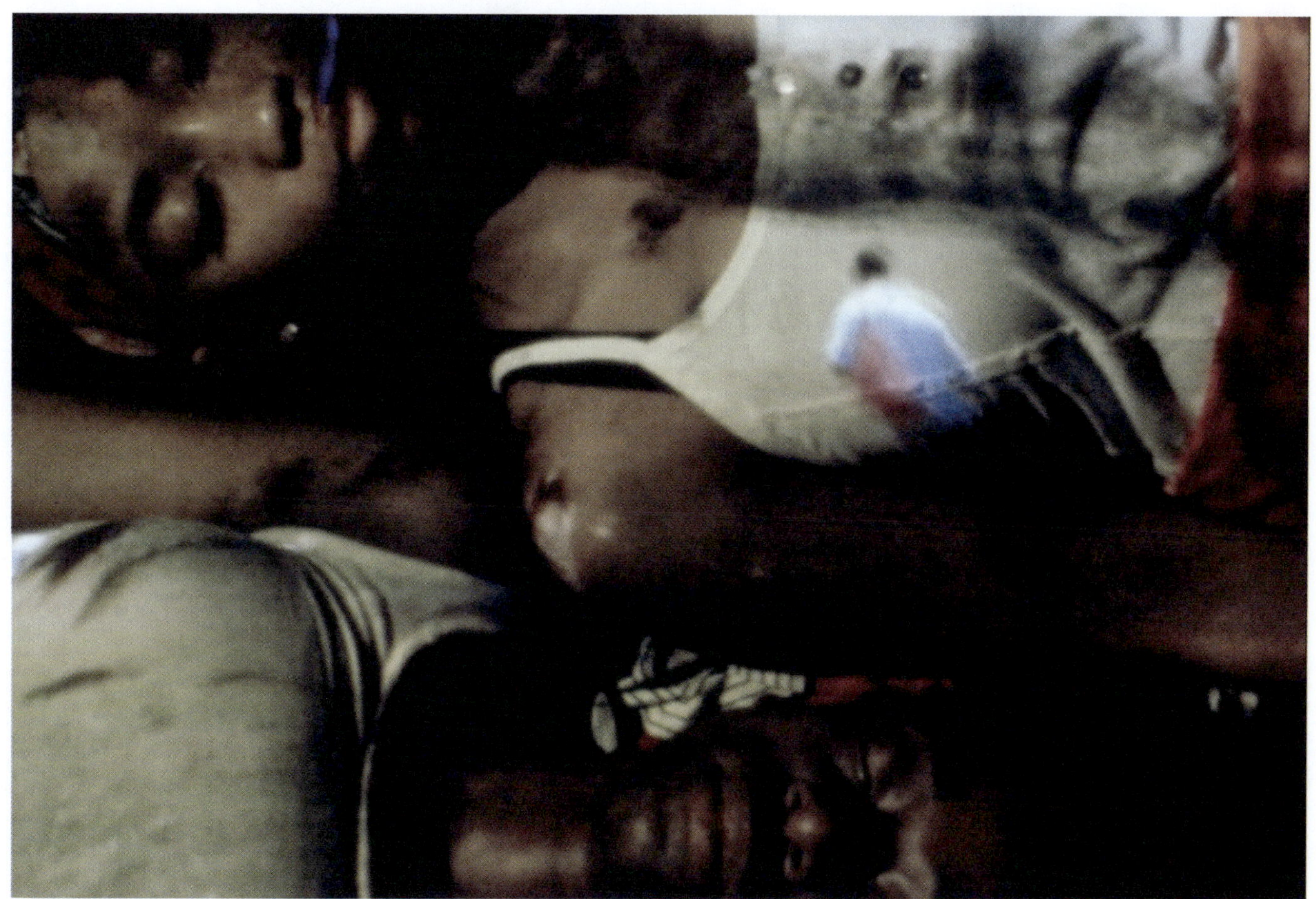

Sonya Mwambu is an experimental filmmaker and editor based in Toronto. She graduated from York University's film production programme where she developed her craft in shooting and experimenting with film to explore concepts of race, language and a connection to her own cultural identity. Although she was born in Kampala, she grew up in Canada and her films are centred on the intersections of her identities.

THE SCHOOL OF MUTANTS
Hamedine Kane (Senegal/Mauritania)
& Stéphane Verlet-Bottéro

The School of Mutants moves between cinema of the real and futuristic speculation, leading into a poetic and political reflection on the mutations of the world. It is part of a collaborative inquiry in African futurism and the possibilities for alternative educational institutions after Senegal's independence. The School of Mutants was initiated in Dakar by Hamedine Kane and Stéphane Verlet-Bottéro as a platform for art, research and activism. The project has been exhibited internationally, with recent shows at Le Lieu Unique, Partcours Festival, Oslo Triennale and Taipei Biennial.

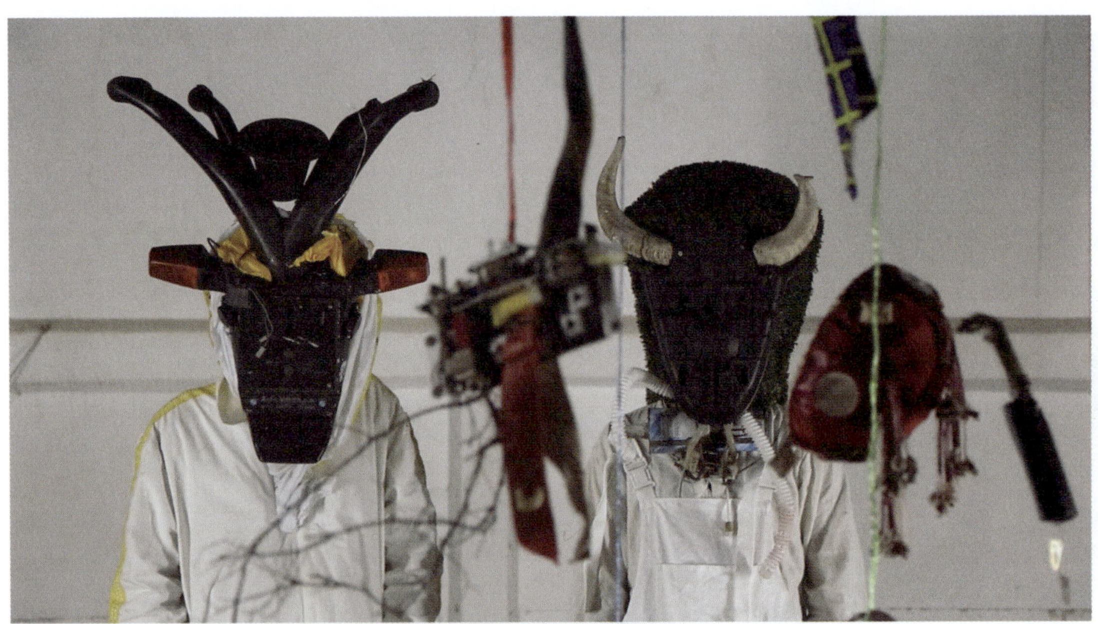

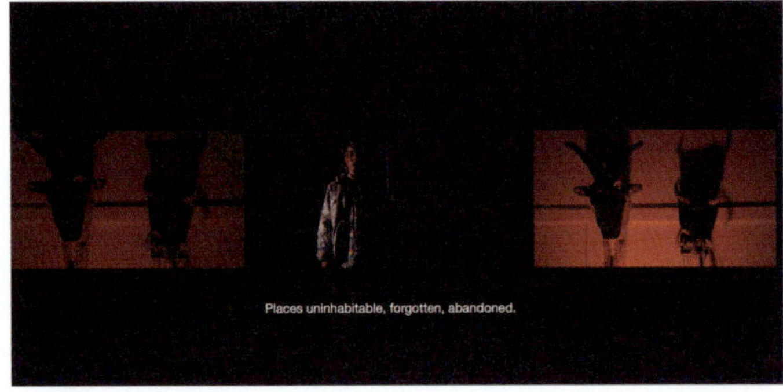

Hamedine Kane is a Senegalese and Mauritanian artist and filmmaker. His film *The Blue House* (2020), which had its world premiere at IDFA in Amsterdam in November 2020, received a special mention from the jury.

Stéphane Verlet-Bottéro is an artist, environmental engineer and curator. He is a lecturer at École Centrale Paris, curator at NA Project, associate researcher at Ensad Paris and researcher at Unbewitch Finance Lab.

'This is Not Your Country' is Inspired by the death of a mother and her children during Christmas 2020. 'This is Not Your Country' is a poem that highlights the effect of migration laws on undocumented citizens. The poem asks the audience to engage with the materiality of crossing the border, as a personal and embodied experience of the migration laws in place.

Tshifhiwa Itai Ratshiungo is a writer and creative from South Africa studying law at the University of the Free State. A selection of his poetry appears in *African Writer* and *History and Imagined Realities: An Anthology of South African Poetry* (Impepho Press, 2021), a project powered by Institut Français d'Afrique du Sud.

Qhakuva tells the story of a distant dystopian future set in South Africa where a space traveller lands in the city of Joburg, wrecking their mode of transport. They begin to explore this foreign land, much to the amazement of the people. It speaks to a certain kind of mobility, and the ability to travel to different dimensions and worlds.

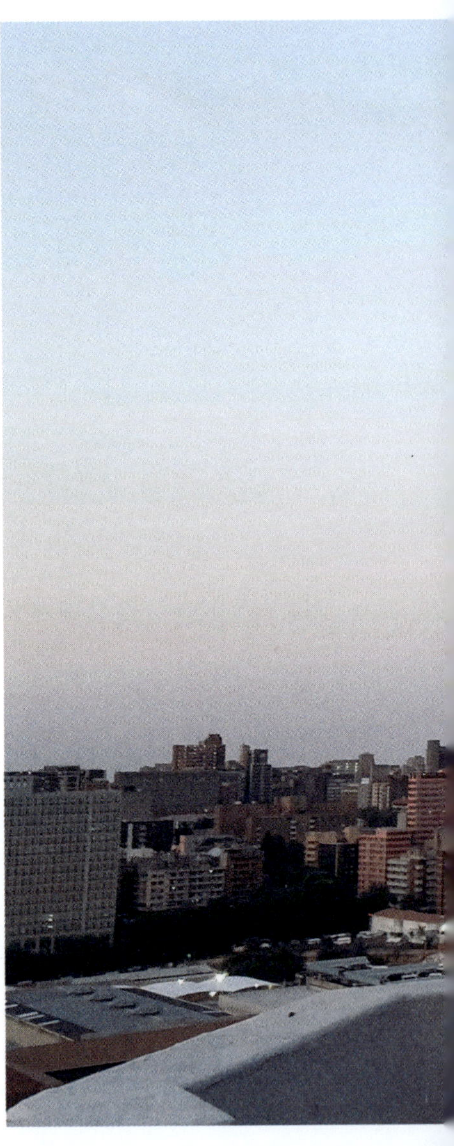

Umlilo, intergalactic shape-shifting kwaai diva, is a genre and gender-bending multi-disciplinary artist. The queer performer and music producer's signature sound dubbed 'future kwaai' explores and pushes the boundaries of electronic kwaito, alt-pop music in contemporary South Africa and has been a regular fixture in the international music community.

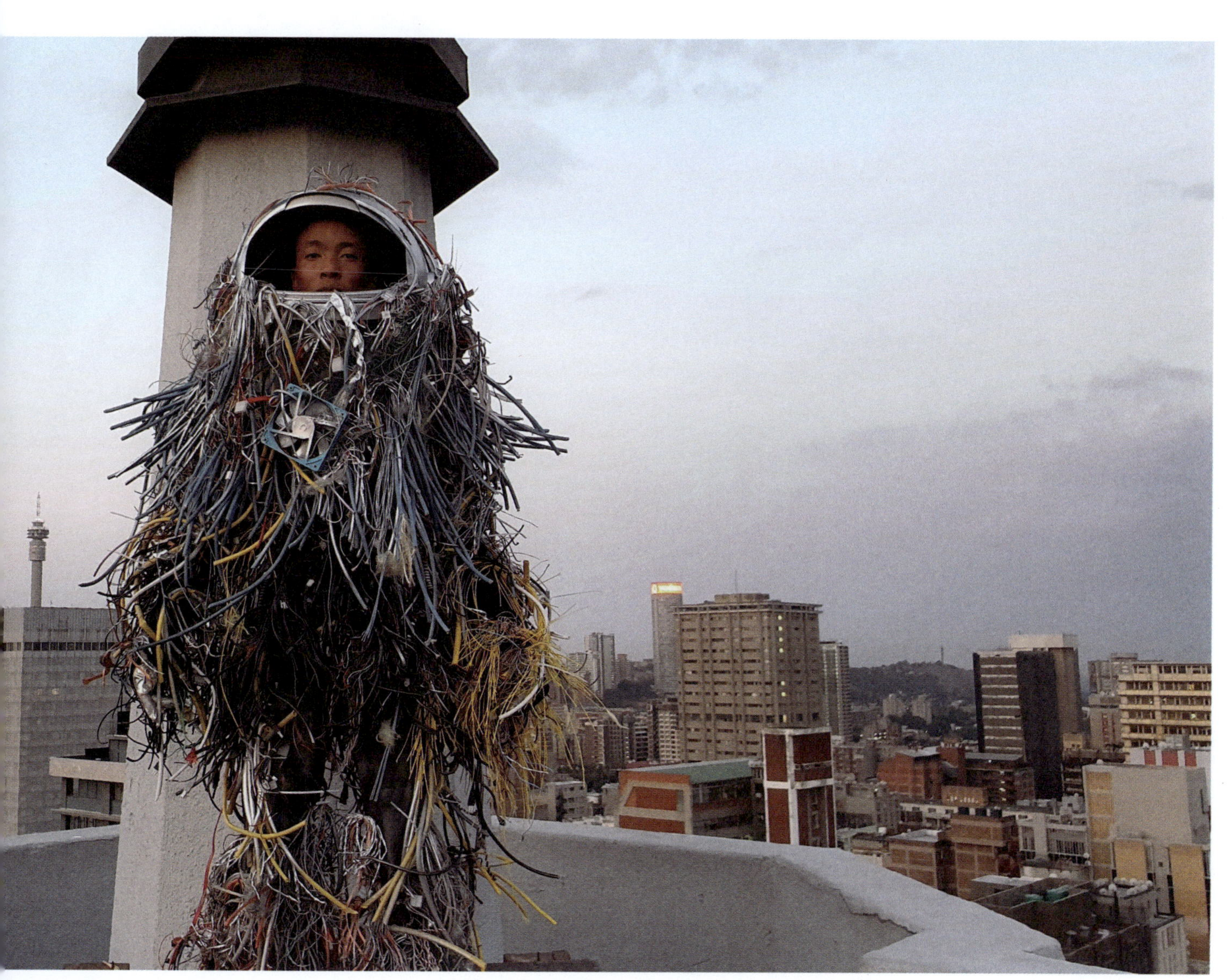

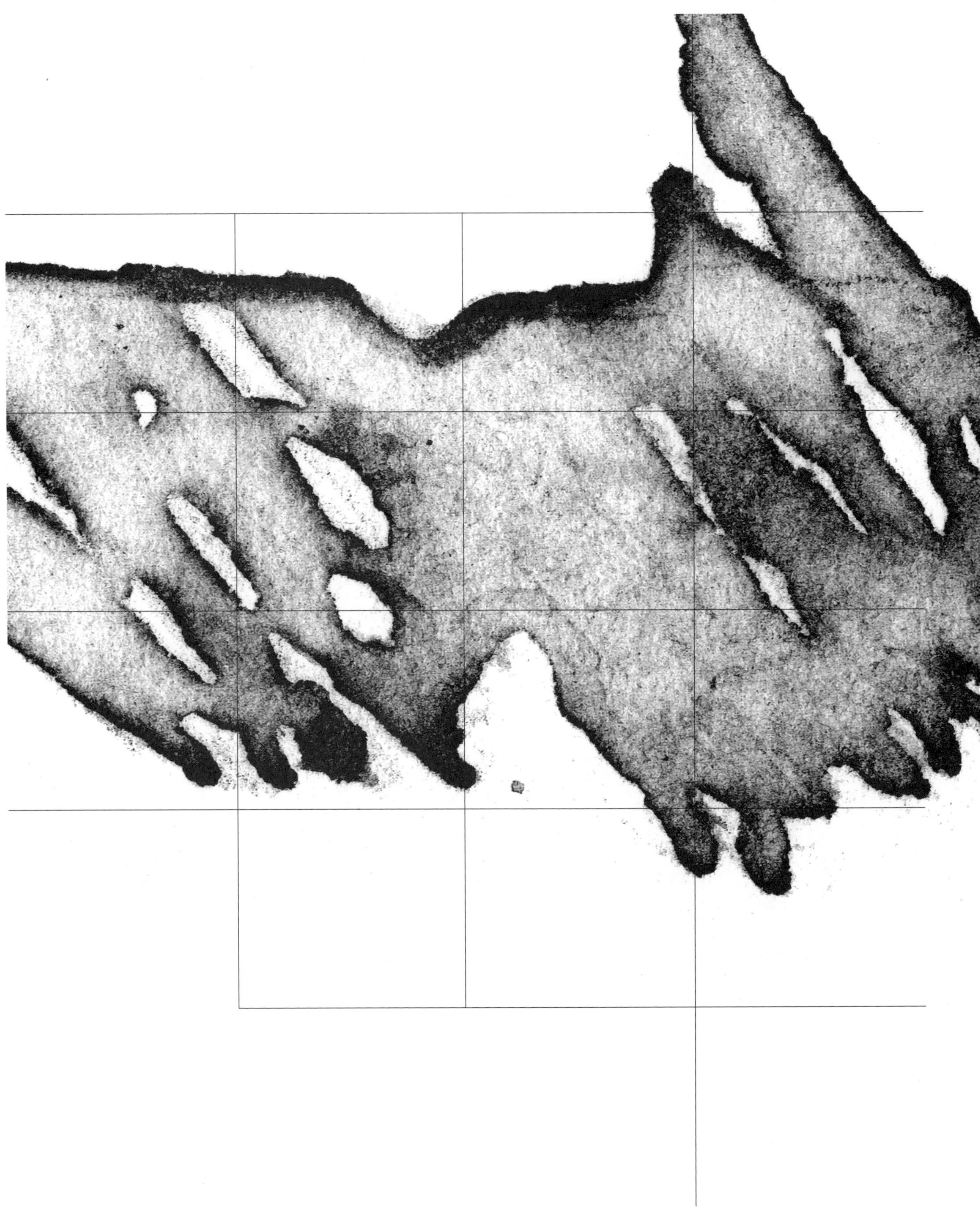

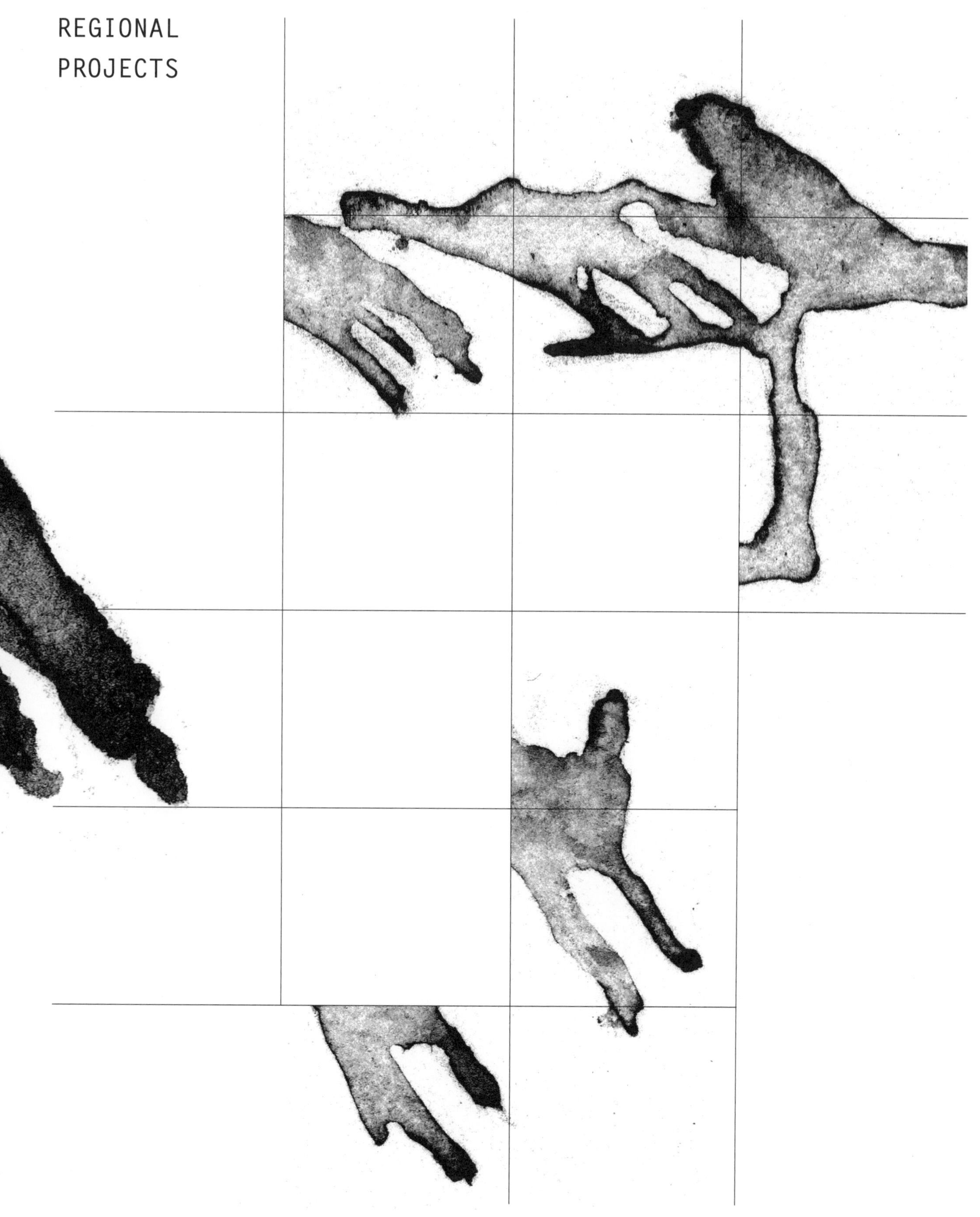

Following the launch of the Archive of Forgetfulness online exhibition in April 2021, six regionally curated projecs were added to the website between May and December 2021. The regional curators, namely Eric Ngangare, Princess Zinzi Mhlongo, Jumoke Sanwo, Omnia Shawkat, Ali Al-Adawy and Zoubida Mseffer, have been involved since the 'Neighbourhoods' phase of this project in 2019. The work has changed over time, taking on new lives and direction, while acting as an important narrative and conceptual bridge across the different phases of the larger project. Each of these regionally curated works offers a different perspective on archives, archival modalities, and questions around remembering and forgetting.

Released in May 2021, Eric Ngangare's film, *My Karitsye,* gives the viewer glimpses into moments of time and experiences of urban life in Kigali and Bujumbura. The film speaks to the author's own movement, alongside a collage of voices from these two cities. In June, Princess Zinzi Mhlongo's *Izibongo* questioned 'where do we go to remember who we once were?'. Mhlongo draws on a personal experience as the starting point to collect clan praises, Izibongo and Izithakazelo, as a recognition of oral history. These twenty-five collected voices and stories point oral history as simultaneously rooted in time and place, and changing, adaptable and fungible. Mhlongo's offering is both an archive of memory and a practice of memorialisation that lives through sound and voice. In July, Jumoke Sanwo's work *Dúna Dúra [The Negotiation]* unfolded over the website and in Obalende market in Lagos, Nigeria. A live performance by Jelili Atiku was live-streamed via the Archive of Forgetfulness homepage, allowing a remote audience a brief glimpse of the night market. The live performance was prefaced with a series of talks, interviews, an installation and spoken-word performance; an active and direct negotiation with space and time, the real and the digital simultaneously. In August, Omnia Shawkat released 'Art Blooms in Uncertainty: Sudan'. Her bilingual text offers a temperature reading in a fast-changing Khartoum of the role and presence of cultural providers and practitioners. Her essay shared online prefaced a series of in-person events in Khartoum, as a means to engage with the on-the-ground growing challenges of the arts context. October and November saw Ali Hussein Al-Adawy's launch of *When the Archive is Speculative, Fatigue with Visualising the Future may Fade*, a two-part event series in Alexandria, Egypt, with an online film screening and essay. Al-Adawy deliberately stages the works as an epistemic and aesthetic intervention, drawing in artists, researchers and thinkers. In December, drawing the year to a close, Zoubida Mseffer delved into forgetfulness through a search for Yasmin, a slave and the wife of her great-grandfather. This deeply personal search unearths absences and silences, and is a reminder of the violence of history.

These wide-ranging projects draw, disrupt and build on questions raised in the *Archive of Forgetfulness*. As with many of the artworks, they ask us to continue to work through deeper histories, think across genres and practices of memory-making, and speculate on future possibilities. The *Archive of Forgetfulness* has been a platform to bring these together and put them into conversation, yet it is important to note that these projects also have other lives beyond this project and the website. There were in-person events in Lagos, Alexandria and Khartoum; and all of these works exist as lived and embodied parts of wider and dispersed relationalities that are mapped and experienced. Unfolding in both time and space, they also point to the political urgency of many of the questions in the *Archive of Forgetfulness*, and the constantly emerging difficulties and repeated crises of making creative work on the African continent. They provoke us to engage with difficulties, poetics, crisis and possibility all at once; and point to an imperative to listen closely and to acknowledge and build on the immense work of radical practice, always already happening.

MAY 2021: MY KARITSYE
Eric '1Key' Ngangare

'Karitsye' is the new slang for 'kartiye', which is derived from the French word 'quartier' (neighbourhood / quarters) and possibly came into Rwanda with the return of the former Rwandan diaspora from the French-speaking Democratic Republic of the Congo or Burundi in the late 1990s. *My Karitsye* is a film that embodies the mixualities of English, French and Kinyarwanda, and captures the spirit and pulse of Kigali and Bujumbura (the capital cities of Rwanda and Burundi). The short film engages with various artists, including poets, rappers, dancers, painters, performers who 'represent' their karitsye. The images and sounds of Kigali and Bujumbura depict a collage of voices, telling the stories of people and the spaces they navigate, bringing to light the many celebrations and struggles of living in these fast-evolving cities.

Eric '1Key' Ngangare is an independent poet, spoken word artist, emcee, performer, actor and blogger from Rwanda exploring various formats of storytelling. His work deals with issues of identities - individual and collective - power systems and societal dynamics. His second album, *Mwiru,* was released in 2021 and offers a mix of genres, styles and languages.

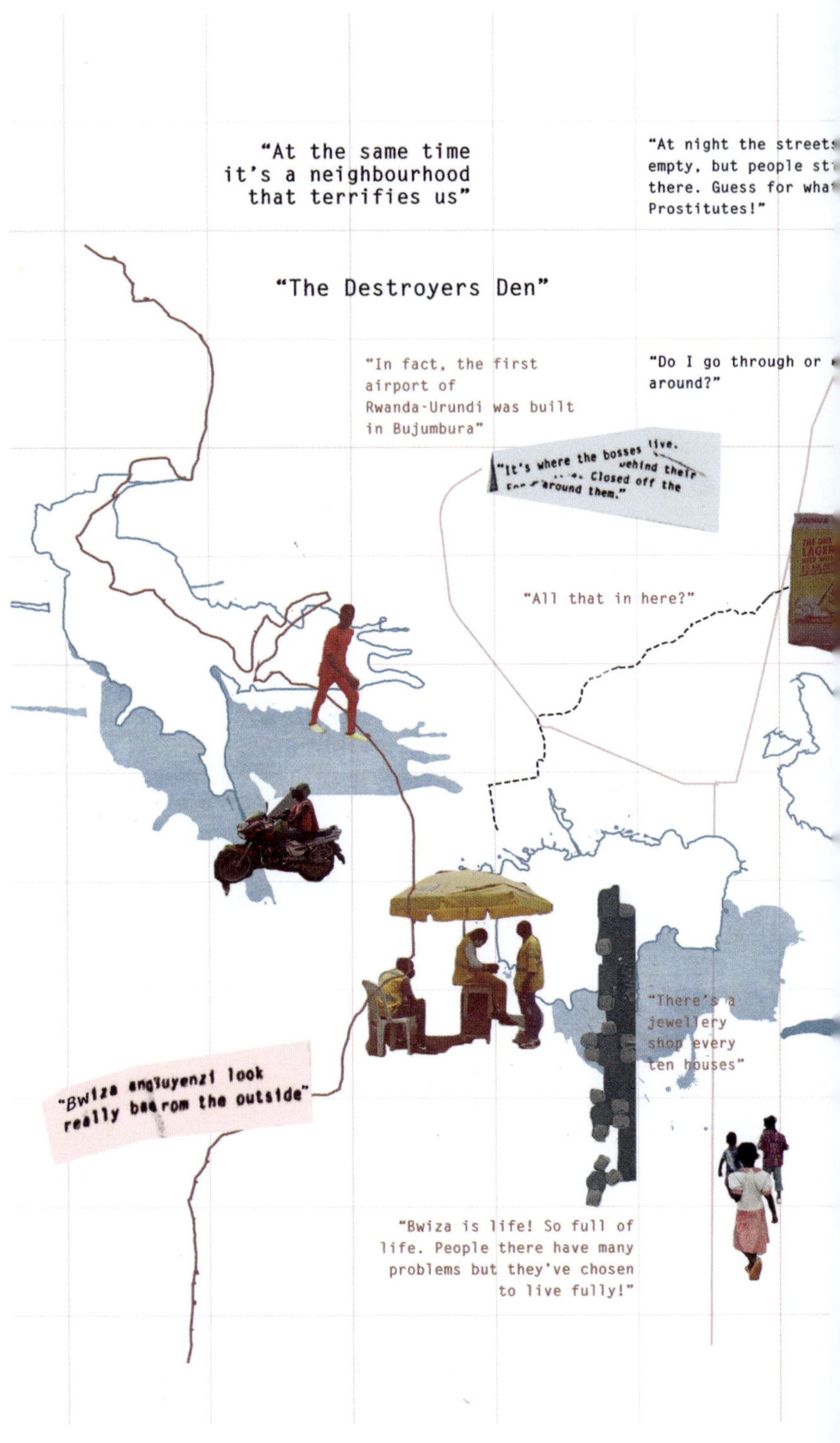

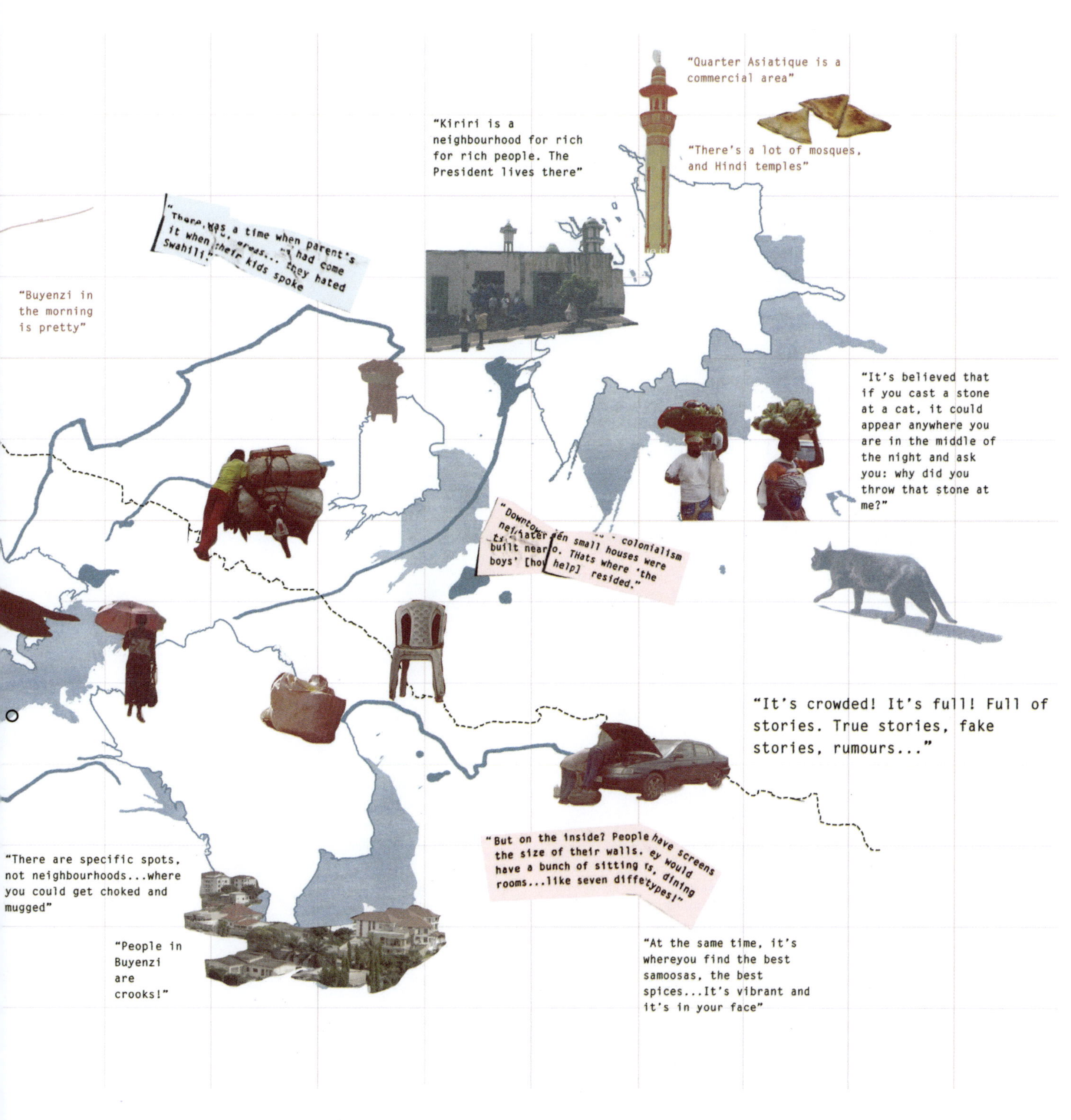

"Quarter Asiatique is a commercial area"
"Kiriri is a neighbourhood for rich for rich people. The President lives there"
"There's a lot of mosques, and Hindi temples"
"There was a time when parent's it when their areas... had come Swahili" they hated their kids spoke
"Buyenzi in the morning is pretty"
"It's believed that if you cast a stone at a cat, it could appear anywhere you are in the middle of the night and ask you: why did you throw that stone at me?"
"Downtown... - colonialism negliater sen small houses were ts. built near o. THats where 'the boys' [hou help] resided."
"It's crowded! It's full! Full of stories. True stories, fake stories, rumours..."
"There are specific spots, not neighbourhoods...where you could get choked and mugged"
"But on the inside? People have screens the size of their walls. ey would have a bunch of sitting rs, dining rooms...like seven diffe types!"
"People in Buyenzi are crooks!"
"At the same time, it's whereyou find the best samoosas, the best spices...It's vibrant and it's in your face"

History, culture and languages have evolved over time, and cross-cultural interactions shape our identities and futures. *IZibongo* (Praises) and *Izithakazelo* (Clan Praises) have formed an important role in oral lore for Bantu people of Southern Africa. Praise poems present themselves as vehicles to archive past memories, which represent indigenous wisdom, cultural identification and personal identity that can be carried through into the future. *IZibongo* and *Izithakazelo* are praises that one carries as they navigate and move to different parts of the world serving as a reminder of their roots. Can these roots help trace origins? What happens when the *IZibongo* you hold does not belong to you? How important is it to carry the praises? In sharing our stories, we create a collective archive of memories, a platform where cultural heritage and history can be held.

       IZibongo consists of twenty-five personal stories collected and curated by Princess Mhlongo. The individual narratives explain and present understandings of family history, identity and migration. Listen to Mabena who has lost his surname when his family migrated to South Africa from Mozambique. Or to Mothibi, who is currently based in Emalahleni, but originally from Lesotho. Due to wars and migration his people are found in Botswana, North West, Limpopo and the Free State.

Princess Zinzi Mhlongo is a theatre director and the co-founder of *The Plat4orm*, which for many years provided an alternative space for artists in the theatre industry to develop new uncensored work. She directed her first professional production, *And the Girls in Their Sunday Dresses*, in 2008. Since then, her work has toured internationally, and she has received numerous nominations and awards, including the prestigious Standard Bank Young Artist of the Year Award for Theatre in 2012. She is a recipient of The Laboratory for Global Performance and Politics 2020-21 fellowship at Georgetown University, Washington DC. In 2020 she launched *Exhibit*, a digital platform that showcases upcoming or unfinished work by an artist seeking funding.

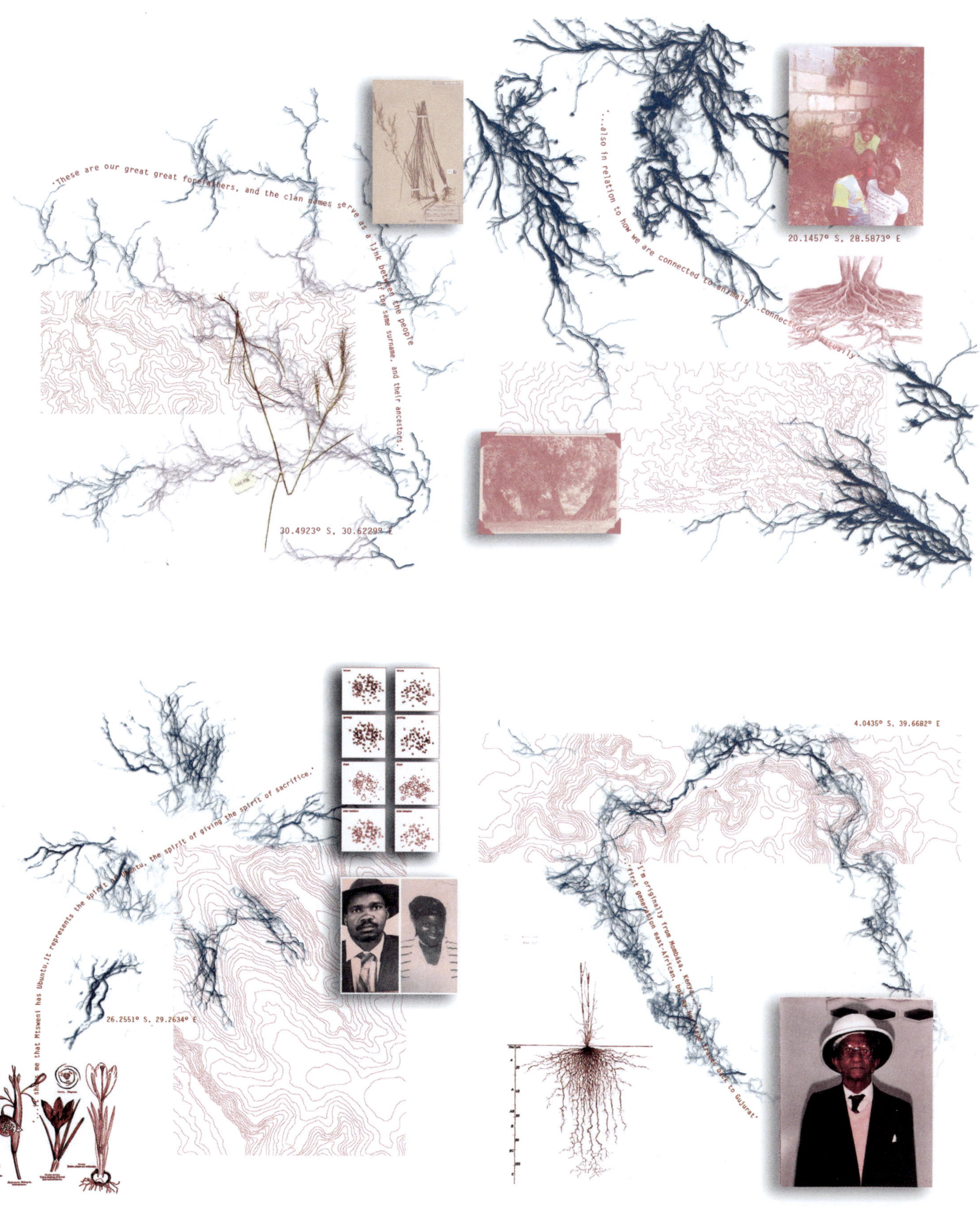
·These are our great great forefathers, and the clan names serve as a link between the people of the same surname, and their ancestors.·
...also in relation to how we are connected to animals...connected directly
30.4923° S, 30.62299 E
20.1457° S, 28.5873° E
4.0435° S, 39.6682° E
26.2551° S, 29.2634° E
·she showed me that Mtsweni has Ubuntu, it represents the spirit of Ubuntu, the spirit of giving the spirit of sacrifice.·
·I'm originally from Namibia, Kenya, first generation east-African, but...one to Gujarat.·

Jumoke Sanwo

In the year 2020, the dissolution of the world as we knew it, with global lockdowns induced by the coronavirus pandemic, took centre stage. This cataclysmic event forced many to critically engage with the new world set to emerge post-pandemic; the Indian author Arundhati Roy described the pandemic as 'a portal, a gateway between one world and the next'.[40] Since then, there has been an evident shift in how we live in the 'Now', and confront realities, exchange knowledge and engage physical and social spaces. The transpositions are also evident in how we now confront the local and the traditional, vis-a-vis the global and the modern.

This shift marginally impacted the 'global South', a space already deemed as existing within the effects of what Boaventura de Sousa Santos coined as the 'abyssal lines', where 'the forgotten' indigenous knowledge systems directly impact and shape lived experiences.[41] Artistic productions are potential entry points into these past erased histories and alternative knowledge systems without the burden of preconceptions. The late author, Chinua Achebe, in his last novel, *There Was a Country*, suggested that artists exist within such liminal zones, where they have the artistic freedom to channel abandoned indigenous knowledge systems, challenge normative assumptions and re-think how to engage memory and history. Artistic and cultural productions hold the potential of creating spaces of encounters and the re-experiencing of a society's abyssal line: that side of 'non-existence', shifting the mind and body from 'place', associated with the world of the past, to 'space', which is synonymous with the world of the present and future. He opined that artists are connected to their community, 'not just the community of humans, but communities of the ancestors, the animal world, of trees, and so on. Everything plays a part'.[42]

It is within this context that we reflected on embodied and spatial memory using the Yoruba religious belief system surrounding the night market - as a portal between the living and the dead as a point of entry. On 9 June 2021, we instigated a spatial intervention called Dúna Dúrà, at the Obálendé Ijeh Oluwaloseyi night-market, located between the Obalende transportation hub and the Ikoyi Cemetery on Lagos Island in the city of Lagos Nigeria. The name, Obálendé, can be translated as 'the place where the king chased us to'. The site-specific re-imagination was an evening of performative encounters, a coming together of artists, and intellectuals channelling the discourse on embodied and spatial memory.

The evening began with what Aremo Gemini termed the 'Sermon from the Dead', Èjìgbèdè, spontaneous poetry performance and 'introspection into the constant visits and intercessions of the ancestors, through dreams, daydreams, spectacular events, other nature beings like wildlife, the aquatics, whirlwind, storms'. Ejigbede by Yusuf Àlàbí Balógun (alias Aremo Gemini), prepared the space for multimedia artist Jèlílì Àtíkù's Ẹmí l'olóọjà ara, a channelling and embodying the spirits of the guiding deities of the market Èṣù (preeminent primordial divinity) and Ajé (deity of wealth and patroness of trade and economic prosperity). The deities were activated through a call by Àlàbí Balógun to intercede in acts of remembering and forgetting. Gbànjo gbànjo, a call for bargaining, opened up a space for the renegotiation

Jumoke Sanwo is a storyteller, cultural interlocutor and creative director of Revolving Art Incubator. She works primarily in photography, video art and extended reality (XR), and her work engages the bodily, spatial and temporal realities and complexities in postcolonial societies. She lives and works out of Lagos, Nigeria.

40   Roy, A., 'The pandemic is a portal', *Financial Times,* 3 April 2020.

41   De Sousa Santos, B., *Epistemologies of the South*, Routledge, Abingdon, 2014.

42   Achebe, C., *There Was a Country*. Penguin Books, New York, 2012, p. 60.

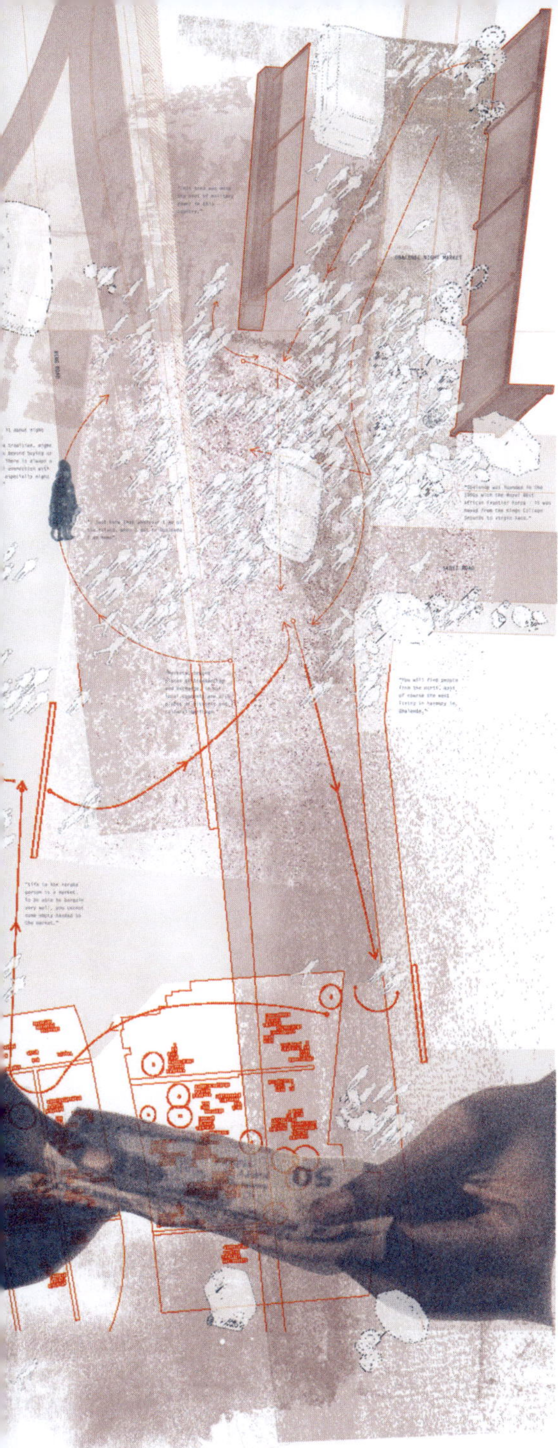

of histories between the global North and South.

    Àlàbí Balógun and Gemini's role as mediums, between the corporeal and incorporeal worlds, transformed the night market into a mystical space with many entry points, an overlapping of the corporeal and the incorporeal worlds. The three-part performance engaged acts of remembrance and forgetting, digging into cultural and ancestral memories, through a constant dialogue between the performer, the space and the audience. The intervention, set in motion, through conversations a day prior, with Prof. Moyo Okediji, Steven Ajadi, Dr Taibat Lawanson and Dr Monsuru Olalekan Muritala on Zoom followed by conversations with Adeboye Martins, Oludamola Adebowale, Adun Okupe, Sola Akintunde, Idris Adewale (Baba Ojá), and Fatimoh Balogun, and then the site-specific introspection Dúna Dúrà, all led by Obasola Bamigbola, created an opportunity to engage what Henri Lefebvre termed a 'third space', a spatio-temporal site, which confronts the notion of embodied and spatial memory, its dislocation and interdependencies.

    Dúna Dúrà asks for relooking and re-engaging the methodologies underpinning memory and in turn archives, as a practice central to decolonising the archives of the future.

السودان: الفن يزدهر في حالة عدم اليقين

Omnia Shawkat

Sudan is going through a period of transformation: in 2018-2019, a popular uprising toppled a system defined by corrupt governance and injustice that had reigned for three decades. During the revolution, neighbourhoods were strengthened with a renewed sense of organised work and collaborative action, consolidating networks of trust to build certain areas as safe spaces for people in tumultuous times. Art was at the heart of the revolution in Sudan between 2018-2019, with pop-up events, mass concerts, poetry, music, graffiti and multidisciplinary performances taking over neighbourhoods along with the Qiyada sit-ins that popped up across different states between April and June 2019.

Since 2019, Sudan has experienced an explosion of artistic spaces, projects and initiatives, after more than 30 years of repressive Islamo-Arab governance that systematically oppressed arts and culture. Although the COVID-19 pandemic ground activities to a halt in some instances, 2020 and 2021 saw many more initiatives pop up due to more donor funding and general economic and political circumstances pointing towards Sudan's rebirth and re-entry into global spheres. Once the COVID-19 lockdown was eased, the country's socio-economic, security and political transitions sprang into action, and artistic players followed suit.

Nonetheless, the fact remains that Sudan was ruled by a fragile partnership between a civilian government and the military for nearly two years until 25 October 2021, when a military coup reversed many accomplishments and thwarted the progress of the revolution. During the joint partnership and after the coup altercations with artists and activists continued, the most prominent being the Feed Arts case, where artivists were imprisoned for weeks following a neighbour reporting their theatre performance rehearsals. In this current situation, artistic hubs and cafes, many owned, founded and run by activists, are easy targets for an oppressive authority that still lurks within the government. To date, the challenges are plenty. Sudan still faces security threats and frequent flareups, an economic collapse has gripped the country further since the coup. Moreover, the government is not committed to any rehabilitation of the art and culture sector that was decimated by the toppled regime, neither through funding, material or formal support of grassroots initiatives taking shape. How does the sector then look in such times of uncertainty?

Cultural hubs, cafes and inter-sectional programmes are not new in Sudan, but the spirit they are carrying now is different than during the Inqaz (previous dictatorship) era. No longer are such spaces open to a certain demographic, holding secretive events and afraid of the notorious Public Order forces that were abolished post-revolution. The spaces are open for dialogue, debates, indie bands and poets, libraries and craft classes. Importantly, spaces are largely able to criss-cross between art, culture and politics thus, cementing the importance of governance in youthful dialogues, using modern and engaging tools to widen the net for discussing topics of importance to the current political transition in Sudan.

يمر السودان بفترة انتقالية: أطاحت الانتفاضة الشعبية ما بين 2018 –2019 بنظام فاسد وظالم استمر لثلاثة عقود. وخلال الثورة بُعثتْ الأحياء السكنية في مشهد جديد عبر التنظيم والعمل المشترك، بانيةً علاقات ثقة وخالقة من أماكن معينة مساحات آمنة للناس في أوقات الشدة. كان الفن جزءاً أصيلاً من الثورة في السودان مع فعاليات الموسيقى الشعبية والحفلات الجماهيرية والشعر والموسيقى والجداريات وعروض فنية متنوعة في الأحياء تزامناً مع الاعتصامات التي انتظمت في عدد من ولايات السودان ما بين أبريل ويونيو 2019.

يشهد السودان منذ 2019 ازدهارًا في المساحات الفنية والمشاريع والمبادرات، وذلك بعد ثلاثين عامًا من حُكم النظام الإسلاموعروبي القمعي، والذي اضطهد الفنون والثقافة بشكل ممنهج. وعلى الرغم من تسبب جائحة كورونا في توقف الأنشطة على الأرض في بعض الحالات، إلا أن العامين 2020 و 2021 قد شهدا ولادة المزيد من المبادرات، نسبة لزيادة الدعم من المانحين والظروف الاقتصادية والسياسية العامة التي مهدت لولادة السودان من جديد وعودته إلى المجالات العالمية. وانطلقت، بمجرد تخفيف الإغلاق الذي تسبب به جائحة كورونا، التحولات الاجتماعية والاقتصادية والأمنية والسياسية في البلاد، والتي سار في طريقها الفاعلون الفنيون.

لكن بالرغم من ذلك، تظل الحقيقة أن السودان كان محكوماً بشراكة هشة بين الحكومة المدنية والجيش لقرابة السنتين، حتى الانقلاب يوم ٢٥ أكتوبر ٢٠٢١ و الذي أدى لتوقف الكثير من الخطوات الإنمائية. و لكن المشاحنات بين الفن و السلطة استمرت في الفترة الانتقالية، و أبرزها قضية مجموعة 'فيد للفنون'، حيث سُجن عدد من الفاعلين الفنيين لأسابيع بعد بلاغ تقدم به أحد الجيران بشأن بروفات أداء مسرحية نظمونها. المساحات الفنية والمقاهي تتميز في أن الملاك والشركاء والعاملين هم من النشطاء، مما يجعلهم أهدافًا سهلة للسلطة المستبدة التي ما تزال متخفية في الحكومة. وإلى تاريخ اللحظة، هناك الكثير من التحديات، ولا يزال السودان يواجه تهديدات أمنية وتصعيدًا متكررًا ، وقد اجتاح الانهيار الاقتصادي البلاد بصورة أكبر خلال العامين الماضيين و بسرعة أكبر بعد الانقلاب. وفوق ذلك، لا تلتزم الحكومة بأي إعادة تأهيل لقطاع الفن والثقافة الذي أفسده النظام السابق، لا من خلال التمويل أو الدعم المادي أو الرسمي للمبادرات الشعبية التي تتخلق. كيف يبدو قطاع الفن إذن في مثل هذه الأوقات من عدم الاستقرار؟

المساحات الثقافية والمقاهي والبرامج متداخلة المجالات ليست جديدة في السودان، لكن الروح التي تحملها الآن مختلفة عما كانت عليه في عهد الإنقاذ (الدكتاتورية السابقة). لم تعد هناك أماكن تفتح أبوابها لمجموعة ديموغرافية معينة، تنظم فعاليات سرية وتخشى قوى النظام العام سيئة السمعة، والتي ألغيت بعد الثورة. المساحات مفتوحة للحوار والنقاشات والفرق المستقلة والشعراء والمكتبات ودروس الحرف اليدوية. والأهم من ذلك، أن هذه المساحات قادرة إلى حد كبير على التقاطع بين الفن والثقافة والسياسة، وبالتالي، ترسيخ أهمية الحوكمة في حوارات الشباب، باستخدام أدوات حديثة وجذابة توسع من شبكة مناقشة الموضوعات ذات الصلة بالانتقال السياسي الحالي في السودان.

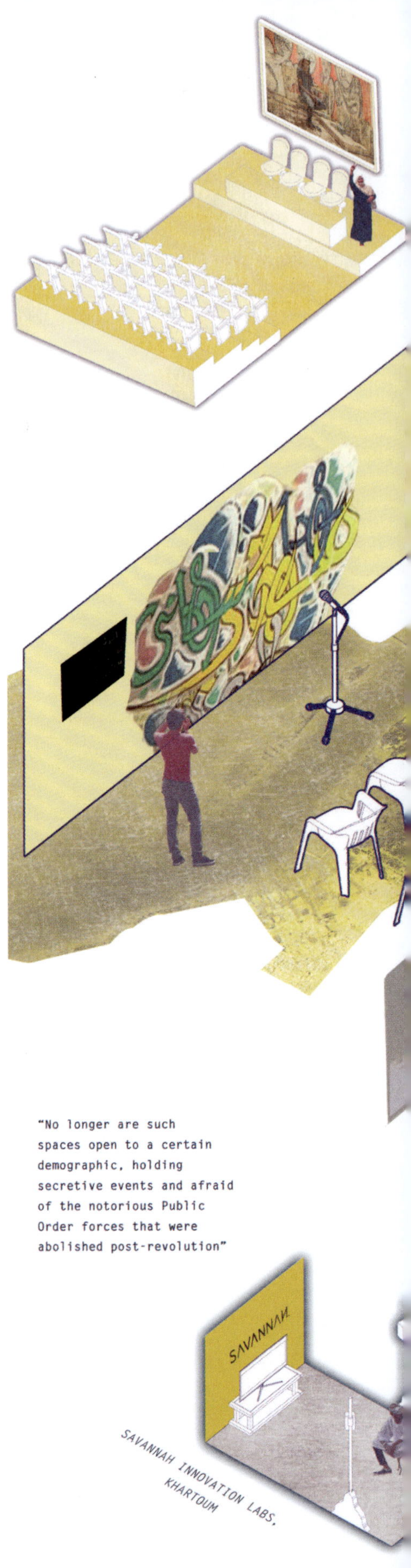

Omnia Shawkat graduated with a
BSc in Biology with a focus on
environmental studies from the
American University in Cairo in
2008. She has a Master's degree in
Environment and Resource Management
with a focus on water and climate
policy from the Vrije Universiteit
in Amsterdam, the Netherlands.
After six years in development and
environmental management, Omnia
rerouted her career to become
a digital storytelling curator
and cultural manager. Omnia is
one of two founders of Andariya,
a bilingual digital multimedia
cultural platform, research and
cross-cultural enterprise launched
in 2015 in Sudan and South Sudan,
and in Uganda in 2018. In 2021,
Andariya entered nine new countries
in the East and Horn of Africa
regions, creating and curating
content and common projects.

"The spaces are open for dialogue, debates, indie bands and poets, libraries and crafts classes. Importantly, spaces are largely able to criss-cross between art, culture and politics" 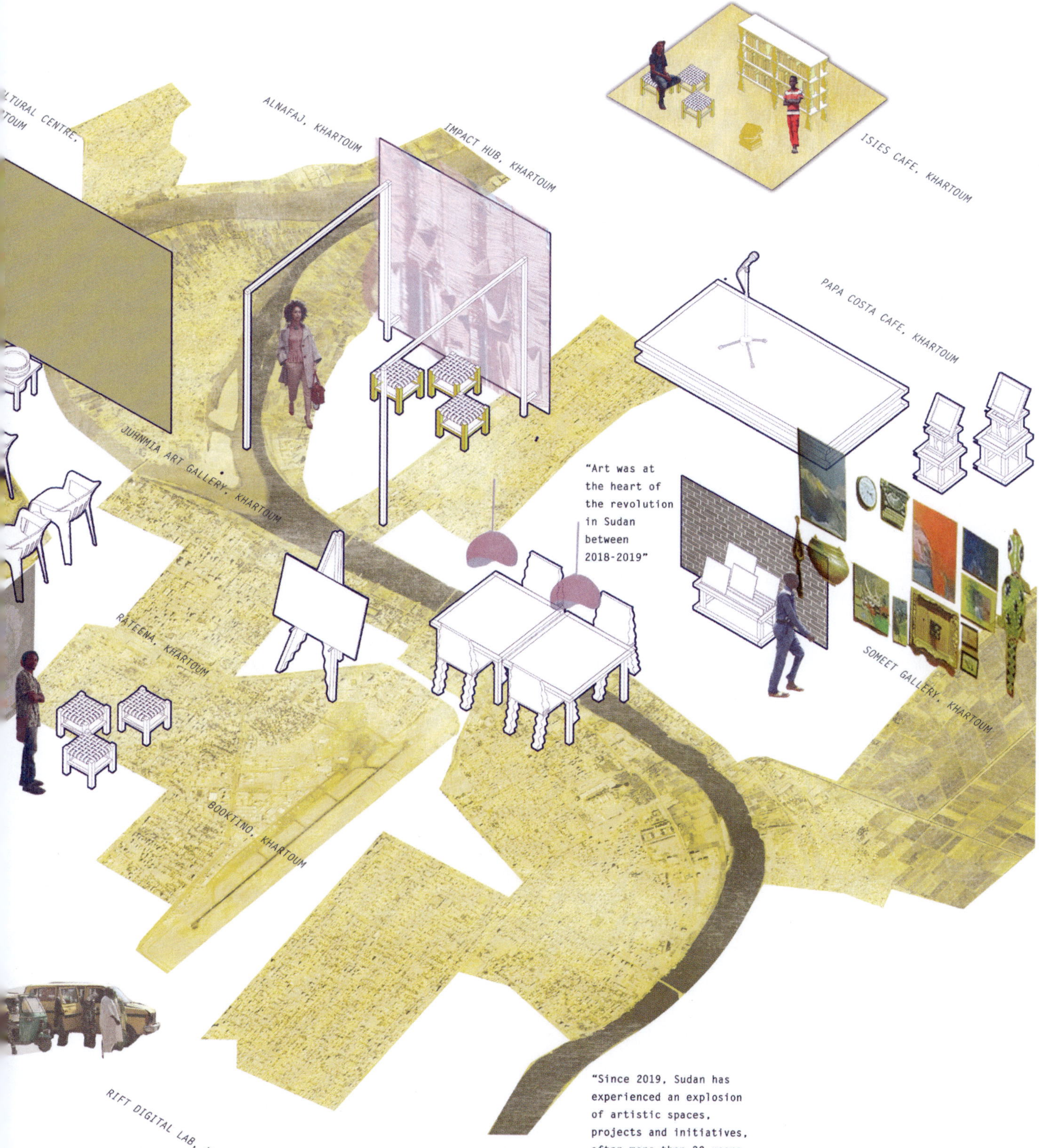
CULTURAL CENTRE, KHARTOUM
ALNAFAJ, KHARTOUM
IMPACT HUB, KHARTOUM
ISIES CAFE, KHARTOUM
PAPA COSTA CAFE, KHARTOUM
JUHNMIA ART GALLERY, KHARTOUM
"Art was at the heart of the revolution in Sudan between 2018-2019"
SOMEET GALLERY, KHARTOUM
RATEENA, KHARTOUM
BOOKTINO, KHARTOUM
RIFT DIGITAL LAB, KHARTOUM
"Since 2019, Sudan has experienced an explosion of artistic spaces, projects and initiatives, after more than 30 years of repressive Islamo-Arab governance that systematically oppressed arts and culture"

حينما يأتي الأرشيف كخيال،ربما يتبدد عناء تصور المستقبل

Ali Al-Adawy

> *'The future has not been canceled. The future is where we will
> live and grow, but first we need to catch up to the present.'*
> - Benjamin H. Bratton[43]

*'Imagine a team of African archaeologists from the future -
some silicon, some carbon, some wet, some dry - excavating
a site, a museum from their past: a museum whose ruined
documents and leaking discs are identifiable as belonging to
our present, the early twenty-first century. Sifting patiently
through the rubble, our archaeologists from the United States
of Africa, the USAF, would be struck by how much Afrodiasporic
subjectivity in the twentieth century constituted itself
through the cultural project of recovery. In their Age of
Total Recall, memory is never lost. Only the art of forgetting.
Imagine them reconstructing the conceptual framework of our
cultural moment from those fragments. What are the parameters
of that moment, the edge of that framework?'*
- Kodwo Eshun[44]

In this project, we imagine and work with a group of futurologists who
try to escape ready-made designs produced by and for a trend-factory,
in order to draw futures based on speculative/archives instead. This
project is understood as a major epistemic and aesthetic intervention,
through three commissions: a text, a short video and a DJ set concert.
These three commissions aim to stimulate discussion and debate, in order
to question and dismantle authoritarian histories of the postcolonial
state in the Egyptian context, as part of an African neighbourhood.
These works can all be accessed online at archiveofforgetfulness.com.

'I Almost Forgot The Roving Body...Let's Call It The Future'
Video, 7 minutes, screened at the Goethe-Institut Alexandria,
29 September 2021, by Mohamed AbdelKarim.

A commissioned video on the disappearance of the Mediterranean. How
could we imagine/map/build a potential world without the Mediterranean,
which goes beyond modern and contemporary histories of colonial/
postcolonial-national imaginaries? How might we problematise utopian/
dystopian easy speculations that often forget to navigate immigration
and ecological questions from the shores of planetary unfair division
of labour, as situated within a socioeconomic/political/technological
complex?

Mohamed Abdelkarim considers performance as a research method
and a practice through which he produces texts and images that embody the
forms of poetry, scripts, sound and video. As part of his performative
practice, he established 'Live Praxes' - a performative project that
brings together lectures, debates, readings, critical responses and
creative quests, alongside organising performance nights.

Ali al-Adawy is a
curator, researcher,
editor, writer and
critic of moving images,
urban artistic practices
and cultural history.
He has curated several
film programmes and
seminars such as *Serge
Daney: A homage and
retrospective* (2017)
and *Harun Farocki:
Dialectics of images…
Images that cover/
uncover other images*
(2018). He also curated,
together with Paul
Cata, the exhibition
*The Art of Getting Lost
in Cities: Barcelona &;
Alexandria* (2017). He
was one of the founders
of *Tripod*, an online
magazine for film and
moving images criticism
(2015-2017) and was
part of the editorial
team of *TarAlbahr*, an
online platform and a
publication for urban
and art practices in
Alexandria (2015-2018).

43   Bratton, B., 'The new normal: Essay', *Strelka Mag*, 2 December 2020. Available at: https://
strelkamag.com/en/article/the-new-normal-essay-bratton.

44   Eshun, K., 'Further considerations on Afrofuturism', *CR: The New Centennial Review*, 3, 2
(Summer 2003), pp. 287-302.

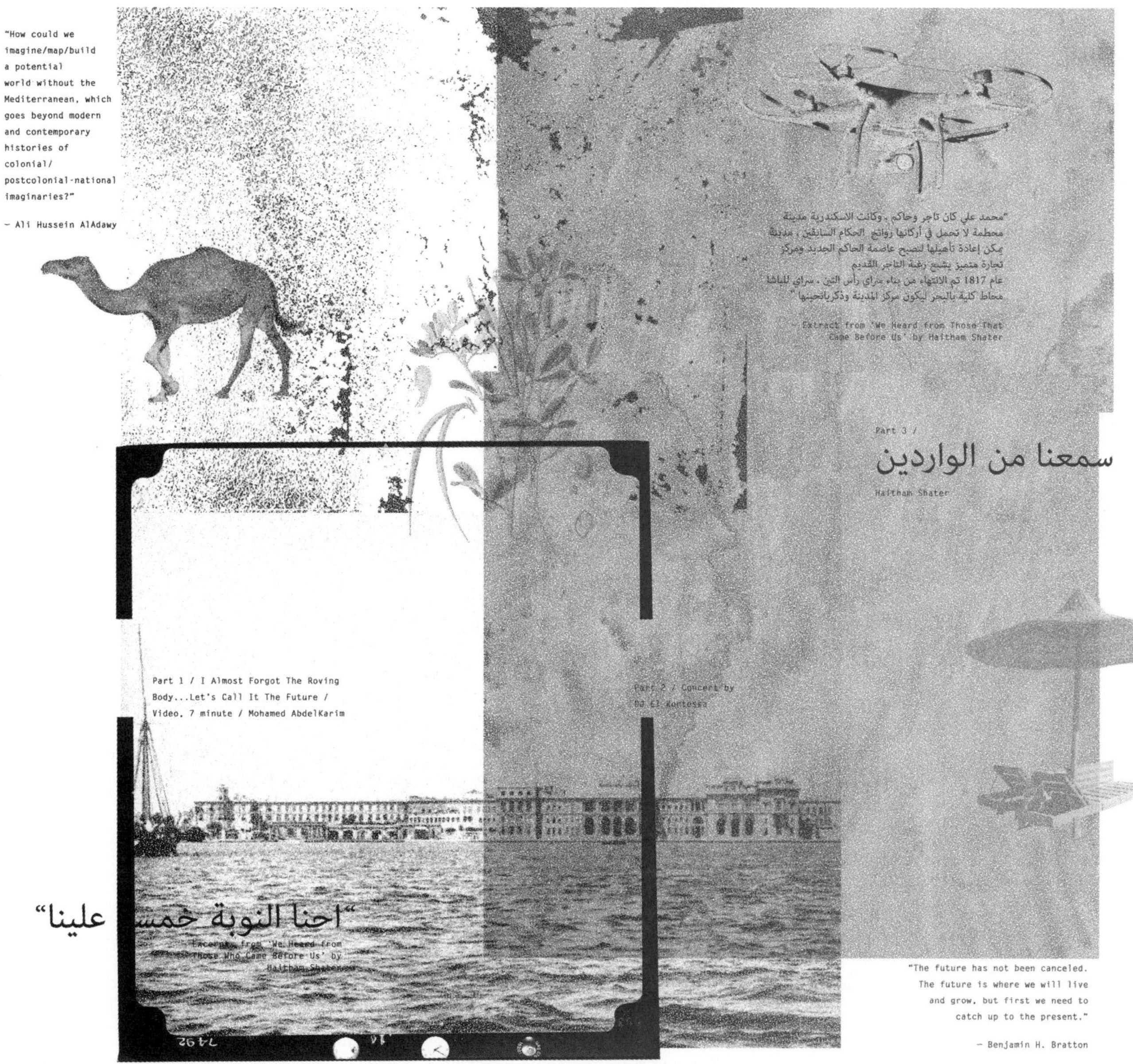

A DJ set by El Kontessa was performed on 27 October 2021 at the Goethe-Institut Alexandria, by DJ El Kontessa. This Dj set is a sonic fictional jamming encounter in outer space between Sun Ra, Salah Ragab and AlBahr Abu grisha.

El Kontessa is a Cairo-based DJ and music producer who mixes mainly Egyptian Mahraganat music, as well as experimenting with different electronic beats.

'We heard from those who came before us' / سمعنا من الواردين

Published on 2 November 2021, this essay by Haitham Shater imagines the city of Alexandria with a Nubian majority population since 1915. It can be read at archiveofforgetfulness.com in Arabic and English (translated by Katharine Halls).

Haitham Shater is an engineer and writer interested in exploring the multiple histories of the city, as well as the veiled-face lady from Koshtamna village, except for the elevator rest time, when he gets busy blogging.

These works can all be accessed online at archiveofforgetfulness.com.

Zoubida Mseffer

The history of Yasmin, my great-grandfather's concubine, is a story I first heard from my grandmother. Lalla Hajja liked to talk about her father, PPa, who, before her birth, had lived 18 years in Manishisteer with Dada El Yasmin. I loved sitting between Lalla Hajja and my mother, wrapped tight in a kitsch, flowery, shimmering blanket, listening to them recount family stories. In particular, the story of Yasmin resonated with me. It was like the start of a novel or a movie. I was intrigued and fascinated by the life of this young woman who had travelled and seen the world. I felt closer to Yasmin than to my great-grandfather. About five years ago, one of my aunts brought home proof of Yasmin's existence from her travels. The document my aunt obtained, the extract from the 1911 Manchester census register, is the only tangible record of Yasmin's life. On seeing this record, I wanted to understand more of her life. To know who this woman was. I wanted to record her story. To not let her be forgotten. I therefore began retracing her journey by collecting memories, family photos and other archives. I followed in her footsteps to places she had known. And I tried to fill in the gaps and the silences left by holes in memories, in an attempt to hold on to fragments of her life story.

What I had thought was a love story, if love could count for something at that time, is actually the story of a young girl whose body bore the marks of a history of subjection. Her story mirrors that of countless women, subject to men's games. I see in Yasmin the shadow of the dada, khadem and abid, silent witnesses to the culture of slavery and the enslavement of bodies for which Moroccan society has long been the setting. I also see the shadow-lives of my great-grandmother, of my grandmother, and of all the women of this era, who lived as prisoners in the lives they led, with no alternative choices. Yasmin's story is nonetheless unique because it is also that of a young woman who wanted and claimed her freedom. Her life begins at the end of the 19th century and ends around 1960. For me, this work is just the beginning of a deeper search.

This project is in French and English and can be engaged with further at archiveofforgetulness.com.

L'histoire de Yasmin, la concubine de mon arrière grand-père, est un héritage légué par ma grand-mère. Lalla Hajja aimait parler de son père, PPa, qui, avant sa naissance, avait vécu dix-huit ans à Manishisteer en emmenant avec lui Dada El Yasmin. J'adorai m'asseoir entre elle et ma mère, enveloppée toute entière sous une de ces couvertures kitch aux motifs fleuris et éclatants, et les écouter dire et redire les mêmes histoires. Celle-ci raisonnait tout particulièrement. C'était comme le début d'un roman ou d'un film. J'étais intriguée et fascinée par la vie de cette jeune femme qui avait voyagé et vu le monde. Je me sentais proche de Yasmin, plus que de mon arrière grand-père. Il y a environ cinq ans, ma tante a rapporté d'un voyage à Manchester la preuve de l'existence de Yasmin et l'unique trace tangible de sa vie. L'extrait du registre du recensement de 1911. J'ai voulu en savoir plus et enquêter sur la vie de cette femme. J'ai voulu consigner son histoire. Ne pas la laisser s'échapper. L'attraper au vol tant qu'il est possible d'en saisir quelques bribes. Je cherche et collecte les souvenirs et les photos de famille. Je recycle d'autres archives et assemble des fragments pour combler les manques et les silences laissés par le récit familial.

Zoubida Mseffer lives in Rabat, Morocco. She is an independent consultant specialising in social development. An anthropologist by training, she has more than 10 years' experience in supporting associations and cultural and social projects, through fundraising, project management, facilitation of spaces for participation and dialogue and research. She is particularly interested in issues related to women and feminism, youth, disability and migration.

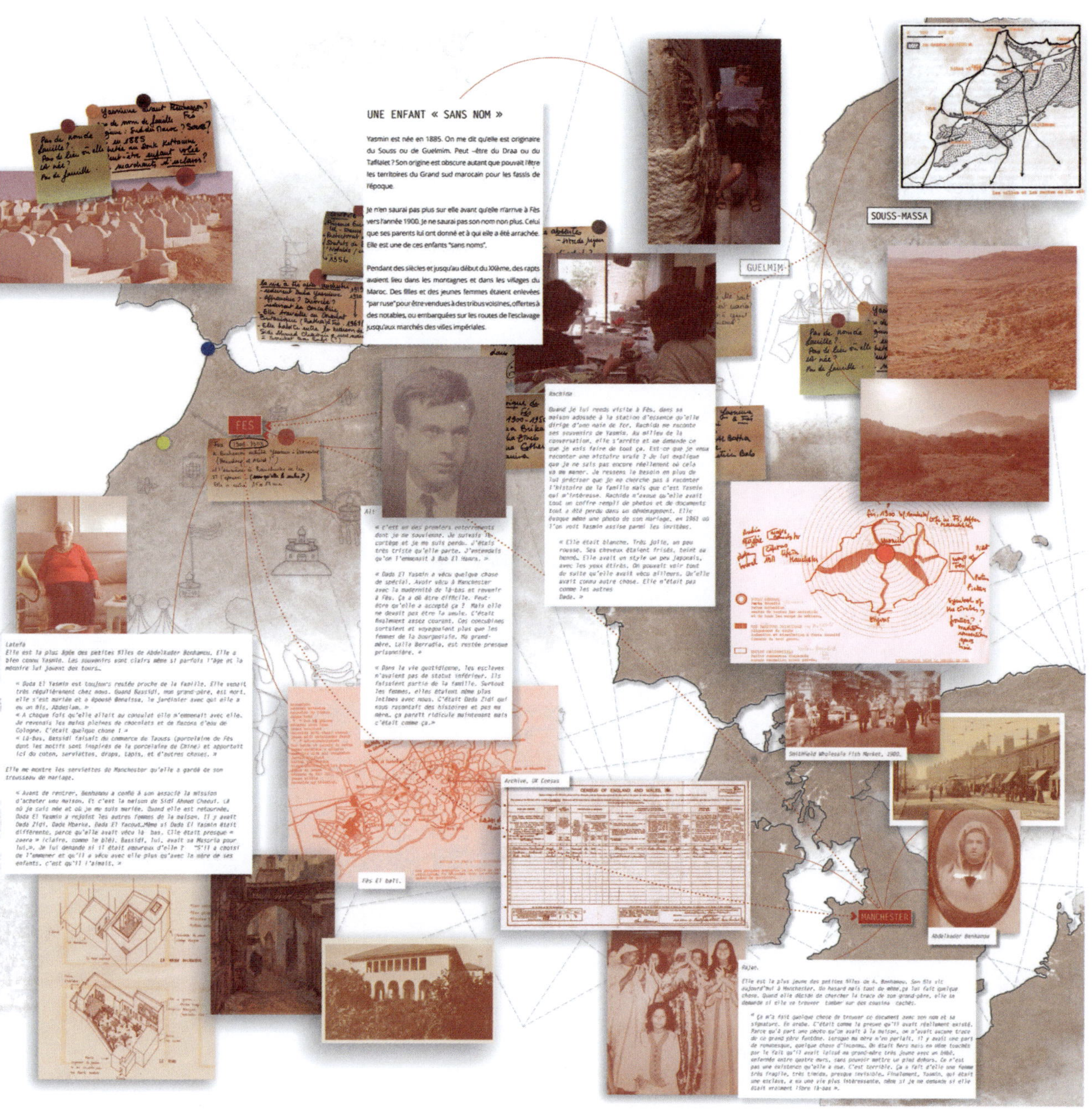

Ce que je pensais être une histoire d'amour, comme si l'amour pouvait compter pour quelque chose à cette époque, est en réalité l'histoire d'une jeune fille dont le corps porte la marque d'une histoire qui dure depuis des siècles. Celle d'innombrables femmes soumises aux jeux des hommes. Je vois en Yasmin l'ombre des dada, khadem, abid, témoins silencieuses de la culture de l'esclavage et de l'asservissement des corps dont la société marocaine a été longtemps le théâtre. Je vois aussi l'ombre de mon arrière grand-mère, de ma grand-mère, et de toutes les femmes, prisonnières dans des vies qu'elles consentent à mener parce que « c'était comme ça à l'époque ». L'histoire de Yasmin est singulière parce que c'est celle aussi d'une jeune femme qui a voulu et qui a réclamé sa liberté. Sa vie commence à la fin du XIXème siècle et s'achève vers 1960. Pour moi, l'enquête ne fait que commencer.

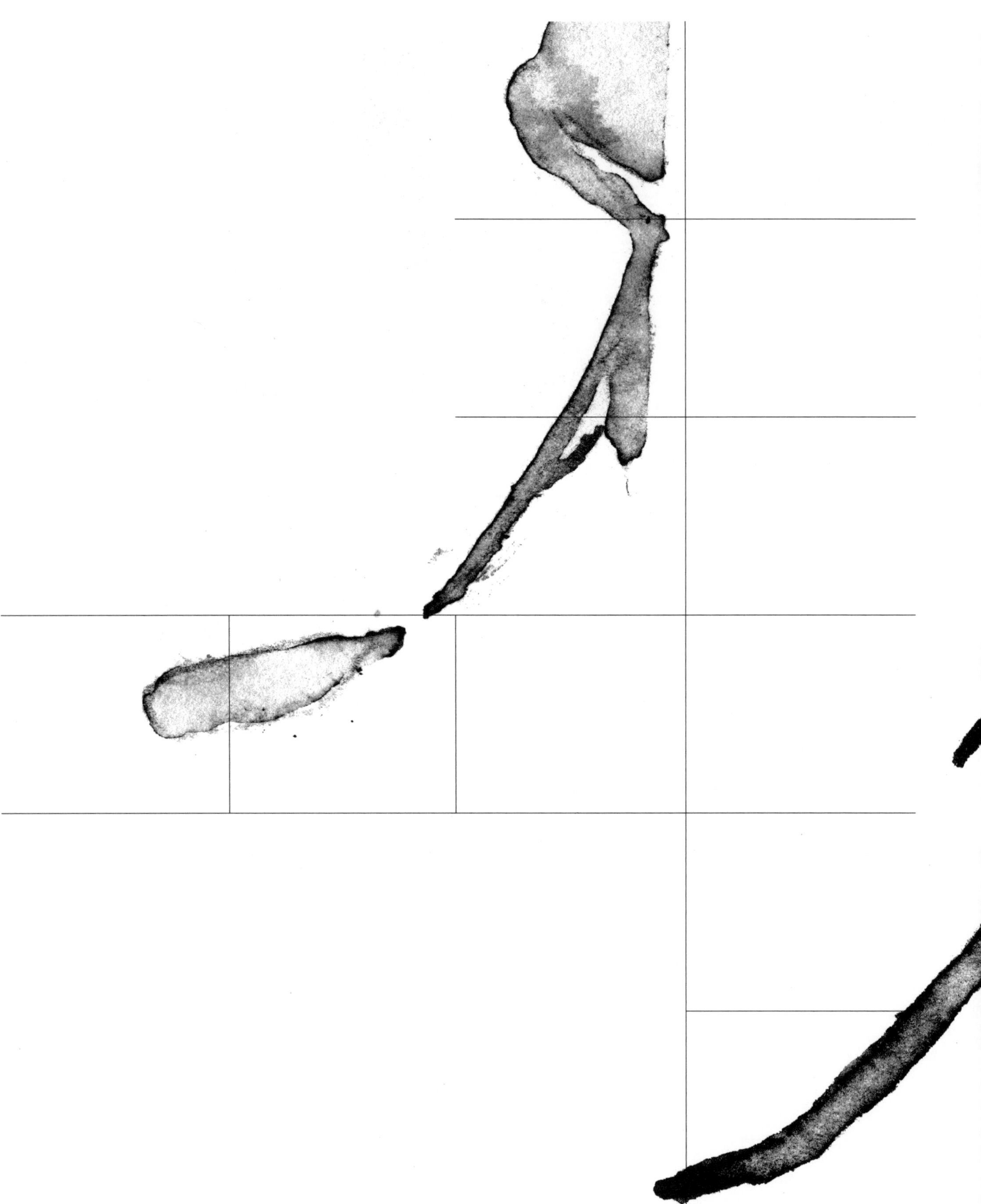

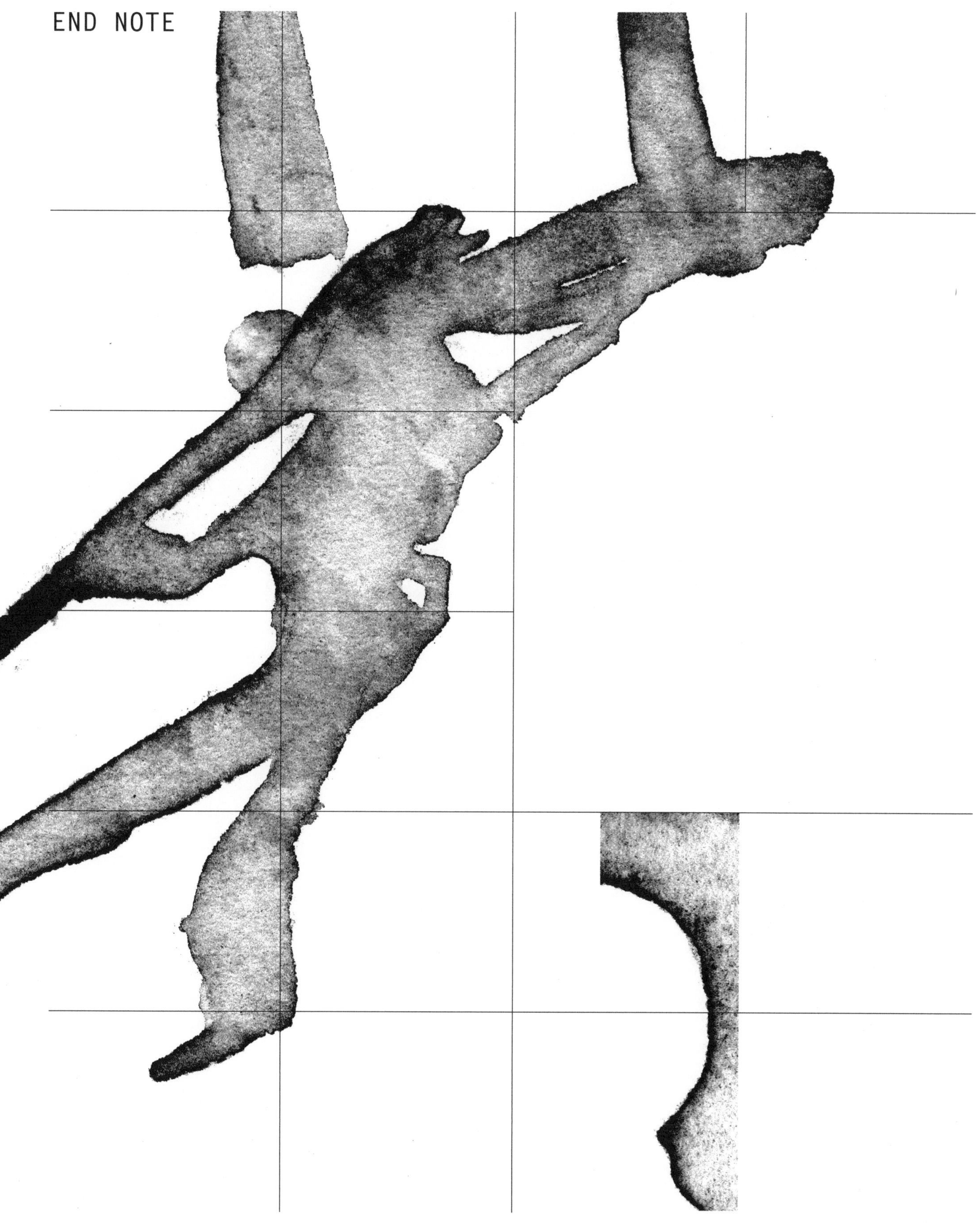

END NOTE

Huda Tayob

Revisiting the many stories gathered and generously shared with the *Archive of Forgetfulness* in this catalogue is a journey through intimate and vast terrains. This publication is a material trace of the multitude of voices, generosities, thinkers and worlds shared, contributed, engaged with. Beyond the specificities and details of histories, gestures, bodily acts of remembering and searching for names that have been forgotten, the conversations within the podcasts, artworks, essays and regional projects point to questions around archival labour and the many forms it might take, and ways it might live. The works suggest an epistemic praxis that is decidedly un- and anti-disciplinary. They argue for an engagement with what might otherwise be an assumed absence, through resurfacing lines of connection that may have been forgotten, but have not been lost.

Archival work is a labour of maintenance against silencing and neglect. In the first episode of *Conversations with Neighbours* Ali Al-Adawy and Jumoke Sanwo draw attention to archives as holding future possibilities, where archival work is always situated. As Sanwo noted, the Yoruba translation for an archive, 'itoju', is 'care'. In the context of a creative project such as this one, archival care must contend with the violence of the present, to move beyond the captured past, and to imagine alternative possible futures together. This labour involves an understanding of time as stretched and circular, and always returning. In working across, and beyond, the African continent, the *Archive of Forgetfulness* suggests ways of reading and writing across south and north, centre and periphery. The work questions whether returning to sites and stories often overlooked by disciplining borders can enable us to move beyond the repetition of inherited violences, in response to active and transitive silencing.[45]

Following Stuart Hall, 'archives are not inert historical collections. They always stand in an active, dialogic, relation to the questions which the present puts to the past; and the present always puts its questions differently from one generation to another.'[46]

---

45   Trouillot, M. *Silencing the Past: Power and the Production of History.* Beacon Press, Boston, 1995, pp.49.

46   Hall, S., 'Constituting an archive'. *Third Text*, 15, 54 (2001), pp.92.

Through body, text, voice, gesture and sound, the works are an embrace of the partial, momentary and not yet complete. In the strands and threads, loose and tightly woven, is a practice of gratitude for those who came before, acts of caring to listen and hear, and acknowledgment of sites and spaces of resistance and refusal.

Remembering, and archival work, can be a choice to carry or a weight to bear. In *Memory for Forgetfulness* (1982), Mahmoud Darwish moves from the urgent to mundane in the midst of crisis, to the aroma and smell of coffee, the sound and sense of a siege, alongside the weight and depth of history. He writes, 'It has had a long history, this double operation of searching for a place or a time on which to put a signature and untie the knot of the name facing the long caravans of oblivion.'[47] Forgetting is not only the shadowy underside of memory, but defines the contours of what is recalled and preserved, what might be deemed minor or trivial. The shape of those contours of futures past and present, however murky or distant, is where potential of the *Archive of Forgetfulness* is sited, rejecting the assumed transparency of the binary position. For Édouard Glissant, 'There is opacity now at the bottom of the mirror, a whole alluvium deposited by populations, silt that is fertile […] with an insistent presence that we are incapable of not experiencing.'[48] Opacity suggests a necessary engagement with relationality, 'a total (dreamed-of) freedom' of possibilities. Beyond momentary engagements to draw out direct connections among works is the importance of the positional and relational field of adjacent work that has been collectively built and assembled through the *Archive of Forgetfulness*. A fragmentary archive of contestation against lines of force, positioned in relation to both futurity and contingency; an engagement and an interruption into a far from settled field; and an insistent presence in the face of imposed forgetfulness.

47   Darwish, M., *Memory for Forgetfulness: August, Beirut, 1982* (translated by Ibrahim Muhawi), University of California Press, Berkeley, 1995.

48   Glissant, É., *Poetics of Relation* (translated by Betsy Wing), University of Michigan Press, Ann Arbor, 1990, pp. 111.

THE ARCHIVE OF FORGETFULNESS TEAM

LEAD CURATORS

Huda Tayob is an architect, architectural historian and curator. Her research is focused on migrant, minor and subaltern architectures and the politics of urban space, alongside architectural ghost stories and other archival silences. She is a CCA Mellon Fellow on the project Centring Africa, is co-curator of Racespacearchitecture.org with Suzi Hall and Thandi Loewenson, and was the project manager for the *Archive of Forgetfulness* project.

> **Bongani Kona** is a Cape Town-based writer and contributing editor at *Chimurenga*. He studied creative writing at the University of Cape Town and is editor of the short story collections *Our Ghosts Were Once People* (2021) and co-editor of *Migrations* (2017). His work has been broadcast on BBC and has appeared in a variety of publications and anthologies including *The Baffler, Safe House: Explorations in Creative Nonfiction* and *The Daily Assortment of Astonishing Things*. Kona was shortlisted for the Caine Prize in 2016 and the True Story Award in 2020/21.

REGIONAL CURATORS

Ali Hussein Al-Adawy is a curator, researcher, editor, writer and critic of moving images, urban artistic practices and cultural history. He has curated several film programmes and seminars such as *Serge Daney: A homage and retrospective* (2017) and *Harun Farocki: Dialectics of images… Images that cover/uncover other images* (2018). He also curated, together with Paul Cata, the exhibition *The Art of Getting Lost in Cities: Barcelona &; Alexandria* (2017). He was one of the founders of *Tripod*, an online magazine for film and moving images criticism (2015-2017) and was part of the editorial team of *TarAlbahr*, an online platform and a publication for urban and art practices in Alexandria (2015-2018).

> **Eric '1Key' Ngangare** is an independent poet, spoken word artist, emcee, performer, actor and blogger from Rwanda exploring various formats of storytelling. His work deals with issues of identities - individual and collective - power systems and societal dynamics. His second album, *Mwiru,* was released in 2021 and offers a mix of genres, styles and languages.

Omnia Abbas Shawkat graduated with a BSc in Biology with a focus on environmental studies from the American University in Cairo in 2008. She has a Master's degree in Environment and Resource Management with a focus on water and climate policy from the Vrije Universiteit in Amsterdam, the Netherlands. After six years in development and environmental management, Omnia rerouted her career to become a digital storytelling curator and cultural manager. Omnia is one of two founders of Andariya, a bilingual digital multimedia cultural platform, research and cross-cultural enterprise launched in 2015 in Sudan and South Sudan, and in Uganda in 2018. In 2021, Andariya entered nine new countries in the East and Horn of Africa regions, creating and curating content and common projects.

Jumoke Sanwo is a storyteller, cultural interlocutor and creative director of Revolving Art Incubator. She works primarily in photography, video art and extended reality (XR), and her work engages the bodily, spatial and temporal realities and complexities in postcolonial societies. She lives and works out of Lagos, Nigeria.

Zoubida Mseffer lives in Rabat, Morocco. She is an independent consultant specialising in social development. An anthropologist by training, she has more than 10 years' experience in supporting associations and cultural and social projects, through fundraising, project management, facilitation of spaces for participation and dialogue and research. She is particularly interested in issues related to women and feminism, youth, disability and migration.

Princess Zinzi Mhlongo is a theatre director and the co-founder of *The Plat4orm*, which for many years provided an alternative space for artists in the theatre industry to develop new uncensored work. She directed her first professional production, *And the Girls in Their Sunday Dresses*, in 2008. Since then, her work has toured internationally, and she has received numerous nominations and awards, including the prestigious Standard Bank Young Artist of the Year Award for Theatre in 2012. She is a recipient of The Laboratory for Global Performance and Politics 2020-21 fellowship at Georgetown University, Washington DC. In 2020 she launched *Exhibit*, a digital platform that showcases upcoming or unfinished work by an artist seeking funding.

GOETHE-INSTITUT COORDINATORS

Asma Diakité heads the cultural programme department of the Goethe-Institut for Sub-Saharan Africa. After studying theatre, film and media studies, philosophy and cultural anthropology in Frankfurt and Cairo, she founded the artist network 'Revolution Divine' and did her doctorate on the concept of exuberance in the performing arts. With her team in Johannesburg, she conceptualises and produces cultural events, creates platforms for discourse and cultural exchange and supports the South African art scene. She is currently working among other things on a discourse series titled, 'Power Talks'. Power Talks seeks a critical reflection on the role of European cultural institutions in Africa.

Lilli Kobler is currently the director of the Goethe-Institut in Khartoum, Sudan. After studying cultural anthropology, psychology and Arabic language at the Free University in Berlin, she worked for the Goethe-Institut in Cairo, Johannesburg and Munich and is currently in her second term in Sudan (2010-2014 & 2018-present). Through her experience of working in volatile contexts and during the revolution in Sudan in 2019, she is particularly aware of the importance of spaces and networks to strengthen discourse and accompany positive transformation through long-term engagement and sustainable project designs. Her next posting starting in the summer 2022 will be Nairobi, Kenya.

Zakiyyah Haffejee is currently a student at the Royal College of Architecture, London. She is a graduate of the University of Johannesburg and has worked at the Johannesburg-based practice, Counterspace Studio. Her work draws on themes of gender, identity and spirituality, and often focuses on rituals and uncovering meaning through language, history and religion.

PODCAST PRODUCTION

Andri Burnett is a producer, audio editor and all-round creative. Along with Vasti Calitz and The Book Lounge she started *A Readers' Community* podcast and has since produced and edited numerous podcasting projects including a podcast with PEN South Africa called *The Empty Chair*, as well as the *Open Book Podcast* and *Climate Frontiers*.

WEBSITE DESIGN AND PRODUCTION

Sarah de Villiers is an architect and designer based in Johannesburg. Her work questions boundaries and borders, and engages with the spatially detectable abstractions of power and economy. She was co-leader of GSA Unit 18 at the Graduate School of Architecture, University of Johannesburg and is the director at Space Kiosk. Sarah designed the graphics for the Archive of Forgetfulness website.

Frederick Kannemeyer earned an MTech in Architectural Technology (Prof)(CW) from the Graduate School of Architecture, University of Johannesburg, in 2019, after gaining two years experience in architectural drafting work, ranging from residential and heritage projects to larger public buildings and industrial architecture. During his Master's thesis work he explored ideas around digital space, queerness, and the politics and technicalities of online knowledge-systems like Wikipedia.

CATALOGUE DESIGN

Fred Swart is a Johannesburg-based graphic designer and director of Ateljee, and is currently director of visual identity at the African Futures Institute. He has created graphic identities and engaged in design work across a wide spectrum of industry and institutional landscapes in South Africa and internationally.

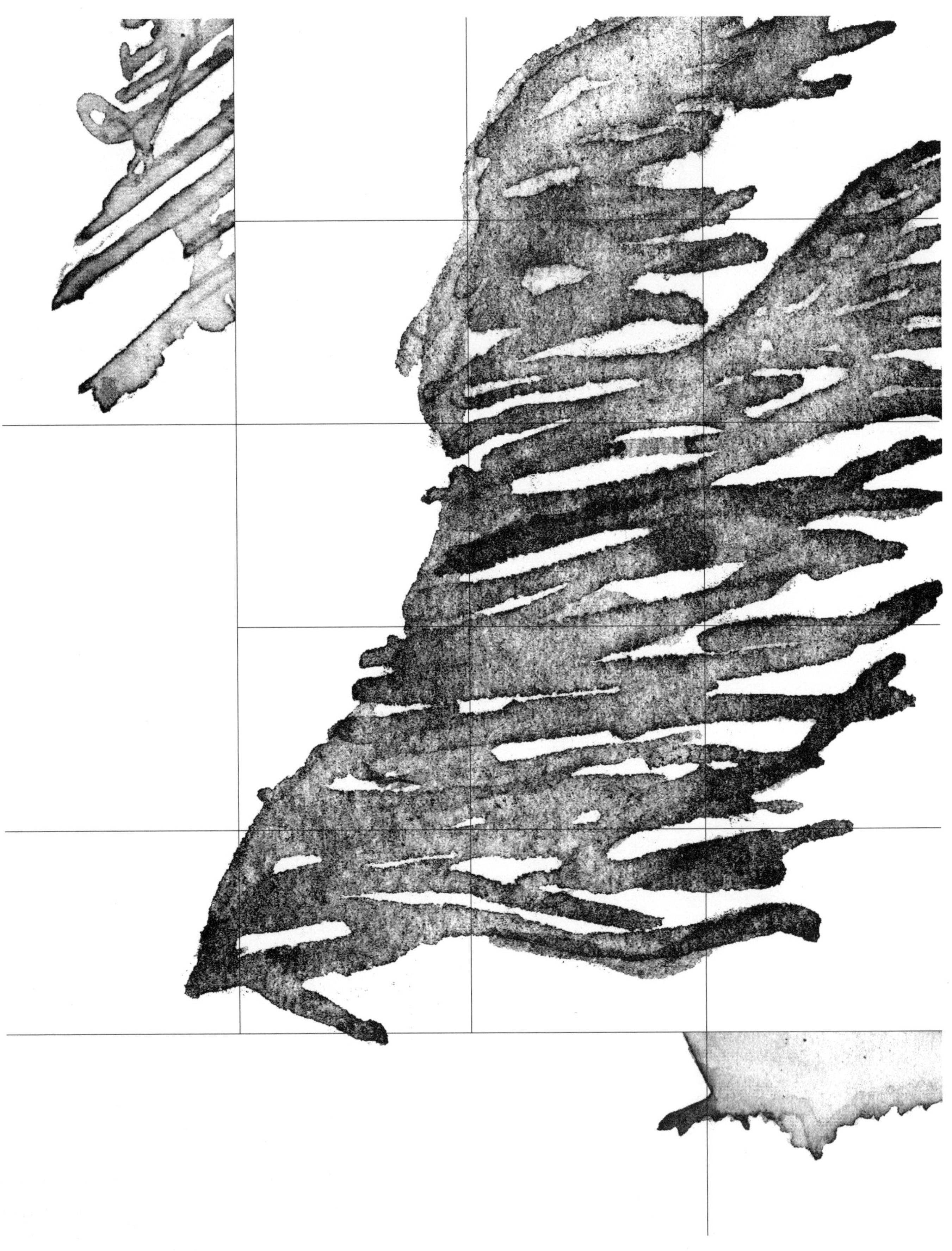